BEING WITH THE DEAD

Cultural Memory
in
the
Present

Hent de Vries, Editor

BEING WITH THE DEAD

Burial, Ancestral Politics, and the Roots of Historical Consciousness

Hans Ruin

STANFORD UNIVERSITY PRESS

STANFORD, CALIFORNIA

Stanford University Press
Stanford, California

Printed in the United States of America on acid-free, archival-quality paper

Library of Congress Cataloging-in-Publication Data

Names: Ruin, Hans, author.
Title: Being with the dead : burial, ancestral politics, and the roots of historical
    consciousness / Hans Ruin.
Description: Stanford, California : Stanford University Press, 2019. | Series:
    Cultural memory in the present | Includes bibliographical references and
    index.
Identifiers: LCCN 2018019691 (print) | LCCN 2018022482 (ebook) |
    ISBN 9781503607767 | ISBN 9780804791311 (cloth :alk. paper) | ISBN
    9781503607750 (pbk. : alk. paper)
Subjects: LCSH: Burial—Philosophy. | Dead. | Funeral rites and ceremonies. |
    Memory (Philosophy)
Classification: LCC GT3320 (ebook) | LCC GT3320 .R85 2019 (print) | DDC
    393/.1—dc23
LC record available at https://lccn.loc.gov/2018019691

Cover design: Michel Vrana

Thus let your streams o'erflow your springs
Till eyes and tears be the same things;
And the other's difference bears,
these weeping eyes, those seeing tears.

—Andrew Marvell, "Eyes and Tears"

Contents

Acknowledgments

More than two decades ago I published a dissertation on the topic of "historicity" (*Geschichtlichkeit*) in Heidegger, where I traced the theme of history, historical understanding, and historical belonging throughout his works, from the early neo-Kantian epistemological analyses to the later ruminations on "the event" (*Ereignis*). In a footnote in that book I mentioned the possibility of an expanded phenomenological social ontology that comprised the living and the dead as a way of capturing the deeper ethical dimension of historical culture and consciousness and thus also of hermeneutic philosophy at large. *Being with the Dead* is a belated fulfillment of this promise. It was conceived and mostly written in the context of the large multidisciplinary research program "Time, Memory, and Representation," generously supported by the Swedish research foundation Riksbankens Jubileumsfond (2010–2016). In this program, twenty-five researchers from thirteen different human and social science disciplines collaborated in an effort to map recent transformations in historical consciousness. This multidisciplinary context and its many extraordinary seminars over the years provided a crucial inspiration for how the book project developed, in particular for how it gave me the courage to move into fields with which I was previously not very familiar. I am deeply grateful to all my colleagues in this group, many of whom will recognize the mark of their own work and personal conversations in the finished text. My gratitude also goes to the members of our international board of scholars, who participated in some of our seminars over these years, sharing their work and commenting on our efforts, in particular Joan Scott, Aleida Assmann, Frank Ankersmit, and the late Hayden White.

As I embarked on this task, I was led away from my original background in phenomenology, hermeneutics, and deconstruction into the sociology and anthropology of mortuary culture, burial archaeology, philology, historiography, and cultural memory studies. But what started as an aspiration to broaden my knowledge and understanding of mortuary culture for a philosophical purpose gradually also opened my eyes to an inner lacuna in how earlier theoretical efforts to account for how humans have engaged with their dead often tended to neglect to theorize the nature of their own existential-ontological commitment to the dead. Thus, the book began to take on the form of what could perhaps be called a metacritical thanatology, that is, an exploration of the social ontology of being with the dead mediated through critical analyses of the human-historical sciences themselves. Or in other words, a series of meditations on how the theoretical eye comes to grief.

Parts of some of the chapters have been presented at conferences and as guest lectures and have also appeared in journal articles and book chapters, notably "Spektral fenomenologi: Om historien och de döda hos Derrida och Heidegger," in *Tid för Europa*, ed. J. Wittrock (Göteborg: Daidalos, 2011), 193–222; "Om graven som minneskonst," in *Minneskonst*, ed. S. Arrhenius and M. Berg (Stockholm: Bonniers, 2014), 33–44; "Spectral Phenomenology: Derrida, Heidegger and the Problem of the Ancestral," in *The Ashgate Research Companion to Memory Studies*, ed. S. Kattago (Farnham, UK: Ashgate, 2015), 61–74; "Life after Death (on Patocka)," in *Transit Online* (Vienna: IWM, 2015); "Housing Spirits: The Grave as an Exemplary Site of Memory," in *Routledge International Handbook of Memory Studies*, ed. A. Tota and T. Hagen (New York: Routledge, 2015), 131–140; "Speaking to the Dead—Historicity and the Ancestral," *Danish Yearbook of Philosophy* 48–49 (2016): 115–137.

BEING WITH THE DEAD

Introduction

Home is where one starts from. As we grow older
The world becomes stranger, the patterns more complicated
Of dead and living.
—T. S. Eliot, "Four Quartets"

In *The Phenomenology of Spirit* Georg W. F. Hegel describes how the collective human spirit over the course of its gradual externalization falls apart into two separate ethical substances, manifested as *human law* and *divine law.*[1] Human law is the expression of a universality embodied in the state, whereas divine law is connected to an individuality manifested in the family. In the moral order of the state the individual recognizes itself as a universal being under universal obligations, whereas the system of the family binds the individual to an inner or "unconscious" ethical order. The obligation of the family members toward one another is said to be concentrated in one particular act: the proper handling of the body in death, in other words, in *burial.* When a citizen dies, he reaches universal fulfillment as a member of his political community. But from the viewpoint of the family this death also makes him into an "unreal impotent shadow."[2] The universality reached in death is from the viewpoint of the deceased a non-action. It is in relation to this passive subjection to nature's course that the specific obligation of the family manifests itself, or as Hegel writes: "The duty of the member of a family is on that account to add this aspect, in order that the individual's ultimate being, too, shall not belong solely to nature and remain something irrational, but shall be something done, and the right of consciousness asserted in it."[3]

By providing a proper burial for its dead member, the family can thus be seen as unconsciously carrying out a work of the rational universalization of spirit. What nature takes away from the individual in death—activity and initiative—the family members symbolically restore through a proper burial. But since destruction is inevitable, the work of the family vis-à-vis the dead cannot ultimately work against nature. Instead it will fulfill the work of nature, but now *as a conscious and willing act*. In the place of "every lower irrational individuality"—Hegel's euphemism for maggots and worms—it thus keeps the body from being dishonored by "unconscious appetites."[4] For Hegel it is significant that the body is ritually placed in the *earth* with which it will eventually unite, but the principal argument could carry over to cremation.[5]

In being bound by divine law, the members of a family are also bound to and by the dead themselves, in relation to whom their obligations are articulated. Since these obligations are generally not articulated as such but rather work as *forces* in relation to which the individual family members experience and perform their actions, they have the character of a *call* from the underworld, as a social pact between the dead and the living. Throughout this account, Hegel is glancing toward one particular narrative, Sophocles's *Antigone*. The tragic heroine is mentioned only in passing, but her destiny guides the argument. She is the sister of the dead Polyneices, who is refused burial by King Creon as punishment for having conspired against the state. She challenges the decree under the threat of the death penalty in order to give him a funeral, if only symbolically by strewing earth on his decaying body. In and through her destiny we have the most compelling testimony from Greek and ancient literature of the compulsion experienced by family members to bury their dead, even at the risk of their own death. In the case of Antigone, the urge to give honors to her dead brother ultimately leads her to being buried alive, which is the punishment given to her by the unyielding king. In Hegel's interpretation, Antigone's destiny bears testimony to the essential confrontation between two legal spheres and thus the two dimensions of spirit, the universal and the individual, as expressed in the state and the family.

Her tragic-sacrificial death is thus inscribed in a reconciliatory account of Spirit, which falls apart and unites again.

In the context of Hegel's social-political philosophy the analysis of the conflict between Creon and Antigone holds a central position. It captures a key movement in the dialectic of Freedom, which will gradually lead up to the development of the modern legal state in which the law of the family and the law of the polis come together, as developed in *The Philosophy of Right* (1821). In this work Hegel does not recall the analysis of burial, and in most accounts of his social philosophy it plays a marginal role, if it is even mentioned. Still the ethical dilemma posed by Sophocles's original drama and highlighted by Hegel's philosophical interpretation points toward a phenomenon with far-reaching implications: the relation to the dead as a foundation for sociality as such. When Antigone defiantly calls out: "I have longer to please the dead than to please the living here," she is speaking both of herself and of her dead brother, with whom she *is* at this point joined in a shared being.[6] How can and should we think of this allegiance? Is she simply "mad," as Creon repeatedly claims in the drama, or is there also a *truth* in her wild and uncompromising commitment to the dead? From the viewpoint of Hegel's reconciliatory dialectic, there is indeed a certain truth in her action, as she fulfills the duty of a family member vis-à-vis its dead. The fact that Creon does not recognize the relative legitimacy and necessity of this allegiance is also what leads to his own downfall, as he is later punished by fate in the drama. Thus, the drama and Hegel's analysis point toward the basic socio-ontological predicament *that humans live not only with the living but also with the dead.* There is a peculiar *being with* the dead that determines human existence down to its basic condition and sense of self.

When questioned by her sister, Ismene, Antigone defends her decision by declaring: "More time have I in which to win the favor of the dead, than of those who live; for I shall rest for ever there." When her sister tries to win her over to consider her obligation to the living and to herself, Antigone is unyielding. Her thinking and her action are already oriented and determined by the sense of loyalty to the dead. The commitment to the no-longer living expresses a temporality in which her own actions and life occupy but a small part. Her brother and her parents are gone. The dead are *past*. But it is a past that is open to a future in the sense that she, in and through her own mortality, is also *part of that which will have been.* In this sense her life is also a *historical* life as she lets her actions be oriented by a time *shared* across present, past, and future. In being led by a loyalty to *ancestors* rather than complying with the juridical-political power of the king, Antigone stands out as an exemplary *necropolitical* heroine, in her uncompromising commitment to caring for the dead in burial.

With the terms and expressions "being with the dead," "ancestrality," and "necropolitics" I have circumscribed the territory of the investigations that follow. They all point toward how what we often casually refer to as "historical consciousness" involves and implies a social ontology of the living and the dead, epitomized in the ritual of burial and a care for the dead. From a commonsense sociological perspective, the role and meaning of burials and graves may seem fairly innocent at first, as simply ritually organized ways of disposing of bodies in acts of social healing. But as we move closer, they become increasingly enigmatic and more difficult to delimit within conventional sociocultural-anthropological frameworks.

It was often stated as a universal anthropological fact that *humans bury their dead* (in the extended sense of caring for the bodies of the dead). Still, the interpretation of the *meaning*, origin, and inner teleology of this practice continues to challenge a conclusive theoretical grasp. A reason for this is that the limited spatiotemporal act of disposing of corpses (in whichever way it is performed) becomes meaningful only in a larger social context of what it means to be *with* the dead. Ultimately it points toward the open horizon of what we are accustomed to thinking of as historical culture and historical consciousness and the different ways in which humans have and inhabit a past. Reciprocally this also implies that the techniques and institutions through which historical culture maintains itself are also part of a larger legacy of continuing to *be with* and *care for* the dead. As humans seek to understand the past, they also continue to explore ways of inhabiting this past as ways of being with the dead.

It is Martin Heidegger who, in passing, and in a section of *Being and Time* that deals with how human existence or *Dasein* responds to the death of the other, first coins the expression "being with the dead" (*Mitsein mit dem Toten*) as an existential-ontological term.[7] But by juxtaposing this short passage with his more extensive description of historicity as constituted through an existential responsive confrontation with the dead as with those *having-been*, the analysis locates the problem of the historical as a "spectral" space between the living and the dead, in the sense given to this term by Jacques Derrida in his *Specters of Marx*. Through Emmanuel Levinas's and Derrida's critical confrontation with Heidegger's understanding of death and finitude it shows how the death of the other can no longer be contained as a marginal phenomenon on the fringe of authentic finite existence. Instead, it opens the space of historicity and of the historical as a social ontological, and thus also as a *haunto-logical*, problem of how humans are with those *having-been*.

To think history and historical consciousness through the category of *being with the dead* and through the exemplary phenomenon of burial is not to reduce history to a culture of piety, remembrance, or duty toward a particular community and their dead. Instead, it permits us to move across the border between the *ethical* and the *ontological*, as well as between the *practical* and the *theoretical* past, and also between *memory* and *history*. From the viewpoint of this domain, these dichotomies can be visualized as different aspects of a more fundamental existential condition. It is also important to maintain a cautious philosophical attitude toward what has become a common trope in the contemporary study of mortuary culture, which seeks to "reenchant" a "disenchanted" modernity that has presumably lost the sense of the natural bond between the living and the dead, captured by Zygmunt Bauman's description of how modernity "banished death and the dying out of sight and thus hopefully, out of mind."[8] Western modernity certainly displays many examples of a disenchanted, technical, and anonymous conception of death and of responses to it. But the philosophical task here is not to resacralize or reenchant a bond that was presumably broken or to invent or posit new forms of material agencies. Instead the challenge is to deepen our understanding of the domain of being with the dead as an existential apriori that can comprise different and even contradicting cultural responses. Looking beyond the critical arguments of Michel de Certeau and Pierre Nora, we also argue that history in its scholarly-academic sense does not simply mark the end of a living relation with the dead, just as it does not mark the end of an organic culture of memory. Instead the human-historical sciences should be seen as disciplined ways of inhabiting a more fundamental existential domain of being with the dead.

As the modern human sciences emerge in the eighteenth century and as they turn their interest toward the culture of death in the study of ancestor worship and burial rituals, they activate a politicized vocabulary that separates a presumably rational cult of the dead from its irrational counterpart. It was through their approach to the culture of death and the spirits of the dead, more perhaps than in any other area, that scholars became complicit in the system of colonial violence in ways that became apparent only in recent decades through the tormented necropolitical struggles over the remains of the dead in anthropological and archaeological archives. In this domain, scholars often found themselves stumbling intellectually without a clear orientation in their attempts to repair what was broken, sometimes professing the "respect for the dead" as a unique privilege of the culturally *other*, sometimes searching for an ethics of respect for the universal "rights" of the dead. The argument here is that only through a deeper understanding and articulation of the social-ontological phenomenon of being with the dead is it possible to address anew what it could possibly mean to live "authentically" in relation to the dead as also a question of what the living "owe" to the dead.

Creon's refusal to let Polyneices's body be buried is a *political* refusal, since it concerns the posterior having-been of a person within the community, in other words how he will be seen in the future. The actions in the play converge around the body-corpse of the dead, but they also concern the dead *himself* in a struggle of how this dead *person* will take part in the shared world of the dead and the living. The struggle is thus a paradigmatic necropolitical situation—of which we shall encounter several—where the fate of the community becomes concentrated in a dispute of how to care for its dead. Thus, it is also a *historical* situation as another name for the *having-been* of the other. Antigone comes on the stage with a clear sense of purpose. Her commitment to the dead is stronger than her commitment to the living. But her voice is not the only family response to the situation. Early on in the play Ismene tries to convince her not to challenge the king and to risk her life. Antigone scorns her for not respecting the holy allegiance to the dead. Later, and in a moment of desperation, Ismene calls out: "What comfort is my life if you leave me?" But Antigone remains cold and full of scorn for the sister, whom she leaves behind to mourn her.

The dialogue between the sisters gives us a concentrated microcosm of the inner pathology of how the living can be *claimed* by the dead and forced to choose sides. History and the past constitute a space from the outset surrounded by deep and powerful affects and emotions, not only of grief and mourning but also fear, revenge, and anxiety and of a sometimes overwhelming and uncompromising sense of responsibility and duty. But rather than speak of *responsibility*, it is perhaps more appropriate to speak of *responsiveness*, since the word "responsibility" promises to translate into moral and legal rules. In the domain of being with the dead there is no certainty or definitive rules. In the end, we can never really *know* what we owe the dead or what they demand from us. All we can see is that here we are confronted with questions of *justice* and of *obligation* that show how we belong to a polis not only of the living but also of the dead.

The term "necropolitics" was first introduced by Achille Mbembe in an article in 2003, as a complementary term to Foucault's concept of "biopolitics" and primarily as a name for the sovereign's right to kill, expanding an analysis from Agamben, who had already coined the notion of "thanatopolitics" in *Homo Sacer*.[9] Mbembe analyzes the different ways in which individuals and communities under such "necropower" can also turn themselves into vehicles of death in suicide and suicide killings, blurring the "lines between resistance and suicide, sacrifice and redemption, martyrdom and freedom."[10] He sees that such a politics of death can take different forms, depending on whether we follow Hegel or Bataille. Either death is seen as the ground for self-conscious action, or it is actualized as a foundation for an unlimited expenditure.

Here I use the concept in a different and more general way, not to designate the political control and mastery of death and dying but to encircle the sense and implications of how the political space is constituted and upheld by both the living and the dead. Politics—as communal organization and action—*involves* the dead through the ways in which the living community situates, responds to, and cares for its dead. It can have the forms of political burials and rituals of commemoration. But it can also involve the different ways in which legacies are created and maintained, so as to bind the living and the dead together in mutual commitment. It is not just a question of how the living *use* the remains of the dead for this or that purpose but of how the social bond between the dead and the living is maintained. This meaning of *necropolitics* also brings us closer to the original sense of *necro-polis*, the Greek word for "cemetery," as not only a space where the dead are hidden and stored away but as a political space in its own right, a polis of and for the dead, in relation to which the polis of the living continues to uphold and to maintain itself and in relation to which it orients its actions, and *on* which it sometimes literally bases and erects itself.

Chapter 1, "Thinking after Life: Historicity and *Having-Been*," gives the philosophical-phenomenological framework for the ensuing explorations. In its classic definition, phenomenology is the project of explicating the meaning of a phenomenon through an analysis of how it is constituted in and through intentionality. From the viewpoint of this methodology, the peculiar absent presence of the dead other marks both a limit and a challenge to develop new types of analyses. The chapter starts off from a marginal and posthumously published text from the late 1960s by the Czech phenomenologist Jan Patočka that seeks to address a "phenomenology of life after death." How can we have a secular and nonsuperstitious account of the way that the dead are somehow still there, or at least of the way in which they are not simply nothing? From Patočka's attempt to capture the core of this experience, I move to Derrida's preoccupation in his later years with the experience of mourning and memory and the strange present absence of the dead, for which he would develop a whole neogothic philosophical vocabulary of specters, ghosts, revenants, and hauntings that found a wide resonance in cultural theory in the last two decades. In his book *Specters of Marx* he indicates the possibility of a fully developed "phenomenology of spectrality," a promise that he never fulfilled but that he left as an open legacy.

For both Derrida and Levinas, Heidegger's account of death and finitude in *Being and Time* was paradigmatic for its philosophical significance but also for how it revealed an ethical and ontological lacuna in regard to the death of the other, a topic to which Heidegger devoted only marginal attention. Their joint verdict was that "Heidegger will have nothing to do with the revenant and with grief." According to Levinas, the experience of the death of the other goes deeper than the experience of our own finitude, since it opens a responsibility for the other's afterlife, which he exemplifies precisely with caring for the dead in burial. Against the backdrop of this important critique, I return to the sections on mortality in *Being and Time* to show how its attempt to describe the death of the other in fact does trigger a series of tentative phenomenological concepts for the ontological *claire-obscure* of life after death. Heidegger refers to "unliving" and "still remaining," and most important, he speaks of a peculiar existential mode of *Dasein*'s "being with the dead." On this basis I then move on to the main point of the chapter and to a key argument for the overall idea of the book, that it is in the existential-ontological analysis of *historicity* and of historical existence that the full implications of this existential predicament of being with the dead is made visible through his concept of *Dasein* as "having-been" (*Da-gewesen*). To be historical is to live with the dead. And at the core of this wide-ranging intergenerational intersubjectivity we find the question of burial as a generic term for caring for the other in and across death. This entire analysis requires that we read Heidegger against the grain, moving beyond his closed economy of authentic repetition and stressing the inescapable ethical ambiguity of our condition vis-à-vis those who have been. Once we recognize that we always live with the dead, the question returns: What do we owe them? Antigone's choice to die for the dead concentrates this dilemma. The chapter ends with a critical comparison between the analysis in *Being and Time* and Heidegger's own explicit interpretation of Antigone in a lecture series in 1942.

The book then proceeds to a multilayered discussion of how the phenomenon of burial in particular and mortuary culture in general were analyzed and understood in the human sciences. According to Hegel's interpretation, Antigone is acting in the interest of the survival and freedom of *spirit as such* when she professes her loyalty to the dead rather than to the living and in displaying it through an act of burial. This implies that there is already a posited metaphysical sociality that comprises the dead and the living in the form of *Spirit*, as the name of that which survives and transcends individual finitude and mortality. This way of looking at burial, as issuing from communal spirituality that transcends the individual, is not confined to Hegel's idealist speculation. On the contrary, it can also be detected as the underlying framework in the single most quoted text in the sociology of mortuary culture, an essay written by Émile Durkheim's most gifted young student Robert Hertz in 1907. In this text Hertz develops the idea that "death has a specific meaning for the social consciousness as an object of collective representation."[11] Chapter 2, "Thanatologies: On the Social Meanings of Burial," is entirely devoted to an analysis of this canonical text in the study of mortuary culture or thanatology. It focuses on the significance of Hertz's distinction between a "first" and "second burial" and how it points toward a larger temporal and historical framework for understanding mortuary culture in ways that also challenge the "reconciliatory" sociological model and its Hegelian foundations. In bringing out the underlying philosophical schema of this theory, the interpretation also contrasts the Durkheimian theoretical response to death with the existential grief of the scientific community in the wake of the war and its dead, including Hertz himself, as expressed in a remarkable obituary by Marcel Mauss.

In Chapter 3, "Ancestrality: Ghosts, Forefathers, and Other Dead," the disputed phenomenon of so-called ancestor worship is addressed as a mode of being with the dead. In summarizing the origins and transformation of this topic in the human sciences from Hegel onward, the analysis shows how the colonial distinction between civilization and savagery was partly enacted as a "politics of the ghost." A philosophical hierarchy of types of ancestral piety was established, where a culture of "spirit" was deemed superior to cultures that worship the "ghosts" of ancestors, exemplified in particular in the work of James Frazer. Ultimately this theoretical-hierarchical depiction of modes of being with the dead would be located by Freud in the interior of the self as its own primitive core. The chapter discusses how the attempts among self-critical anthropologists to distance themselves from the colonial legacy of the discipline by reconceptualizing the ontology of ancestral ties also led to an inverted primitivization of the other, in an upgrading of traditional piety per se. In its place, I argue for a transcultural understanding of *ancestrality* as a generic dimension of being with the dead, with an open agenda and where the question of how to interact with the dead is never decided once and for all.

Chapter 4, "Necropolitics: Contested Communities and Remains of the Dead," focuses on the topic of necropolitics through a wide array of examples of contemporary political burials and reburials and how they challenge standard sociology to encompass not only the living but also the dead. In their attempts to theorize phenomena that range from the grave of the unknown soldier, to the recovery of the bones of ancestors stored in museums, to the restoration of cemeteries of oppressed minorities, social scientists and anthropologists often found themselves grappling for explanatory schemata taken from ancient and primitive layers of human religious sensibility. And often these analyses were accompanied by an explicit wish to challenge "Weberian disenchantment" and introduce new types of "agency." But as we face a surge of necropolitical activism, it is not to a neo-enchanted sociology or to theories of material agency that we should first turn. Instead, we need to develop a social ontology that includes what it means for humans to also be *with* the dead. Here I return to the social phenomenology of Alfred Schütz and his theory of the world of "predecessors" as the most elaborated attempt to link Weberian sociology with Husserlian and existential phenomenology on this question. In a final section I confront Schütz's analysis of the world of predecessors and the space of history with the theory of spectral historicity, building partly on the implicit philosophical consequences of how he himself worked and wrote *in the wake* of Weber, as a paradigmatic predecessor in his own right.

Chapter 5, "Ossuary Hermeneutics: Necropolitical Sites of Archaeology," is devoted to archaeology as the discipline most deeply involved with graves, both theoretically and practically. It is built around three "sites," or case studies, that display how burial sites constitute neutral scientific facts and containers of historical material. But these complex and many-layered phenomena also expose the discipline of archaeology itself in its ambiguous necropolitical position as both observer and participant, as both caretaker and desecrator of graves. The first site discusses the evolutionary anthropological approach to mortuary culture and how it seeks to locate the "origin" of burial through the study of nonhuman primates. It leads up to the problem of the *symbol* and of *symbolization* as the arch-gesture of caring for the dead. The second site recapitulates how the field of archaeology from the 1970s onward fell apart along its social-scientific and humanist-hermeneutic fault line precisely over the issue of how to conceptualize graves and burials. Through the critical elaboration of the meaning of ancient burials the temporal and the historical within history itself gradually emerged, highlighting the question of what it means to be situated within the space of being with the dead as also an archaeological predicament in its own right. The third site recapitulates how burial archaeology from around the same time became involved in necropolitical struggles over human remains that challenged its entire ethos and sense of self as a cultural-historical endeavor. Here I critically analyze the responses to these challenges and, in particular, how this struggle resulted in the remarkable composition of the first document in human history that explicitly speaks of the universal "rights" of the dead.

Chapter 6, "Visiting the Land of the Dead: History as Necromancy," presents Odysseus's travel to the underworld and his confrontation with the Sirens as a poetic anticipation of historical sensibility and historiographical writing as it is subsequently developed by Hecataeus and Herodotus. The ultimate deed of the hero is to travel across space and time to the domain of those having-been in order to bring back their voices to the living. From there I move to an extended critical discussion with Michel de Certeau, who in *The Writing of History* presented the historian as a melancholic necromancer who operates on the threshold of the living and the dead that he both "seeks, honors, and buries." In the end I argue that Certeau's compelling analysis remains restricted by a structuralist and constructivist framework that presupposes a too strict limit between the living and the dead. He is also guided by a conventional contemporary understanding of burial as "disposal" and as a way to do away with death. The strict anthropological-philosophical distinction between cultures that presumably live with their dead and cultures that no longer "believe" in this bond has to be rethought. It is as a continuation and modification of a culture of death and communication with the dead that historiography is understandable and, thereby, also its inner disputes over how to access the past. The last part of this chapter discusses the so-called Homeric question as an exemplary illustration of this dilemma.

The chapter thus moves in a loop. First Odysseus's journey to the land of the dead is presented as the original site of the historical imagination and desire. Then the very nature and standing of the Homeric epic as a historical source is presented as a case in point that shows how the historical imagination both sought and shattered its access to the presumed origin of the text and its historical author. In doing so, however, it also reveals how it continues to inhabit the world with the dead.

Among contemporary historians of antiquity, the person who has perhaps thought most deeply on this intersection between history and caring for the dead is the German Egyptologist and co-originator of cultural memory studies Jan Assmann, whose joint work in these fields gives him a particular place in the context of the questions that occupy us here. Chapter 7, "The Tomb of Metaphysics: Writing, Memory, and the Arts of Survival," brings together his work on Egyptian mortuary culture and cultural memory. It shows how the two are inextricably related and how the project of a theory of cultural memory emerges from the attempt to understand the workings of technologies of survival beyond death in this ancient context. Within Greek culture, historiography emerges as a genre of writing after only a few centuries of literacy. In the Egyptian context, however, three millennia of writing did not generate a single work of historiography comparable to that of the Greek historians. This motivates the question concerning the site and representation of historical time as the transindividual space of the *having-been* in the Egyptian context. From Egypt we have a large body of artifacts that show how the new technology of *writing* was integrated from early on within mortuary ritual and culture as a supreme medium of spiritual preservation. The art of embalming and saving bodies and the construction of stone burial monuments blend with pictorial and alphabetical writing as means of symbolization.

As a theory explicitly concerned with the inner structure and technical means of maintaining the link between the dead and the living, the theory of cultural memory is the most important among contemporary attempts to chart the existential-ontological domain of being with the dead. Yet in its philosophical positioning of itself, and in particular in its response to Kierkegaard's and Heidegger's account of mortality, it also displays the inherent tendency in the human sciences of objectifying through anthropologization the nature of this domain. The chapter recalls the early explicit connection between deconstruction and cultural memory studies and then shows how the latter move in the direction of a more Hegelian and Durkheimian notion of collective spirit. Ultimately Assmann disparages modernity for having lost the living link between the living and dead that presumably prevailed within Egyptian culture. Instead of confronting the precarious transcultural "hauntological" predicament of living *after* as also a living *with*, the theory thereby turns into a theory of distinct and relative cultural formations. The chapter concludes that with the theory of cultural memory we come closer to the inner workings and dynamics of being with the dead than in any other current theoretical pursuit, yet at the same time we are shielded from its more difficult transcultural ethical and political reality.

In the current predicament of the human sciences and in politics and religion in general, often plagued by destructive pathologies of traditionality and ancestrality, there is a need to reflect deeper and more critically on what it means to inhabit the earth as a place where life *has been*. There is a need to see and find words that can respond to the ontological reality of being with the dead. There is a need to resist the temptation of objectifying the lives of the dead as the political, cultural, or spiritual property of the living, just as there is a need to move beyond an unreflective awe before their shadowlike being and demand. Seen from the perspective of the present, the dead are pitiable, always weaker than the living whose blood their shadows need in order to be heard. But from the perspective of the dead and the dying, the living are just short, flickering lights waiting to take their place among them in the temporality of *having-been*.

Philosophy is the art of dying, Socrates declares in the *Phaedo*. To this we should add: it is also the art of learning how to live with the dead and to share the earth with those who have been. Life is a life *after*, as inheritance, ancestry, legacy, and fate. All wounds are not healed by time. Time itself is a wound within which life prevails. We do not overcome the finitude of death; we share it, as we share it with the life to which we give birth and for which we too will belong along with those having-been.

Thinking after Life

HISTORICITY AND *HAVING-BEEN*

> Death is a Dialogue between
> The Spirit and the Dust
> "Dissolve" says Death—The Spirit "Sir
> I have another Trust"—
> Death doubts it—Argues from the Ground—
> The Spirit turns away
> Just laying off for evidence
> An Overcoat of Clay.
>
> —Emily Dickinson, Poem 976

A Phenomenology of Survival

Among the posthumously published papers by the Czech phenomenologist Jan Patočka, there is a short and unfinished piece titled "Phenomenology of Life after Death," probably written in the late 1960s.[1] Here Patočka raises the question, How can we speak consistently about life after death without presupposing the existence of some kind of "substantial carrier" and "double" of this life, as "soul" or "spirit"? How can we as phenomenologists, with our strict demand to stay with the things themselves in their immediate givenness, speak of something nonexistent and nonevidential without giving way to a "metaphysical fiction"?

The first and preliminary response to such a temptation would be to simply say, no, this is a territory on which no meaningful discourse can legitimately be pronounced. To speak as a phenomenological philosopher is essentially to speak from the viewpoint of the living, of and for the living. The dead are no longer here. They have no presence. They offer no evidence. Yet, he adds, we cannot deny that the dead do not "entirely disappear, for the other continues to live in us. . . . It is of course only a precarious life, dependent on us, not immortality, but a simple living on that does not last longer than we live." The life of the dead other is not an independent self-sustaining life, and still it is not nothing. So far, he adds, no one has tried to give a phenomenological account of this strange phenomenon of how the dead other somehow continues to live and how in a certain sense there is "life after death." For such a phenomenon exists; indeed, he says, it exists "without any doubt." Therefore, it also deserves to be made into a theme of phenomenological analysis.

One reason that this has not been attempted before, Patočka suggests, is that it provides "so little comfort." But through phenomenology, as the unique method available for such an enterprise, the continued life of the dead shall now be made visible in its peculiar presence. As his starting point, he then turns to intersubjectivity. Human existence does not exist on its own and by itself. We are beings for ourselves, but we are also beings for the other. From the viewpoint of original temporality we are in a strict sense "totally private" and inaccessible to the other, who reaches us only from an "outside." Yet the image we have of ourselves is constituted through the other. Indeed, it is only the other who can see us, as it were, "objectively." In this sense our lives are already from the outset mediated, exteriorized, and thus in a sense "alienated." Patočka vacillates in his formulations as he tries to express this enigma of the self through the other, where the self finds itself as both an original experiential pole and as always already deferred in relation to itself. This is also true of the other, whose existence is dependent on me through the images and representations I have of him or her, and vice versa. In this sense, humans live and become manifest *through* each other.

When the other is dead, he or she continues in me, in what from his or her own viewpoint amounts to a "nonexistence" and for me a "nonoriginarity," yet as somehow being there. This "somehow" is the crux of the whole issue: In what form of being does the other continue to be? As long as the other lives, there is a reciprocity where we live and exist through each other. With death, this reciprocity is canceled. The dead do not respond; they do not collaborate, for "they accomplish nothing at all" (*il n'effectue rien du tout*). Referring explicitly to the memory of his father, Patočka states that all that remains are certain "characteristics" that somehow retain the "essence of a person," a look, a voice, a gesture, and so forth. The individual person is gone, yet in this diluted form he remains in the memory of the son. He even states that those who have been close to a person have the special task of "incorporating the other in some form or other in their lives." In this phenomenon of *incorporation* of the dead in and by the living, we come across what he refers to as an "original consciousness of life with the dead," which guarantees that the nonexistence of the other is not just a non-being but also a *positive* continuation of life.

This tentative formulation of a continuation of the dead among the living through "incorporation" marks the speculative peak of this short sketch. The rest of the unfinished article contains a discussion of Kojève and the dialectics of desire and a critical reflection on Sartre and his exaggerated subjectivism. Against Sartre, Patočka states that we reach authenticity not just through ourselves but also through each other. And at the very end of the text he returns again to the experience of death of the other, but now explicitly as also a problem of *grief* and *mourning*. These affects can induce a false consciousness of a continued reciprocity where there in fact is none, which he likens to the phenomenon of "phantom limbs." In response to this pain of loss, human existence must ultimately regain its sense of reality and continue its life without the full reciprocity of the other.

In her editorial comment to the text, Erica Abrams mentions an unverified "rumor" that it was composed following the death of Patočka's wife, which would date it to 1967. Part of its content, especially the criticism of Sartre, would suggest an earlier date. A letter to Walter Biemel indicates that the topic was still on his mind as late as 1976, shortly before his own premature death, and that he was planning to write more about it. Whichever is true, it seems clear that Patočka's thoughts are at least partly motivated by a personal experience of loss. This is suggested by the references to the memory of his father and the remarks on the need of incorporating and caring for the dead other. Seen from this perspective, the text could also be read as a philosophical work of mourning, a reflexive attempt to come to terms with personal loss and its reverberations in memory, where the dead other is internalized and somehow maintained after death in and through a truncated reciprocity.

Other Phantoms

As a philosophical work of mourning Patočka's sketch anticipates Jacques Derrida's thoughts on the workings of memory in relation to the dead in his *Mémoirs for Paul de Man* (1987). There Derrida also tries to articulate the peculiar and ultimately paradoxical experience of what it means to preserve someone in memory.[2] When we experience painful loss, he writes, we say to ourselves that the departed is not fully departed but that somehow he or she *lives on in our memory*.[3] Yet at the same time it is clear that memory cannot keep or preserve the other, who is irrevocably gone. Should we then, he asks, with an implicit reference to Freud, look upon this ambition to preserve the dead other as only a "narcissistic refusal" to recognize inevitable loss? His answer is no, because the structure of this relation between subjectivity and the dead other and memory is more complex. The presence of the other in the self is the experience of something that is "greater" than the self. And the possibility of mourning someone is ultimately a dimension of and even co-constitutive of what it means to be a self.

"Memory" thus becomes a name not just for an inner trace of the other in the self but also for the possibility of subjectivity as such. It is by being outside itself, in a continued relation to what is other than oneself, that human existence is what it is. Patocka never found the opportunity to develop these ideas further, but in the case of Derrida it would gradually emerge as a central theme in his later work, notably in *Specters of Marx* (1993), *Aporias* (1993), and *The Gift of Death* (1995). In *Specters of Marx* he recalls that the existential imperative to *live* also implies an imperative to address *death*.[4] Learning to live is learning to exist between life and death, in the existential stretch constituted by one's own life span, from not yet being born to no longer existing, but also to learn to live in relation to those no longer there. In order to describe this existential in-between, he suggests that we think of it in terms of "the phantom" (*le fantôme*). Unlike in Patočka's text, the *phantomatic* here is not simply the name of an illusion to be overcome by a rational work of mourning. Instead it is presented as a positive phenomenological category in its own right, as designating a mode of being shared between the living and the dead.

Even though Derrida does not address it explicitly in the book on Marx, the idea of the *phantom* and the *phantomatic* had first come to him through his collaboration with the Romanian-French psychoanalysts Nicholas Abraham and Maria Torok.[5] In Abraham and Torok, the "psychic phantom" is the name of a sealed remnant of a traumatic event that exists as a separate and ultimately inaccessible "crypt" within a psyche, manifested only indirectly through its somatic and psychic effects. It is a structure that can be inherited and passed from generation to generation while becoming increasingly inaccessible, moving from the silenced to the unthinkable. At the center of this theory are the experience of death and the challenge of having to handle the loss of close kin. In Abraham and Torok the basic difference in ways of mourning is between "introjection" and "incorporation" (concepts that they take over and elaborate from Ferenczi and Freud). To normal mourning belongs the "introjecting" not only of the person but also of the realization of the loss as such. An incomplete work of mourning, however, can take the form of an "incorporation" where the survivors believe themselves to somehow be capable of "saving" the dead by interiorizing the lost other within themselves as the other's keeper. The refusal to let the loss have its way can result in the other being hidden in an interior as something to return to in a secret, forbidden, and even possibly lustful communion. Opposed to this inner and perverse death rite, Abraham and Torok see the supposedly more authentic and introjective mourning as characterized by the ability to accept, contain, and hold absence and loss.[6]

While being inspired by Abraham's and Torok's work, from which he inherited the concepts of the "phantom" and the "crypt" as ways to depict phenomena of survival and continuity, Derrida also distanced himself from their thinking on some points. This is true in particular of what he found to be their too-rigid distinction between introjection and incorporation. He asks if it is not the case that also "normal" grief in a certain sense preserves the other precisely as other (a living dead person) inside the self. The question could always be asked, he writes, "whether or not 'normal' mourning preserves the object *as other* (a living person dead) inside me."[7] While being loyal to the overall way of analyzing the process of grieving in its complex affective and semantic vicissitudes, he senses something more in these concepts that take them and the whole problem beyond the more strictly defined psychological-psychoanalytical context. For Derrida, *the phantomatic* becomes a way of reaching into an absent presence, an ontological shadow zone where the living and the dead cross, or rather from the point where the separation between them can be thought differently, not just as an *affliction* but as an ontological-ethical category in its own right.

Levinas and the Temporality of the Dead Other

The lectures that Levinas presented as his last course at the Sorbonne in 1975 and published in 1993 as *God, Death, and Time* also provide important background for how this theme was developed by Derrida.[8] Through a detailed critical reading of Heidegger's analysis of death in *Being and Time*, Levinas explicitly sought to move beyond what he found to be its too-restricted conception of authentic finitude as understandable only from the perspective of individual mortality. Instead he too sought to approach death from the experience of the dying other, insisting that death does not simply reduce the other to corpse or decomposition but instead lets the other be "entrusted" to me, as my "responsibility." Thus, he could argue for the need to move beyond the supposedly solipsistic and subject-centered analysis of personal finitude in Heidegger, toward a domain of shared finitude, and ultimately also a more profound experience of personal finitude. And here he suggested that it is perhaps only the death of the other that truly reveals the temporal in life and that it is the care for the dead other that "opens thinking" toward the infinite. When the other moves out of time, into the time of the past, making the survivors responsible for this passage, then a new kind of relation is also established to something wholly other, to a time beyond time and to transcendence, forging a new community between the dead and the living, a world where the dead can prevail and where the living can be with them.

Like Patočka, Levinas is looking for ways of transforming the experience of loss of the other into a phenomenology of *living-after*, while avoiding commitment to a metaphysical belief in afterlife.[9] More radically than

Patočka he seeks to let the unique experience of the death of the other become a critical lever for destabilizing the experiential horizon of the subject itself. At the heart of this experience is the standing before a *non-response* that is at the same time a *responsibility* and a duty to a living spirit or "soul" of the other. This experience does something to the subject; it affects and ruptures its identity, exposing it to a passivity in itself where it is affected by a non-presence. In the end "intentionality" is no longer the final word on human existence, since it is not only a future-oriented drive or conatus but also "a disinterestedness and adieu."[10] It is not its own mortality that exposes the ego to its ultimate fate but its exposure to what transcends it in the gesture of farewell.

In his detailed critical reading of Heidegger's analysis of death in *Being and Time*, Levinas repeatedly returns to what he diagnoses as the latter's inability to understand death as anything other than annihilation and end of being-in-the-world.[11] There is, he argues, a sharing of the other's death that goes deeper than one's own mortality, precisely through this shared responsibility. It is when looking for other ways to conceptualize this relation that he also comes upon Hegel's analysis of burial. In caring for the dead through burial, Levinas writes, the subject demonstrates that the "act of burial is a relationship with the deceased, and not with the cadaver." It is an act whereby the family makes the dead a "member of a community" and thus is also a way of transforming the dead into "living memory."[12] But whereas Hegel saw the act of burial as a way of symbolically manifesting the universal and free nature of spirit across the threshold of individual death, Levinas is here pointing toward another dimension. In his reading, the encounter with the death of the other and with the other as dead reveals a unique temporality at the heart of subjectivity that is connected precisely to a responsibility for the one no longer there.

Aporetics and Mortuary Culture

In the same year that saw the publication of Levinas's lectures, Derrida published the small book *Aporias*, which is a series of meditations on death, partly motivated by his reading of Philippe Ariès's monumental anthropological study of death, *L'homme devant la mort*.[13] Here he returns to Heidegger's analysis of mortality as a critical lever against the anthro-pological and historical claim to speak authoritatively on death. He also distances himself from a critique voiced by many historians and anthro-pologists from the 1970s onward against a purported cultural "silence" on matters of death and the ensuing aspiration to restore death to its "rightful place."[14] This project will be in vain, he writes, since ultimately there is no *natural* way of dying and even less of caring for the dead, just as there is no pure culture of death, since "dying is neither entirely natural, nor cul-tural." Seen from this critical perspective, the existential-ontological anal-ysis of finitude developed by Heidegger "includes beforehand the work of the historian."[15] In order to have a cultural history of death, we already have to presuppose the concepts of culture and history. And still respond-ing to Ariès, he states that "culture itself, culture in general, is essentially, before anything, even a priori, the culture of death."[16] Culture is a his-tory of death, and culture always involves some cult of ancestors, some ritualization of mourning and sacrifice, including institutional places and modes of burial, even if "only for the ashes of incineration."

Throughout the book he gives credit to what he sees as the unsur-passable originality of the analysis of death in *Being and Time*, especially for its strict adherence to the *finite* perspective and how Heidegger, as opposed to Hegel, thinks from within finitude and not from a position where death and finitude have always already been overcome. But in the end he too marks his distance from Heidegger and the existential analytic when it comes to the question of *the death of the other*. In these passages, which explicitly recall Levinas, Derrida echoes the latter's words that "it is for the death of the other that I am responsible, to the point of including myself in death." And just like Levinas he concludes that Heidegger and the existential analytic "does not want to have anything to do with the revenant and with grief," suggesting that if Heidegger were ever to touch upon such topics, he would most likely reduce them to psychological aber-rations.[17] In a similar vein as his critical remark concerning Abraham and Torok, Derrida wants to retain the possibility of seeing "mourning and ghosting (*revenance*), spectrality or living on, surviving" as "non-derivable categories" in their own right. He points in the direction of what such an analysis could contain by just listing a series of topics: "there is no politics without an organization of the time and space of mourning, without a topolitology of the sepulcher, without an anamnesic and thematic relation to the spirit as ghost (*revenant*), without an open hospitality to the guest as ghost, whom one holds, just as he holds us, hostage."[18]

In *Specters of Marx*, written around the same time, Derrida experiments more extensively with these postphenomenological terms in an attempt to address the intersection between the living and the dead as a way of approaching the constitution of political and historical communities. The "spectral" is here one name for this indeterminate space between the dead and the living and also a distance or difference within time itself and that which is never fully itself but always divided, carrying a past and anticipating a future. As in many of the later texts, the topic is not systematically developed but only hinted at and suggested as a future task. In a footnote to the last section in *Specters of Marx* he suggests the possibility of a "phenomenology of spectrality" that should be carried out "with good Husserlian logic, cutting out a limited, relative field within a regional discipline" and that should explore systematically the "original experience of haunting."[19] In the end, however, it would be more than just a regional ontology, since the problem of the spectral is said to point to the fundamental phenomenological themes of ideality, intentionality, and the very idea of an intentional object. The latter does not belong to the world nor to the mind but to a third and indeterminate space of "meaning." With such a radicalization of the phenomenological enterprise, Derrida writes, "the possibility of the other and of mourning" would be written into the very phenomenality of the phenomenon. In *Specters of Marx* all of this remains a tentative anticipation of something yet to be developed. Husserl is mentioned in the quoted footnote, and in that book Heidegger is recalled only in passing. As it stands, the book therefore leaves open the question of how and to what extent the question of the spectral is indeed possible to develop further in phenomenological terms.

Partly as a direct consequence of Derrida's book, the last two decades have witnessed an invasion of "ghosts," "revenants," and "hauntings" in cultural theory.[20] But throughout these new experiments in "hauntology" there were no real attempts to develop Derrida's idea of a phenomenology of the spectral, and in this literature the references to the phenomenological-hermeneutic background of the topic are mostly absent. For both Levinas and Derrida—and at least implicitly for Patočka—Heidegger is the primary reference point in their attempt to develop an understanding of finitude. They all stress what they take to be a decisive lacuna and maybe even a structural limit in his exposition. Still they seem to agree that it is only from the perspective of the existential analytic that the phenomenological question of death and finitude can initially be posed in an illuminating way.

The idea here is to return to this ambiguous and disputed legacy of Heidegger's analysis of finitude and the death of the other in *Being and Time* in order to see how it responds to the criticism leveled against it. It is true that the experience of mourning and the "ghost" of the dead other are largely absent in Heidegger, as claimed by both Levinas and Derrida. Yet the underlying phenomenological movement of his analysis is less clearcut. It is after all in *Being and Time* that the existential category of "being with the dead" is first introduced, if only in passing and in a context intent on downplaying its significance. In order to elicit and trace the presence of this topos in Heidegger's work, we therefore need to read him partly against the grain of the manifest text, exploring the existential-analytical link between the question of the dead other and the problem of the meaning and possibility of history.

The purpose of such an exercise is not to restore Levinas's and Derrida's critical interventions back to their Heideggerian roots. It is an attempt to let their criticisms resonate in relation to the question of historicity as the existential foundation of history and historical awareness, especially in relation to the dubious ideal of "authentic historicity" as ultimately a question of our ethical responsibility toward the dead. What we find when we trace the question of the dead and being with the dead to the core dynamic of human historicity is not just a purified and authentic individual and collective resoluteness as suggested by Heidegger's analysis. Instead, we are led to a contested space of conflicting loyalties where the subject is always already called to respond to the dead—indeed where its historical belonging and historicity can be thought only within the larger existential domain of a being-with that it can never fully master but only hope to inhabit in a responsible way.[21] In this territory Heidegger also operated and navigated, exploring and succumbing to its passions both in his personal and political life and in his philosophical choices. The latter is witnessed not least in his troubling reading in 1942 of Sophocles's *Antigone* and of Antigone's and Ismene's confrontation on the issue of the loyalty to the dead.

Heidegger and the Death of the Other

The overall argument of *Being and Time* rests on the premise that even though human existence is always closest to itself, it tends conceptually to misrepresent itself and live estranged from its own basic existential condition. This is the reason that the *constructive* enterprise of developing an existential analysis must also run parallel to a *destructive* dismantling of the tradition of metaphysics and of inherited theories of human being and existence. A genuine and authentic (*eigentlich*) understanding of existence requires us to move beyond the alienated and alienating objectification of life and its inclination to represent itself through that which is not itself, what the book also speaks of as "falling prey" to inherited modes of discourse. Instead of relying on explanatory schemata that concern objects in the world, human existence should try to understand itself through concepts that are generated from within the movement and potential of existence itself as lived, from the perspective of *possibility* rather than *actuality*, and thus ultimately from the perspective of the temporality of *becoming*.

Throughout its different stations one and the same argument is rehearsed in new constellations, where objectified and objectifying conceptions of existence are contrasted with new and critical terms through which life can presumably grasp itself in a more "authentic" way. Already at the outset of the book, Heidegger questions that what is simply given as present objects (*Vorhanden*) is ontologically primary by showing how they presuppose the primordial givenness of meaningful and useful things to hand (*Zuhandenheit*). In a similar way objective physical space is reinterpreted as in fact secondary in relation to lived spatial structures where *Dasein* orients itself in de-distancing (*Entfernung*) and directionality (*Ausrichten*). And the everyday experience of being an "ego" is shown to rest on a deeper and enabling structure of "self" and of "being-with." In the most important part of the analysis he challenges the conventional ways of designating and understanding *time* as the objective framework of events. In its place, he develops the account of existential temporality (*Zeitlichkeit*) as the most primordial level of meaning formation and as the culmination of the entire existential analytic.

The persistent challenge throughout the book is to conceptualize life from the perspective of its *potentiality* rather than through the categories of its objective being. Nowhere is this challenge more acute than in the sections that explicitly try to think the nature of finitude and mortality.[22] Here the issue at stake is to think human existence or *Dasein* as a whole. After having determined its essence in the first part of the book as being-in-the-world and as care (*Sorge*), Heidegger raises the question of how this presumed totality could be conceptually grasped and articulated. Existence is delimited by birth and death, thus constituting what appears as a finite stretch of life. To really think its totality, however, we cannot simply rest with an understanding of it as a life process, delimited by death, as if death were somehow outside life or simply its outer limit. Death *belongs* to life, and life is a being-toward-death in being permanently open to the possibility of its nonpossibility. This motivates him to pose the question. What would a proper and presumably authentic way of conceptually grasping death amount to? In other words, what is it really to *know* death? We think that we know death simply because we experience it all around us. But what we experience is always the death of the other, not death as our death or as *my* death. We should not simply take the medical, biological, and social "fact of death" for granted as our source of knowledge and reflection when we seek to understand mortality because death, as he writes, is ultimately a phenomenon of "Dasein as possibility."[23] Somehow death must be grasped and conceptualized as a phenomenon of life, of this life itself from the viewpoint of the living as their utmost possibility, indeed as the "possibility of impossibility" as the definition reads.[24]

From this perspective, the question of the death of the other will appear only as a negative limit phenomenon, a distraction from the genuine realization of inescapable individual mortality. But in the course of this brief outline of the meaning of the death of the other Heidegger also comes across a phenomenon that challenges the methodological confines of his argument. When the other *Dasein* has reached its "completion" (its *Gänze*), he writes, it becomes a "no-longer-being-in-the-world." But how is it that we can understand this phenomenon of having left the world? On one level it means that something simply no longer is there. Yet on another level it still is there, but now as *a being no-longer-alive*. In the dying of others, Heidegger writes, a "remarkable" phenomenon occurs: the sudden transition or reversal (*Umschlag*) of *Dasein* or *life*—to a "no-longer" *Dasein*. It is as if the end of *Dasein* were suddenly the beginning of another type of being but now in the order of a purely present entity, as *corpse*. But, he continues, even if the dead body can become the concern of a "pathological anatomy" that will always be oriented by an idea of the living, this description does not exhaust its phenomenological meaning. For it fails to capture the peculiar sense in which this being "is still remaining" (*nochverbleibende*) and thus is not representable by the purely corporeal. It is "more" than lifeless (*leblose*). It is something "unliving" (*Unlebendiges*), and as such it can be the object of multiple concerns, "as in funeral rites, burial, and cults of graves."[25]

The mourners are still with the other, in the mode of a care that is characteristic of being-with others, not the kind of care that is given to objects. A dead body is not taken care of in the same way we take care of artifacts. We continue to be with them, in a world that continues to give meaning and significance to our peculiar mode of being with those no longer there, even though they have, as it were, "left" this world "behind" (*zurückgelassen*). In "lingering together with him in mourning and com-memorating, those remaining behind *are with him*, in a mode of concern which honors him" in a way that should not be confused with a caring for things at hand.[26] And to this Heidegger adds, "In such a being-with the dead [*Mitsein mit dem Toten*] the deceased himself is no longer factically 'there.'" To be sure, being-with in a genuine sense always means to be with-the-other in one and the same world. And the one who has died has left our world, the world from which the ones that live can be with him. Therefore, this being-with could never qualify as being-with in the full sense of the word. And yet it is not nothing. Thus, Heidegger's existential analytic had already pointed out, or perhaps stumbled across, almost as if in passing, the same strange and uncertain sociality that we found in the works of Patočka, Levinas, and Derrida.

After this excursus, Heidegger returns to the principal theme of the paragraph, to show that the true meaning of death and finitude cannot be grasped via such a being-with the other as dead. The loss that belongs to and defines death is here not the loss of the being who really dies but the loss of the one who remains in the world that the dead have left. And the fact that we, as mourners, are still there in this same shared world in our grief for the other is also what prevents us from truly grasping what it means to die. For we do not truly experience the death of the other; at most we only witness it because we are with them in their death, as it were "near by."[27]

These reflections sum up what he has to say in this particular part of the book concerning the dead other. As already stated, the primary purpose of the analysis was never to provide a separate phenomenology of the deceased or of an existential category of being-with the dead but rather to serve as a critical introduction to the question of the existential meaning of individual finitude and being-toward-death. Its purpose was to establish that the death of the other cannot ultimately help us understand what it means for us to die. Instead, this is something that we must approach from the experience of anticipating our own end as the permanent possibility of nonpossibility or impossibility. The genuine existential truth of death is not the general truth that "one dies" but that *I am mortal.*

This overriding purpose of the analysis and its stress on individual mortality stand at the center of Levinas's and Derrida's critiques and their conclusion, quoted previously, that Heidegger "does not want to have anything to do with the revenant and with grief." But even though the death of the other from the perspective of the overall direction and thrust of the analysis is of subordinate significance when elaborating a nonobjectifying phenomenological description of human finitude, we have seen how it nevertheless leads Heidegger toward the same elementary phenomenon that Derrida will later speak of as *spectral existence.* The dead are not just possible *objects* of concern for the living. They have a peculiar mode of being that leads him to introduce a series of new phenomenological concepts in this particular section of the text, of the "still-remaining" (*noch-verbleibenes*) and "un-living" (*un-lebendiges*), that anticipate both Patočka's and Derrida's analyses.

For Levinas the crux of the matter ultimately turns on the chiastic reversal of Heidegger's dictum that finitude is constituted by "possibility of impossibility," which he wants to replace with the "impossibility of possibility." The two formulations could appear interchangeable, yet they bring out two very different dimensions of the temporality of finitude.

Whereas the first expression captures finitude from the active and pro-active perspective of life as it reaches toward its utmost limit, the other captures finitude as a *passivity* that is shared between the living and the no-longer living. It is precisely this sense of a *solidarity* with the dead other that Heidegger ultimately sets aside in his ambition to grasp the genuine and authentic sense of finitude. This is at least one way of summarizing the difference between him and Levinas on this pivotal issue.

While recognizing the validity of Levinas's (and Derrida's) criticism, it is important to see how Heidegger in his own way thereby also opens the door toward an exploration of a peculiar and irreducible intersubjective ontology of a being with the dead. The very expression "being with the dead" is his after all, and it occurs just at the point in the argument when the topic of the care for the other in death is actualized, even though the context is meant to question the ontological priority of the death of the other.[28] For Heidegger it is essential that his analysis is an analysis on the basis of and from the perspective of *this* world. In a later section, he even states this explicitly: "Our analysis remains purely 'this-worldly.'"[29] Yet through his own observations and reflections, he has come across the question of what it means that within this world there is also a being-*with* those who have left it. What happens to these other dead in the continued argument of *Being and Time*? Is there a way to continue this analysis within its hither-worldly horizon? In no other part of the book does Heidegger explicitly mention the dead other or a being-with those who are no longer there. Yet, as we shall see, they continue to inhabit the argument and the overriding question of *Dasein*'s temporality and historicity.

Historicity as Responding to the Dead

In chapter 5 in the second part of *Being and Time* Heidegger addresses the existential problem of *history* as a problem of how to understand the *stretch* or interconnectedness of life as played out between birth and death. The phenomenological task is first presented as understanding the possibility of this dynamic in-between as an origin and foundation of historical being and awareness, what he also refers to as its *occurrence* or way of *happening*, its *Geschehen* as also another word for its "historicity" (*Geschichtlichkeit*).[30] Following the general pattern of critical-destructive hermeneutics, Heidegger states that for such a pursuit we cannot base our understanding on an actually observed history, with its artifacts, remains, or narratives. Just as the death of the other could not ultimately provide the key to what it means to die, neither can objective history account for the possibility of the historical happening of human existence. The articulation of this possibility must be sought as a kind of critical self-explication of the *historizing* that we ourselves are. This is what it means to have an "ontological understanding of historicity" or of the existential apriori of history.

The first question that opens the analysis of historicity in §73 is what makes something historical? Usually we would answer: its "pastness" or its "being past." But what is the phenomenal content of being "of the past"? "History" in the conventional sense is taken to refer to all that *was*. What is the relation between history in this general sense and human existence? Is it the case that we simply belong to history as somehow contained in it, and that therefore our becoming part of history is something that comes to us from the outside by virtue of being situated in the great river of time? Or is there a more intimate relation between human existence and *the historical* that could be explicated to account for the possibility of there being history in the first place? In other words, is there also an existential historical apriori?

To begin to answer this question, Heidegger invites the reader to contemplate a "historical artifact," a household utensil of the kind that fills our *historical* museums. As buildings devoted to "presenting the past" or of "displaying history," such museums largely rely on material remains, preserved and removed from their original context and placed in cases as objects of historical contemplation and learning. But what is the source of their historicality? In other words, how do certain things obtain the meaning "historical"? Heidegger's response is that this meaning rests on them being perceived as part of a world once lived and a world that no longer is. But what is the nature of a world that is no longer? Should we say that it is simply *past*? Then it too would appear as only an objectified entity among other entities in an objective chronological sequence of events, and we would again have taken for granted precisely what was to be clarified: the possibility of appearing as historical in the sense of carrying or displaying *pastness*. From whence does this meaning of pastness emerge? This, he says, is the real "philosophical enigma" that we face: "On the basis of what ontological conditions does historicity belong to the subjectivity of the 'historical' subject as its essential condition?"

If pastness relied only on *Dasein* that no longer is, then again it would be the objective chronological framework that determines the nature of this pastness, not *Dasein* as past. But what does it mean for *Dasein* to be past? It does not become past simply by disappearing from the present, by no longer being there. The nature of its pastness is not "in [a] strict ontological sense" "past" but "having-been" (*Da-gewesen*), the perfective form of *Dasein*. Just as in the analysis of the nature of the dead other as "unliving," Heidegger does not pause to reflect on the deeper implications of his own term. Instead, he almost smuggles it into the overall argument that is concerned with historicity as an existential apriori that applies to *Dasein* as essentially alive. But with the introduction of the phenomenological category of *having-been*, he has again given expression to a spectral being, since this is a name specifically for the existential nature of life both present and absent. He could have written *Dasein* as *un-living*. But at no point does he explicitly recognize the structural isomorphism between the two analyses. Even though historicity is a category that is applicable to the living, it is the dead, in the peculiar existential mode of having-been, that are the source of the meaning of the historical, precisely by virtue of not being simply past but constituting a middle region of perfective or perhaps ancestral being.

Heidegger does not speak here of *ancestry* or *ancestral*, the standard German words for which would be *Abstammung* or *Vorfahren*. Yet at the outset of the analysis of historicity he does suggest that "the past" does not simply mean that which is located in another temporal region, but rather that it carries the meaning of "derivation" (*Herkunft*). The word *Kunft* or *Kumft* is an older German word for "coming," and thus also for "arrival" or simply "future." *Her-kunft* thus means that from which something has come or originated, which could be described as *ancestry*, that which "comes before" (*ante cessor*). Thus, it is structurally aligned with the term "having-been."[31]

In the analysis of the phenomenological nature of the dead other, Heidegger had introduced—if only in passing—the category of "being with the dead," which was then exemplified primarily through the way that humans care for their dead in funerary rites. But in the analysis of historicity the stakes are higher. Here the question concerns the foundation and possibility of history, historical awareness, and the institutions that maintain a relation to the past. When the dead other makes its appearance here in the form of *Dasein* as *having-been*, it is as a name for the constitutive basis for this whole domain. Just as in the analysis of finitude and the dead other, Heidegger wants to remain strictly within a this-worldly horizon, which in this case means that he wants to find a way of describing the reality and happening of *pastness* in terms of its existential meaning for *present* and living *Dasein*. This is the only way he can remain true to the basic phenomenological imperative that the meaning of a phenomenon should be sought through its lived projection toward a future. But what is so striking in this analysis is that as he seeks to grasp the elementary meaning of pastness, he is compelled to invite the pastness of the dead other, not as an entity from a presumed objective past somehow preserved in the present but as this peculiar pastness in the present to which the living are linked through acts of understanding, repetition, and action with those no longer there. It is as if he is both affirming the irreducibility of this mode of being and at the same time trying to dispel it, only to see it return again. Whereas living and future-projecting *Dasein* is ultimately said to constitute the "primarily historical," his own analysis and conclusion lead him to affirm that this relies on a more elementary exposure to the other as *having-been*.[32]

The inner tension in his argument comes out even more clearly as he turns to the question of what "authentic" historicity could amount to (§74). If the previously recapitulated analysis concerns the presumably neutral structure of historicity, it has left the question open to what extent there is also an *authentic* way of living and enacting this predicament. As he seeks to push his analysis toward the supporting pillar of the structure of historicity, he repeats that all existential comportments ultimately rest on temporality, so much so that the interpretation of historicity is here depicted as only a more "concrete elaboration" of temporality. And since temporality is revealed most fully through "resoluteness" as the authentic projection toward the future in a lucid awareness of one's personal mortality, it is presumably only in such a clarity of our most basic inescapable existential predicament that we also truly touch the root of our historicity.

But as he reaches for this existential zero point, the analysis suddenly shifts focus, when he declares, "The factual revealed possibilities of existence are not to be elicited from death." In other words, our fully realized finitude does not offer us any direction. Or to put it in sharper terms: authenticity as a projection toward finitude will remain an empty formality until it is given a concrete form and content. To find such a concrete form, human existence must open itself not just to the situation but to possibilities handed over to it, through which it can come into its own by committing itself to a "heritage" (*Erbe*) that it takes over. Only from within a handed-over set of existential possibilities can it thus orient and project itself toward a future in and through its "thrownness." But what are these possibilities and this heritage? They do not come from those existing in the present or from the world *but from Dasein as having-been.* And since *Dasein* is always a being-with-others, the constitution of the individual subject through an affirmation of an inheritance is necessarily carried out in a shared space of meaning with the dead others. In acting, Heidegger writes, *Dasein* acts with its "generation," taking over an inherited possibility in the moment of decision. These two levels of the constitution of historicity as future-oriented commitment to a legacy he summarizes as having a "fate" (*Schicksal*), the collective modality of which is "destiny" (*Geschick*).

When life moves toward the authentic individualized projection of its finitude, its phenomenological horizon collapses to reveal it as already claimed and belonging to an inheritance in communion with those having-been. If the explicit purpose of the analysis was to found historicity on individualized temporality, the outcome appears contrary, as if the concrete realization of authenticity were possible only for a being that already belongs and responds to what has enabled it. In the end, however, we need not choose sides in this dialectic. It suffices to note that the movement between radicalized finitude and openness to the past as destiny cannot be sealed and terminated once and for all. The critical moment—the *Augenblick*—in which the authentic historicity is presumably realized is always a moment that is displaced and exposed to the claim from what is other than itself, through the repetition of an inheritance that it assumes as a project for a future.

In moments of decision, when existence is pushed toward its limit and is forced to choose sides and to act, history becomes *practical* in a more fundamental sense. It is no longer a question of taking an interest in this or that or of knowing about what has been in general but of living an uncertain future as the necessity of personal and collective choices that force it to confront and weigh questions of belonging, inheritance, and responsibility. Who we are and what we become are determined by the way that we permit possibilities of the past to resound and to whom we experience loyalty. Heidegger's account of authentic historicity recalls these types of situations where history is realized in the form of decisive choices and commitments. At the same time, it distorts their phenomenological reality by suggesting that individual (as well as collective) human existence could somehow generate a purified and authentic course of action simply by affirming its own mortality in the most radical way. In seeking the right action, in seeking the measure or simply *the just*, life is often forced to confront a conflicting set of commitments, directives, and imperatives where truthfulness and betrayal are not always easy to disentangle and where the very idea of a "right" course may even be detrimental to the possibility of acting wisely in the specific historical moment. Do we speak, or do we remain silent? Do we join, or do we resist? Do we act, or do we refrain from action? Do we go to war, or do we seek another solution; do we cling to the other, or do we let go? These are difficult and sometimes painful choices, where history is enacted in and through a space of conflicting loyalties.

What we think of as history, tradition, and collective memory is constituted in this ambiguous in-between of freedom and destiny in relation to inherited existential possibilities and in response to those who went before, in other words, in relation to the dead. *Dasein* lives its historicity in this openness for an address that has always already reached it from those having-been or from having-been-ness as such. The words Heidegger uses to qualify the peculiar form of "repetition" that characterizes genuine historizing, that it *responds* (*erwidert*) to the possibility of existence that has been-there, are important.[33] It is not a question of a blind repetition or of refusing the historical in the present but of somehow letting it happen through an affirmative response. The historical in life emerges as an inner opening in the direction of the demand of the dead other. It is not properly a "dialogue" since it lacks genuine reciprocity. Here life relates to an address that reaches it both from outside and inside itself, in relation to which it is called to respond and to take responsibility, thus constituting it in its own sense of continuity and identity.

When read through the lens of Derrida's idea of the spectral, and through Patočka's and Levinas's elaboration of the phenomenon of after-life and survival, Heidegger's analysis of tradition as the possibility of an authentic historicity and collective destiny appears in a different light. He too confronted the phenomenological problem of how to understand and properly conceptualize the strange *lingering on* of the past in the present through *Dasein* as *having-been*. The domain of the historical is such a breach or lacuna in the present, an ethical and political existential situation characterized by afterlife, living-on, and spectrality. And contrary to Heidegger's abstracted conception of how personal finitude can provide a directive for how to respond to a historical existence, the implications of his analysis expose the inner pathology of belonging to the past as an ongoing deliberation within the space of being-with the dead, as a domain where political life is shaped, oriented, and led astray.

In his memoirs, Karl Löwith reports a meeting and conversation with Heidegger in Rome in 1936, where he is said to have pointed precisely to the analysis of historicity in *Being and Time* as a key to his political involvement.[34] Löwith does not develop it further, but one possible interpretation, which also corresponds with letters and diary entries from the relevant period, is that in opting for National Socialism in 1933, Heidegger felt that he was being true to a collective national destiny. It was a nationalist-communitarian intoxication that he shared with a large part of the German population that not only clouded his political judgment but also made him numb to the exposure and suffering of many of his Jewish colleagues, students, and friends. This is not the place to address the complex and extensively debated topic of Heidegger and politics, of which I have also written elsewhere.[35] It suffices to note that the existential predicament of historicity points us toward the deeper dynamics of communities built and upheld through a sense of shared commitment across time. Thereby it also highlights the ethical-political-juridical question concerning how and when we can separate a genuine and authentic sense of belonging to a people and a community from just falling for deceptive and destructive myths. When are we truly giving shape to history through our own example, and when are we the vehicles of passively inherited normative traditions?

As we here return to develop and build on the analysis of *historicity* in Heidegger, and thus to a theme that had such an immense impact on ensuing philosophical thought, notably in the work of Hans Georg Gadamer, Paul Ricoeur, and Derrida, we can begin to look at it from new angles.[36] We can see it both as a conditioning framework for the establishment of tradition and cultural memory through dialogical transmission of inheritance and as a name for the inner caesura in the formation of collective consciousness that lets us understand the inner workings of how traditions are shaped, as always involving complex layers of intergenerational commitments.[37]

A Warm Heart for Cold Things

In *The Phenomenology of Spirit* Hegel posited the act of burial as the means of finite existence to save and maintain the continued life of the spirit across individual mortality. In his (mostly implicit) reading of *Antigone*, she is interpreted as an only semiconscious heroine of the life of universal spirit. In *Being and Time* there is no mention of Antigone or of the passion to be with the dead. But as a last point, I turn to a later text by Heidegger where not only Antigone but also the dialogue between her and Ismene concerning the responsibility toward the dead plays a central role. This is found in a lecture course that Heidegger gives in 1942, where the principal topic is Hölderlin's poem "Der Ister." This lecture course is of particular interest in relation to what we have discussed so far, not only for how it touches on the deeper ethical implications of human existence as a being with the dead but also for how it invites us to reflect further on its more troubling consequences.[38]

The lecture series is one of Heidegger's most nationalistic texts, a course in which he seeks to define "the political" and what it means to have a "fatherland" as well as the nature of "Germanness," where Hölderlin is seen as the poet who has articulated most deeply the historical "destiny" of the Germans. All of its topics would deserve a longer commentary, but here I focus in particular on his reading of the figure of Antigone. The lead motif of the course is taken from the first Chorus Ode of Sophocles's drama, which speaks of man as "the great wonder" or "the most uncanny" (*to deinoteron*) as he makes his way across the earth, subduing everything only to be subdued himself by death.³⁹ For Heidegger this text is credited with an unsurpassed philosophical-foundational significance. He carefully circles around its description of human existence as the *deinon*, a term that he renders as *unheimlich*, signifying precisely what is strange and terrifying but also what is *not at home*, what is *unheimisch*. The foremost example of this position is Antigone herself, as she chooses to challenge the king's verdict by caring for her dead brother and, in particular, how this is articulated in the dialogue between the two sisters.

Heidegger rejects the conventional interpretation of this passage according to which Ismene just represents the commonsense view that one should not challenge power to no avail. Instead, he focuses on how Ismene describes her sister: "to commence in pursuit of that remains unfitting, against which nothing can avail" (*archen theran tamechana*).⁴⁰ Contrary to the common view, he reads this not as an accusation against the daring sister but as a *truth* of who she really is. Antigone dismisses Ismene's appeal and declares her hatred for her sister. But for Heidegger the most important line is Antigone's statement that she has a "passion for the strange and terrifying," a *pathein to deinon*. In Fagles's translation this line reads: "to suffer this—dreadful thing." Thus, it is understood as referring to the punishment that she is about to undergo. But in Heidegger's reading the whole interaction between the sisters and its conclusion obtain a different meaning. For him the decision and direction of Antigone mirror and recall how the Ode describes man generally as the most uncanny (*to deinoteron*). In going with the dead, Antigone captures and concentrates the supreme destiny and truth of human existence as also seen and recognized by the sister. In her last words to Ismene, Antigone declares that she will not have a "dishonorable death" (*me kalos thanein*). Heidegger's translation is remarkable, as it also brings out the underlying philosophical thrust of his interpretation. He renders it as *zum Sein gehören muss mein Sterben* (that my death belongs to Being). To belong to being is here explicitly equated with a choice to go with and to die for the dead.

Earlier in their dialogue, Ismene has addressed the unyielding sister with these words (in Fagles's version): "So fiery—and it ought to chill your heart." But the Greek is not only more concentrated; it also conveys a different meaning. In the original it reads *thermen epi psychroisi chardian echeis* (line 98), which literally translates as "you have a warm heart turned toward the cold/dead," which is also how Heidegger renders it: *Ein heisses, doch den Kalten (Toten) zugewandtes Herz hast du.*[41] But when he then goes on to unconditionally affirm her position as the ontological truth of human existence, the terrifying paradox of this description escapes him. He cannot see how Sophocles also depicts and uses the tension between the sisters to say something important about the living and the dead and the limits of the former's commitments to the latter. In his willingness to let Ismene speak the truth of her sister and not just be meek and uncourageous, Heidegger bypasses a profound ethical challenge of the drama, in that it poses the question of what we really owe the dead. Antigone's uncompromising passion is one possible position. She walks with the dead rather than with the living. But in making her into a simple figure of the truth of this predicament, Heidegger disregards the tension conveyed by the text. Instead, her unyielding commitment to the dead is raised to the level of an existential-ontological task.

If we take this summary interpretation of the 1942 lectures and return again to what Heidegger had written fifteen years earlier in *Being and Time* on authentic historicity, the earlier work begins to resonate with a new tone. There he had written that only in being "free for death" is *Dasein* fully exposed to its goal and its destiny. By "grasping our finitude," we can pull ourselves away from the "endless possibilities" and place ourselves in the "simplicity of our fate." And only in this "authentic decision" is the original happening and historizing of human being realized as it plunges itself free for its death, "toward a given and yet chosen possibility" issuing from and called forth by those having-been.[42] Here the figure of Antigone is actually not so far away. By contrasting and comparing the analysis of authentic historicity with the interpretation of Antigone in the Hölderlin lectures, we can sense how the relation and commitment to the dead is at work also in the earlier analyses. An ontology and a politics of the dead are operating and guiding the argument already there.

From here we can also turn back and relate the criticism of Heidegger articulated by Levinas and Derrida from a new perspective. The critique that in Heidegger there is no sense of mourning or of the ghost needs to be modified. If the predicament of historicity is from the very outset connected to a responsive acting in regard to the dead, and if the passion of Antigone to care for her dead brother constitutes an epitome of authentic historicity, then the question of the ghost and mourning has to be given a different formulation. Then it would not just be a question of ghost or no ghost, or grief or no grief, but rather of how to comport oneself vis-à-vis ghosts and of how to properly respond to and care for the dead. Or to put it in the concentrated terms of Sophocles's original drama, what Heidegger's reading of Ismene brings out is a question of the temperature and temporality of the heart, as perhaps a question of the temperature of temporality itself. It is a question of this strange *warm heart for the cold.* It is a heart that in its passion already belongs *to that which will have been*, knowing that it will have "more time in which to win the favor of the dead, than of those who live," since it will "live forever there."

Antigone's passion for the dead and Heidegger's affirmation of the uncanniness of her uncompromising commitment place us right before the ethical abyss of the ontological bond between the living and the dead as also an abyss of history. It invites us to think the bond between the dead and the living beyond the standard socioanthropological and psychological framework. It presents us with an image of the act of burial not just a restricted ritual for handling the bodies of the dead but also the exemplary expression of how the past as the domain of life having-been can lay a claim on the living. The question of the temperature of the heart and its desire here also becomes a question of how to live one's temporal-historical predicament. In its grief and compassion and responsibility toward the dead, human life is not just situated before a choice of mourning or no mourning, or between ghosts and no ghosts, but at the original site of its ontological destiny, as a being with the dead. Life may tell itself, as in the existential purification rites evoked by Heidegger, that a clear-sighted affirmation of its own mortality will somehow secure the authenticity of its choices. It may believe, as in the more melancholic and less heroic thinking of Levinas, that it will be redeemed through the infinite responsibility of memory of the dead. But in the end, no philosophical analysis will secure the validity and authenticity of its choices. At best, it can visualize only the nature of its predicament.

Thanatologies

ON THE SOCIAL MEANINGS OF BURIAL

> At wedding-feasts of sky and earth. Thread
> My hands to spring-rites, to green hands of the dead
> —Wole Soyinka, "O Roots!"

Introduction

In the overall context of Hegel's *Phenomenology of Spirit*, the particular theme of *burial* will first seem marginal to most readers. But as we stop at this particular point in his narrative and focus instead on the broader range of problems that it actualizes, a different story can be told, with wider implications. It starts with the questions that Hegel claims to have answered: What is the *meaning* and existential truth of burial? And why do humans bury their dead? In describing the act of burial not as an exclusively religious or superstitious ritual but as an act of *spirit* and of ethical life, he initiates questions that will continue to work their way through the study of human culture up until the present with an ever-increasing urgency, where the different ways in which humans care for, communicate with, and in general relate to the dead will emerge as a decisive dimension of culture. By connecting the analysis to Sophocles's narrative, Hegel has also pointed to an ethical compulsion and passion among the living vis-à-vis the dead, not just of a *responsibility* but of a potentially uncompromising *allegiance to* the dead.

But what is burial? Is it even one thing or one type of practice? As is generally the case throughout *The Phenomenology*, its descriptions of supposedly essential structures are rarely based on references to specified sources. Instead, they are presented as explicatory schemata with an inner logic and necessity and with a universal reach. Among more recent sociological and anthropological interpretations of human culture and behavior, such philosophical-phenomenological or "intellectualist" analyses were often viewed with suspicion. For the specific case of burial, the problem was articulated in a poignant way by Peter Metcalf and Richard Huntington in their modern classic, *Celebrations of Death: The Anthropology of Mortuary Ritual* (1977). Here they argue that even though we are inclined to see death as a universal event with universal emotional repercussions—notably "horror and grief"—we should be cautious in thinking that we can explain the differences in death practices in terms of one original general pattern. The sociological approach will be reluctant to confirm a general *meaning* as experienced by an ideal individual. Instead, it will seek to ground the analysis in the interpretation of the collective practices themselves. In the first chapter they state, in a graphic passage that was often quoted in the subsequent literature,

What could be more universal than death? Yet what an incredible variety of responses it evokes. Corpses are burned or buried, with or without animal or human sacrifice; they are preserved by smoking, embalming, or pickling; they are eaten—raw, cooked, or rotten; they are ritually exposed as carrion or simply abandoned; or they are dismembered and treated in a variety of these ways. Funerals are the occasion for avoiding people or holding parties, for fighting or having sexual orgies, for weeping or laughing, in a thousand of different combinations. The diversity of cultural reaction is a measure of the universal impact of death.[1]

Their description clearly contrasts with that of Hegel, which spontaneously connects burial with interment or inhumation, as was the common practice in Europe in Hegel's own time. When Antigone speaks to Ismene of her wish to "heap the earth above the brother whom I love," she confirms the exemplary role of *earth*. Yet, as pointed out by Robert Garland in *The Greek Way of Death*, for the Greeks in the classic age the most common form of burial was actually not *inhumation* but *cremation*, as illustrated in the most detailed description we have of early Greek burial practices, the funerary rites for Patroclus as depicted in the last book of the *Iliad*.[2]

The historical record also shows that the form, scope, and even the very fact of burial were unevenly distributed over time. Certain individuals would receive extraordinary burials, whereas others seem to have been handled without ritual. Likewise, the social context of burial obviously changed over time. The practice in Hegel's own time actually marks a significant change in this respect. With the establishment of the Père Lachaise Cemetery in 1804, Napoleonic France took the lead in a process that had been tentatively initiated over the course of the preceding century and that would drastically change Western burial practices, in which the bodies of the dead were moved from the church and inner-city graveyards to state-organized necropolises on the outskirts of the city, and burial was declared to be a "right" for every citizen. This change of responsibility and location was partly motivated by an anticlerical return to pre-Christian Roman and Greek practices. These and other historical transformations were studied by Philippe Ariès in *The Hour of Our Death*, another modern thanatological classic published in 1977. It was an inspiration for many subsequent studies of mortuary culture over the course of the following decades, the most recent of which is Thomas Laqueur's impressive *The Work of the Dead* (2015), which traces the complex connection between political, religious, and practical motives behind the new burial regime of modernity from the second half of the eighteenth century until the present.[3]

All of these studies confirm the need to contextualize and historicize the kind of sweeping interpretations that Hegel represents. Still, they do not invalidate or ultimately transcend the basic question and the underlying problem that he first raised concerning the meaning and significance of burial in the general sense of a ritual caretaking of kin after death. Despite their stress on the historical and cultural diversity of burial ritual and the need to broaden its scope and empirical underpinnings, Metcalf and Huntington ultimately also confirm the continued relevance of this more fundamental question in basing their study on the general concept of "mortuary ritual." The growing body of *thanatological studies*, the entire historical, anthropological, and archaeological literature devoted specifically to the study and interpretation of death and funerary culture, also underscores the relevance and importance of continuing to reflect on this fundamental philosophical and existential-ontological question: Why do humans bury their dead?

In anthropological and sociological studies of burial, Hegel is never mentioned. His short analysis never became part of or a reference within this field. Throughout the nineteenth century, researchers in the human sciences gathered a massive historical record of various ways of caring for the corporeal remains of the dead. But mostly it was not accompanied by a sustained theoretical effort to *think* these practices, which were perceived mostly through an explicit or implicit Christian framework. Only with the rise of the comparative approach to the history of religion and the culture of death toward the end of the nineteenth century did a presumably "secular" theory of burial in general became possible. This modern ethos of the human sciences is represented in an exemplary way by Durkheim and his circle that gathered around *L'année sociologique*, initiated in 1898. An important part of their work was devoted to the sociological and philosophical understanding of religious life and practices.[4] It is therefore not surprising that it was from within this group that the single most important theoretically oriented text on the problem of burial culture emerged, "Contribution à une étude sur la représentation collective de la mort," written by the twenty-seven-year-old philosopher and sociologist Robert Hertz.[5] It was published in the 1907 edition of Durkheim's yearbook. Eight years later Hertz died as a soldier in the First World War. His singular achievement lay mostly dormant for half a century, but in 1960 the essay was translated into English by Rodney and Claudia Needham on the initiative of Edward Evans Pritchard, as "A Contribution to the Study of the Collective Representation of Death."[6] It then became a canonical text within the emerging field of death studies, thanatology, or the study of mortuary culture.[7]

The main topic of this chapter is a critical-philosophical reconstruction of this classic essay in the anthropological literature. This is carried out in a comparison with Hegel and also against a background of the philosophical-phenomenological schema developed in the previous chapter. Burials and graves are acts and artifacts with a peculiar temporality and historicity. With the grave, *the past* is made into an explicit goal of a future-oriented action through a technique that responds and relates to what no longer is, the life of an other as *living-on* and *having-been*. To read Hertz's text from the perspective of these questions permits us to explore the inner continuity between speculative idealism and sociology/anthropology on the topic of death. It also gives us a deeper perspective on the theoretical stakes and implications surrounding the phenomenon of burial for the human sciences at large and how it challenges the limits of their interpretive framework and exposes their own ethos as themselves caretakers of the dead. Thus, a historical loop is disclosed where the presumably limited practice of burial begins to move across its initially established anthropological limits.

Hertz and the Sociology of Burial

At the outset of Hertz's essay, death is presented as both a familiar and an everyday event surrounded by strong emotions. Often it is said to have given rise to ideas of how "the soul has left the body and travelled elsewhere." He notes that burial does not primarily have to do with hygiene but that it is experienced as a genuine "moral obligation" and that the event of death imposes certain cultural specific duties on the living. It is in this sense, he writes, that "death has a specific meaning for the social consciousness" as an "object of collective representation" (27).[8] The study is then devoted to describing and analyzing the elements and the origin of this *representation*. And just as in Hegel a century earlier, its explicit goal is the *general* meaning of burial through a theoretical-eidetic variation of its different empirical manifestations.

According to Hegel, death demands a response in and through which the living show respect for the dead in the form of a burial rite, the underlying purpose of which is to reestablish and secure the autonomy of spirit across the threshold of death. Despite a prevailing Christian confessional bias that structures the overall argument of the book, Hegel is aiming toward a transcultural interpretation. The reference to Greek burial custom through *Antigone* also shows that he is looking for a philosophical understanding of the inner *necessity* of burial through an interpretation of the logic of universal spirit.

In initial contrast to this universal aspiration, Hertz begins his study by discussing how "we" in "our" society tend to see and represent death. As we compare our practices with those of other societies, it becomes clear that "death has not always been represented and felt as it is in our society" (28). It is against the background of this cultural relativization of death and its symbols that the study then approaches its more specific theme and introduces its key conception, the so-called double or second burial. Here he builds mainly on earlier published anthropological reports from the Dayaks of Indonesia, more specifically from the Olo Ngaju population of southeastern Borneo.[9] Even though the study explicitly distinguishes itself as an analysis of an empirically specific and situated material, over and against culturally biased and "intellectualist" generalizations, it makes it clear that the analysis of this remote and particular culture is nevertheless meant to lead us, through a comparative approach, to a more general and valid matrix for the understanding of a transcultural phenomenon. Indeed, the purpose of the study is to see how the extraordinary burial practices among the Dayaks are "not merely local customs." The *social experience* of death and loss as such is said to be represented in rituals that correspond to a process of "mental disintegration and synthesis" (86). In formulations like these, *society* and the *social* do not designate a specific Indonesian community but a general structure pertaining to the "collective consciousness." In relation to this ambition, the Dayaks of Borneo obtain a role and position for Hertz and for the continued understanding of death and burial in anthropology that is methodologically different from but structurally similar to the role of Sophocles's heroine in the *Phenomenology*. I return to the philosophical implications concerning the general meaning of death and its rituals that emerge from such a parallel reading of Hegel and Hertz. But before doing so, we need to look closer at the central concept of "double burial," as this is first introduced and elaborated by Hertz through some of the empirical observations on which it was based. The philosophical and phenomenological implications of this anthropological matrix in the study of mortuary culture are greater than they may first appear.

Double Burial and the Precarious
Temporality of the Dead

Hertz divides his analysis of mortuary rites along three basic dimensions: the *body* of the deceased, the *soul* of the deceased, and finally the *survivors*. At the center of the double burial complex is the transformation of the corpse from living tissue to bones and the different practices that surround this transformation. This can be carried out in many different ways. He describes that among the Dayaks the remains are taken to their final burial place only "after a more or less long period of time during which the body is placed in a temporary shelter" (29). This shelter can be the house of the family, a temporary hole in the ground, a wooden platform, simply a structure with some kind of protective roof, or on branches in a tree. This temporary sheltering of the body during the time of its decay can take place anywhere between a few months and several years before the remains are handled in the final ceremony, the local name of which is *tivah*, a burial feast that often involves great expenditures with complex and excessive social rituals and that sometimes may include human sacrifice. The details of these burial feasts as recounted by Hertz need not occupy us here. What is important for the general interpretive matrix are the meaning and importance of the transformation of the body to its skeletal remains and the cleansing and the drying of the bones. Among the Dayaks, the potentially repulsive process of bodily decay is not concealed but integrated within a ritual form. Hertz lists various ways in which during the course of this process the decaying remains are carefully taken care of and later buried together with the bones and, in certain cases, even partially consumed by the relatives.

The aspects of the burial ritual that concern the actual handling of the body are what can be described most straightforwardly. It is when the analysis moves to the second stage, to the question of "the soul," that it becomes more tentative and involves more interpretation. Hertz begins this part of his essay by equating the two levels: "*in the same way* as the body is not taken at once to its 'last resting-place,' so the soul does not reach its final destination immediately after death" (34, my emphasis). It has to "stay on earth" or "wander in the forest" before it can move to the "land of the dead" with the aid of the proper ritual. To this he adds that the "ideas relating to the fate of the soul are in their very nature vague and indefinite." The soul of the dead is not a unitary entity but is seen among the Olo Ngaju as containing two parts: one has more to do with the "personality" of the person, and the other is more bodily and "unconscious" and connected to the actual decaying corpse. The more genuine soul of the *person* leaves the body at the time of death, but it is seen as occupying a sort of middle region, as in waiting, before the final ceremony is celebrated and through which it can then move safely to be with its ancestors.

Hertz then lists a number of different ways in which this middle period is ritually articulated. It is a time when the soul is understood as remaining among the living: "as long as the temporary burial of the corpse lasts, the deceased continues to belong more or less exclusively to the world he has just left" (36). The ontological instability of the soul during this time is also a source of anxiety among the living since it can be transformed into a "malicious being" that can cause damage to the community, especially if the rituals are not carried out properly. Once the final ritual has been celebrated, the relatives can control the return of the dead, but until that moment the dead are credited with an "initiative" of their own. The middle and transitory period thus captures in a concentrated way the two supposedly basic affects vis-à-vis the dead, "pity and fear." Hertz lists a number of ways in which not just the body of the deceased but also his or her belongings and house become perceived as impure, tainted with the fear of contagion and surrounded with "taboos." This applies also to the relatives who are temporarily isolated from the community in various ways during this transitory period. The time of this perilous middle period is partly correlated with the actual time it takes for the body to fully decompose to a point where "only the bones remain."

What makes the Dayak rituals so striking is how they follow this biological process of decay of the corpse and how they integrate it within their overall response to the death of kin. For Hertz, the essential point is not ultimately connected to any specific process of transformation but concerns the inner logic and meaning of this intermediary period. Even though embalming and incineration are not common among these particular groups, he concludes that "these artificial ways of disposal do not differ essentially from the temporary ways that we have listed" (41). In this way the concept "double burial" also permits him to integrate the practice of Egyptian mummification within a larger anthropological framework, or as he writes, as "a special case derived from temporary burial" (42). The same argument is then applied to cremation, since "far from destroying the body of the deceased, it recreates it and makes it capable of entering a new life" (43).[10] He also mentions the famous practices among the followers of the *Zend Avesta* or Zoroastrianism of letting the bodies be eaten clean by birds and dogs before the purified bones can be buried. He suggests that its theological context can in fact be seen as a "later" construct and that we must "discover what meaning younger societies attach to reducing the body to a skeleton" (45). This remark is followed by a number of examples of similar practices across a wide geographical and cultural array, from Africa to South and Middle America, of different ways in which the body is transformed into its skeletal remains before it can be handled in a final burial. What he is looking for through this "eidetic variation"—to use a term from Husserl—of his material is something he himself refers to as an "essential point" and a "constant theme." And this he finds in the "two complementary notions" that "death is not completed in one instantaneous act" but considered to be "terminated only with the dissolution of the body" and that "death is not a mere destruction but a transition" into a different and sometimes even superior existence (48).

A striking expression of this conception is found in a Maori tradition, where a chief is quoted as having said to his son: "For three years, your person must be sacred and you must remain apart from the tribe . . . for during all that time my hands will gather earth and my mouth will feed constantly on worms and vile food, the only kind that is offered to the spirits of the underworld. Then when my head falls upon my body and when the fourth year has come, waken me from my sleep, show my face to the light of day. When I arise, you will be *noa*, free" (51).[11] The story points to the often strictly regulated period of mourning, which is sometimes directly correlated to that of corporeal decay and transformation. The time between a first and second burial is also a time when the living are required to act in particular ways in relation to the remains of the dead and in relation to the community. For Hertz's overall analysis, this also permits him to integrate those communities that do not have an exterior second burial ritual but can nevertheless have a regulated period of mourning. These rituals can then be interpreted as a sublimated version of a widespread practice of following and culturally integrating the transformation of the body from living flesh to dry bones. Or as he writes, "One would be tempted to answer in the affirmative if our view were accepted that there is a natural connection between the beliefs concerning the disintegration of the body, the fate of the soul, and the state of the survivors during that same period" (53).

A special section in the text is devoted to a comparison of different ceremonies through which the second and final burial is carried out. Sometimes these are lavish feasts that consume huge resources from the family and the community. Their overall purpose is not just to give the dead a final burial and thus to ensure that the souls of the dead pass into the "land of the dead"; they also free the living from the obligations connected to the period of mourning and thus restore the community to its ordinary life. At the center of these feasts are the concrete remains, the cleansed bones that are sometimes also painted or dressed and paraded in public. Parts of the skeletal remains may also be kept by the family, especially the heads of important persons. Hertz lists several examples of decorated skulls becoming part of the family's sacred treasury. The implied parallel to Christian relic ossuaries does not even need to be spelled out, as it would be obvious to any contemporary reader of the text.

The ceremonial feasts and the keeping of body parts confirm the connection between burial practices and ancestor worship. In many of the societies to which Hertz refers, the explicit purpose of the ritual is to enable the dead members of the community to enter the domain of the ancestors. How this domain is visualized can vary greatly, but the general structure has to do precisely with the sense of a parallel community beyond the community of the living and to which the living community stands in a reciprocal relationship. Hertz notes that the societies on which he has focused have moved beyond the supposedly earlier stages of "totemism," where a mythic ancestor is worshipped in an often half-human and half-animal form. He mentions several examples of the second burial rites involving rituals in which the bones of the dead are reunited with the ancestral totem and sometimes believed to be reborn again in other incarnations of this original and foundational force.

Through the different examples it becomes clear how the connection between the dead and their community is often enacted and symbolized through a care for the *bones*, where great efforts are sometimes spent to bring back bodily remains to the land of their origin. Referring to the North American Choctaw, Hertz writes: "It seems that the group would consider itself diminished if it were to admit that one of its members could be permanently cut off from it" (70). As a striking example, he recalls the so-called feast of soul among the North American Hurons that was held every other decade, when individual groups would unearth and bring the bones of the dead to a communal burial feast as a celebration of the nation as a whole (71).[12]

He also mentions several examples from different parts of the world of the fear that the common burial grounds will be disturbed or destroyed by enemies. This fear sometimes even leads communities to conceal the final burial ground so it will not be desecrated. In the extension of this concern one can also interpret the practices of carrying the bones of ancestors as amulets, including the exceptional practice documented among some South American tribes of grinding the bones to a powder that they rub onto their bodies or swallow with drink, thus literally making their own bodies into the burial site of the dead (72).[13]

In a concluding section Hertz tries to summarize the wealth of sources and testimonies that he has mobilized throughout his text (a few examples of which have been recalled here). A principal prerequisite for his analysis is that death is not perceived in these societies as a "natural thing" or as a "natural phenomenon." Instead, it is understood as the action of "spiritual powers." Rather than see these societies as misguided or in "error" in this respect, Hertz interprets it as the "naïve expression of a permanent social need," in other words, as the spontaneous experience within the community of seeing itself as "immortal." The death of an individual is therefore experienced as an attack on the community as a whole. In extreme cases the dead individual and its closest relatives can even be attacked by its compatriots as though the threat to the community came from the deceased body itself.

Ultimately, "collective consciousness" is said not to believe in death. In a very Hegelian turn of phrase, Hertz concludes that the last word *must* remain with life (78). From the "least advanced" societies up to the contemporary Christian Church, this collective life provides a release from the damage of individual death and holds out a promise of a reintegration within itself. At this point in the essay, the Christian context of Hertz's argument is made explicit in a comparative leap between the primitive tribes and contemporary church ministers, in relation to which he concludes that "at whatever stage of religious evolution . . . the notion of death is linked with that of resurrection" (79). The space of the resurrection he calls the "mythical society of souls, which each society constructs in its own image." It is a world that exists "only in the mind" and is therefore said to be "free of all limitations," in other words, "ideal." He then makes the comparison between the rituals of death and other initiatory rites, such as adolescence and marriage. He compares his own type of civilization, where the life of an individual goes on more or less the same way from birth to death with "less advanced societies," where every new stage is said to be perceived as a death and a subsequent rebirth. All of this is brought together in the conclusion that to "social consciousness," "death is only a particular instance of a general phenomenon" (81).

The concluding remarks suggest that burial could be seen as a "rite of passage," as this was subsequently developed by Arnold van Gennep, who is often mentioned alongside Hertz as the other principal theorist of mortuary culture in the anthropological literature. In his book with this title published in 1909, van Gennep devotes one chapter to funerary rites. There he classifies them as a branch of the more general phenomenon of rites of passage, which all presumably seek to handle the transport between different stages in human existence. While using and even repeating parts of Hertz's argument, van Gennep also voices sharp criticism of Hertz just as he criticized Durkheim and his school in general for what he took to be their "social determinism." Even though his work and analytic model are often equated with those of Hertz, and even though they partly overlap in their general orientation in seeing death rites as parallels to rites of initiation and rebirth, van Gennep's study is of less philosophical interest and weight. In its explicit urge to develop the general concept of rites of passage, it overlooks the specificity and thus also the broader implications of the phenomena of death and burial. It does refer to the space of interaction between the dead as a middle ground and as a "special society," but it does not try to develop any ontological understanding of this middle ground. Nor is van Gennep attentive to the deviant cases of the temporal-historical aspect of the phenomenon of burial that emerge when we consider what Hertz has to say about extraordinary and sudden deaths.[14]

On Deaths without End

Whereas the conclusion of Hertz's essay has a distinctly Hegelian ring, with "social consciousness" acting as the role of "spirit" and where life ultimately triumphs over (individual) death, the final remarks of the text open a different trajectory. Here he speaks of the "brute fact of death" as an event that the human mind cannot accept and master in one blow. It is only through a "series of internal partings" that the living can let go of the dead: "We can not bring ourselves to consider the deceased as dead straight away: he is too much part of our substance." The fact of death, Hertz adds, is first contradicted by the flood of "memories, images, desires, and hopes" (82). The "evidence" of death therefore sinks in only slowly and gradually until we reach a point where we give in and believe in the separation as something real. He describes this as a "painful psychological process" that gives rise to the mystical belief in a soul that only gradually sever its ties. The image of the soul that has reached its final destination can then be seen as mirroring the process through which the dead come to obtain a more peaceful and stable appearance in the consciousness and memory of the survivors. In these passages he is presumably not only identifying himself with grieving humanity in general but also thinking of his father, who had died suddenly in a climbing accident ten years earlier, leaving behind his wife and five young children.[15]

In this process of "disintegration and synthesis," a society gradually restores its inner balance before the experience of death. The dead are carried over, as it were, to an imaginary space of the collective representation in and through rites that involve the most stable and solid part of the physical remains, that is, the bones. In a final section Hertz supports his "hypothesis" of the social meaning of the representation of death by listing a number of limit cases among the Dayak and certain Australian tribes. The burial of less significant members of the community, notably children, very old people, and people having died from sudden disasters through accident or childbirth, are not accredited with the extended ritual of a first and second burial. Instead, they are buried more swiftly, surrounded by different rites, and their remains are kept away from those of the ancestors. The strong and sudden emotion of horror and fear presumably generates a different response than in the cases of more "ordinary" deaths. The souls of the former unfortunate individuals are described instead as "roaming the earth for ever." For them there is no transitory period; instead, it extends indefinitely since "their death has no end." The absence of ritual in these cases is not explained with reference to any lack or weakness of emotion among the survivors but instead by "the extreme intensity and suddenness of this emotion" (85).

The possibility of such a "death without end" is here only indicated as a marginal case to underscore his general point that for "collective consciousness death under normal circumstances is a temporary exclusion of the individual from human society" (86). From the perspective of his general theory, burial still marks a passage from one dimension of society to another, from the "visible society" to the "invisible society." To mourn one's kin constitutes a "necessary participation of the living in the mortuary state of their relative." In the very last line of the essay he gathers his thoughts on the collective representation of death with the formulation that it amounts to a "dual and painful process of mental disintegration and synthesis." Only when this process is completed, he adds, can "society triumph over death."

The conclusion is remarkable in several respects. In the culminating moment of this exemplary comparative and classificatory analysis it proclaims the possibility of a "triumph" over a phenomenon that he at the same time has described as a "brute fact" and in the face of which there is no guarantee that it does not become a "death without end." In order to give an account of the meaning of the extraordinary rituals that he has gathered, Hertz is inclined to align himself with what he proclaims to be their *meaning*, that is, "peace" and "triumph." Through this interpretive matrix the ethnographic evidence is organized into a comprehensible whole. How should we view this conclusion in relation to the overall orientation of the analysis? To what extent is this really a depiction of a state of affairs, and to what extent is it itself an expression of a certain rationalistic and perhaps Jewish-Christian bias?

The intellectual context of the interpretation is "secular" in the sense that Hertz, following Durkheim, seeks to be neutral in relation to his

Jewish-Christian upbringing, whose particular doctrinal interpretation of death and the afterlife is interpreted through the general matrix elicited from the comparative approach. The "invisible society" of the souls is part of a social imaginary, and the act of double burial is a complex expression of ritualized mourning. Yet in the end these interpretive explanations continue to rely on the concepts of "society" and "collective consciousness" as designating entities from within which the process can be grasped, understood, and made sense of. Following the general Durkheimian sociological matrix, it is the *whole* and the *general* that ultimately triumph over the *part* and the *singular* in the course of these events. Despite the differences between Hegel and Hertz, in both cases the act and ritual of burial (regardless of how it is carried out) are seen and explained as a manifestation of a collective life that through its different rituals secures its own continuity and survival. Ultimately, burial is not about death but about life, the life of the community or collective and its compulsion *to heal itself* after the wound of a loss of one of its members.

Healing the Wounded Body of Sociology

In April 1915, at the age of thirty-five and eight years after the publication of his essay, Hertz was killed in action on the plain of Woëvre in northeastern France. As a consequence of the outbreak of the war and the death of Durkheim in 1917, the group ceased publication of its yearbook. Only in 1925 did it resume its activities again, and now under the editorship of Marcel Mauss, Durkheim's nephew and intellectual heir. In the first issue Mauss introduced the journal again with a text simply titled "In Memoriam," containing a series of obituaries that marked the death not only of its founder but also of a number of its key members, several of whom had perished in the war. The reopening of its collective efforts thus also became a second intellectual burial ritual, a litany and epitaph in memory of the dead and a celebration of life to come. The longest of the brief obituaries was devoted to Robert Hertz, dead in a "useless assault" and described as the "master among masters." He is depicted as the one who chose the most "difficult topic" among religious and moral phenomena, the "dark side of humanity."[16] In the text Mauss also commits himself to overseeing that the unpublished manuscripts are edited and published, in other words, that his legacy is secured.

All the individual obituaries are short and focused on the work of the members and to the continuation of their efforts. After the list of obituaries, Mauss summarizes in a moving passage the situation for the community of scholars, comparing it to a "devastated forest" where only a few truncated trees are still standing but under which new shoots are pushing forth. The full concluding passage of this preface-epitaph by Mauss is worth reading, as it resonates in profound and unintentional ways with Hertz's conclusion on the meaning of burial two decades earlier:

Let us be courageous and not indulge in our weakness. Let us not think too much about the sad present. Let us not compare it with the forces that have escaped us and with lost glories. We should not cry except in hiding over these friendships and over these impulses that we miss. We should try to go on without them, without the one who directed us, without those who sustained us and those who were meant to take over the relay and replace us. Let us work for yet some years. Let us try to accomplish something that can honor their memory and that will not do injustice to what our master once inaugurated. Perhaps the sap will return. A new seed will fall down and begin to grow. It is in this spirit of faithful memory to Durkheim and to all our dead; it is in continued communion with them; it is in sharing their conviction in the usefulness of our science; it is in nourishing ourselves like them from the hope that man is perfectible through it; it is in these feelings that we are together with them beyond death [*par delà de la mort*]; that we all resume forcefully with our hearts, the task that we never abandoned.[17]

Together with them beyond death; what the text celebrates is the possibility of collective life over and beyond individual loss and a rebirth on the barren soil of death, a rebirth that also keeps the dead with it in "memory" of their lives and in continuation of their work and thus in their continued presence. In the wake of the destruction of this community, including its intellectual leader and several of its most prodigious members, those remaining thereby commit themselves to its continuation through an act of commemoration and commitment to shared ideals. At this point, in this existential moment of vulnerability and loss, there is no room for analysis or for adopting one's distance. The world has been destroyed and the world needs to be re-created. Mauss says and does what he has to do in the somber and passionate mood that the situation requires. Hertz was a great promise and now he is gone.

In this moment of grief over lives, loves, and friendships that have been lost, there seems to be no other discourse available than this commitment to its continuation. Thus, the intellectual memorial services for Hertz, his second burial as it were, confirm in a profound and irrefutable way the topic and theme to which he had devoted his efforts. Through these words the activity of one of the most sophisticated intellectual communities on earth realigns itself with and brings forth the echo of similar rituals that have been celebrated in different ways throughout the course of human history.

But what are we to make of this connection? Where and how do death and its response become *available* to us in understanding and in theoretical-discursive knowledge? How indeed should we *understand* the need for and compulsion to perform burial rites for the dead? Or should we ultimately leave all theorizing aside and simply conclude that in response to death, we as humans simply do this, in different ways and through different techniques but in the shared sense that through these practices we are somehow able to save and serve life in general in the face of its uncompromising individual destruction?

We can compare Mauss's words with the words spoken at the funeral services for Hegel on November 16, 1831, by Friedrich Förster. There Förster—echoing the enigmatic words of Luke 9:60 that Marx would also recall in his *18th Brumaire*—declared that we should "let the dead bury the dead, to us belongs the living; he who, having thrown off his earthly bonds, celebrates his transfiguration."[18] In the case of Hegel, this celebration of a life beyond death is less remarkable, not just in the sense that it manifests a conventional Christian phrasing in accordance with the times but also that it reaffirms the basic ethos of Hegel's own interpretation of the meaning of burial as a way to mark the eternal life of spirit beyond its corporeal destruction. But when the same trope is reinstated a century later by one of the most important representatives of the modern secular social-scientific ethos, it carries a greater theoretical significance and implication.

For Durkheim, the underlying motive and idea of exploring the "irrational" or "dark" dimensions of human behavior from a secular-philosophical-scientific perspective were to "explain" them in terms of their social *function*. In the preface to his great work *The Elementary Forms of Religious Life* he stated his reasons for taking an interest in so-called primitive and simple religious expressions: in these cases we are closer to an explanatory context of the surrounding society. Still, he did not want this kind of study to remain purely historical or of only ethnographic interest. Ultimately, his ambition was not just to explain present social realities but to reveal "an essential and permanent aspect of humanity."[19] His fundamental starting point was that religious representations respond to some fundamental "human need" and thus to some basic aspect of life, whether individual or social. There is a *reason* to be given for everything, since reality is ultimately rational and can be grasped by reason.

As a consequence of this way of examining different religious representations, their specific content is demythologized. Yet Durkheim did not want to see his work as a means ultimately to disparage religion as superstition; instead, he would affirm the fundamentally rational element of religious practices. Or as he puts it in one of his most assertive formulations, "At the heart of all systems of beliefs and of cults there must be a certain number of fundamental *répresentations* and ritual attitudes which, despite the diversity of forms they have each been able to assume, have everywhere the same object meaning and universally fulfill the same functions."[20] Focusing on so-called primitive societies and forms of religion was a "methodological" choice. By analyzing more restricted historical and ethnographic material, it should be possible to access and understand the "origin" of religion. In this basic commitment to the possibility of rationally grasping all forms of human comportment in terms of their inner social logic, a Hegelian legacy is bequeathed to the social sciences of the twentieth century.

This methodological approach is illustrated clearly in Hertz's essay. The explanation of the extraordinary rituals of the Dayak in response to death is accomplished by situating them within a social matrix where they serve the purpose of healing and maintaining the community and where they can be understood as a natural way of articulating an extended process of mourning. The analysis is both compelling and sympathetic in its universal and humanizing way of looking at these extraordinary rituals as "essentially isomorphic" with present-day Christian burials. When looking for the deeper meaning of burial, Hertz can conclude that the Dayak are fulfilling essentially the same social purpose that motivates a modern Western burial, and for the same reasons.

From this viewpoint, the sociological model of interpretation and explanation of burial could seem to have captured the basic meaning and origin of this transcultural ritual. This is also where most writers on this topic end up. When burial and mortuary practices are discussed in theoretical terms, Hertz's contribution will still be recalled as the theoretical framework, sometimes alongside that of van Gennep (which is then hastily taken to say the same thing). But instead of stopping at this point, we can take the analysis one step further. More specifically we need to look beyond the functional-rationalizing sociological (Hegelian) model of explanation. In doing so, we can follow Hertz and his analysis while also pointing out the inner tensions that its overly harmonizing conclusions tend to conceal. In particular, we need to look beyond the conventional sense of burial as a *rite de passage* and as a manifestation of social *healing*, which is a model that too easily fits within a conventional conception and framework of a living society guided by a collective rationality.

Thinking Burial beyond Healing and Rejuvenation

Unlike other rituals that involve only the living, burial is a ritual in and through which the living are explicitly interacting with the dead. A burial is not done for the living but for the dead. In burial, *an expanded understanding of society* is enacted and constituted, that is, a society as consisting not just of the living but also of the dead. When Mauss refers to his dead friends as a community with which he can now be "together beyond death," we should not simply discard this remark as a conventional and ritual phrase evoked by the sadness of the moment, or as a perhaps surprising remnant of Christian metaphysics. Instead, we should take it seriously as a challenge to think what Hertz in his own way had already grappled with. For Hegel, the possibility of such an expanded social body was never a genuine problem. He saw the life of spirit as transindividual, manifesting itself constantly across the finitude and mortality of human beings. The role of burial was to manifest the continuity and life of an essentially collective and immortal spirit.

For the modern sociological approach this conception of a community beyond death, which can relate to itself something that transgresses the event of death, is more problematic. Seen from one angle, such a community should be a nonentity. A community, by definition, consists of the living, for it is only the living who can exist in a mutual relation of exchange and communication. When someone claims to communicate with the dead, this activity is interpreted as a form of superstition, in other words, precisely as an "imaginary" sociality that is not really a sociality but something else. When this "belief" results in rituals and more complex social behavior, as in the case of the rituals analyzed by Hertz, it needs to be interpreted in the context of living society as in fact responding to certain more basic needs and thus as having a rational core. The sociological account that introduces the idea of a society healing itself through these rituals, which are then understood as rituals of mourning and rebirth, purports to think from within the strict confines of the living. But at the same time, it affirms the manifest mythical content of the ritual: that it reflects the establishment of another community beyond death. At the very moment when it manifests its own aspiration to break with the superstitious content of the rituals, the theoretical-rational account reaffirms them on another level in claiming to be able to think from the viewpoint of a totality that comprises the dead and the living. It is in this respect that Mauss's words on Hertz across the threshold of death also obtain a theoretical weight beyond the moving testimony of personal grief. Ultimately, they do not deviate from the sociological analysis; instead, they give a more personal tone to its basic message, that there is indeed such a community of the living and the dead. Thereby the living can indeed continue to *be with* the dead across this limit, as the community heals itself in order to prevail across finitude.

For us, however, even this should not be the final word. Our purpose is to ponder the nature of this spectral "community," of this being with the dead as a social ontological reality in its own right. The discussion so far has exposed a structural ambiguity in the approach of theoretical sociology, which refuses to recognize a communication with the dead as a reality while at the same time, in and through its aspiration to seek a rational understanding of the pretended communication with the dead, introduces a concept of sociality that presupposes the very phenomenon that was to be explained, a society or a community that transgresses the limit between the living and the dead.

As we try to think its structure and dynamic, we can still make use of the remarkable testimonies and interpretations brought together by Hertz. The rituals are performed with and for the dead themselves. During the course of these complicated interactions, the no-longer-living are recognized as members of a society in regard to which it becomes especially important to conduct oneself properly. The rites are animated by a sense of *duty* toward the dead, and they articulate in their different ways what the family and the community feel that they *owe* the dead, who can no longer carry and comport themselves.

To analyze the process as serving social healing captures one aspect of its phenomenality. But in the end this metaphor also conceals an important dimension of the situation that through its many examples exposes an extended and ultimately unlimited temporality of a continued *being-with*. The latter surfaces most dramatically in the concluding remarks on how the community responds to unfortunate and destructive deaths, the so-called deaths without end, where the souls are seen as "roaming the earth for ever." As mentioned in the previous commentary, Hertz saw these deaths as "marginal" cases meant to underscore his more general point that for "collective consciousness death is in normal circumstances a temporary exclusion of the individual from human society." If, however, the marginal case of a death "without end" is seen as signaling a parallel and likewise fundamental aspect of death for a society, then the idea of a healing across death or of death as only a temporary exclusion from collective life will appear in a different light.[21]

The life across and beyond death that has supposedly been celebrated in burial rituals throughout human history is a life that cannot be thought of as a life without death. It is only as a life that has always already been struck by death and therefore has death in it that it can manifest itself as a life beyond death. It is also along these lines that we should think the category of a being with the dead, not as a name for social immortality but for shared finitude, as a shared vulnerability and nonsustainability. This is not a communal existence in full possession of itself. Its experience may take the form and articulation of a final affirmation of life beyond death, as in Mauss's obituary for Hertz and his other colleagues. Yet its deeper predicament is captured in the preceding words of his texts, which speak of an experience of itself as "barren soil" and with the exhortation to "be courageous and not indulge in our weakness" and in the affirmation of a commitment to a *legacy*. The "communion" with the dead to which he appeals is not an expression of the certainty of collective survival but the expression of how the task of living-on is connected to a sense of shared vulnerability, of *being-with* as *inheritance* and as *history*.

When the community of the living understands itself as also a community *with* the dead and across the threshold of death, as in the many examples gathered by Hertz and in Mauss's obituary, it brings forth another and expanded sense of sociality. This evasive community of the dead and living is not something that can be simply captured in terms of the rational *needs* of the living and the *imaginary* space of the dead. The standard anthropological-sociological approach sees burial activity both as based on certain "beliefs" or "conceptions" having to do with "after-life" and as a rational way for society and individuals to "heal" themselves in the face of death and loss. But from our reading of Hertz's essay we can glimpse a more fundamental condition. Even though we tend to experience mortality as a sudden disaster at the moment when it strikes, it is a permanent condition of human life, individually and communally. This is not another way of saying that death is "natural." When death is described as "natural," it is usually with the wish to contain it conceptually within a single economy of being and non-being.

The act of burial is a testing ground for what sociology seeks to contain and master in its conceptualization of *the social* as both comprising and not comprising the dead. Where is this sociality located, and where is it enacted? And from what point can it be conceptualized? As we move closer to this domain, it slips away and loses its clear contours, and the idea of a supraindividual totality from which the whole effort originated becomes more difficult to visualize. In its immediate practices, burial involves the corporeal remains of kin. Yet from their very inception these remains are not just themselves. They become symbols and ciphers for what they are not. In death, the other is not simply there in his or her corporeality. She or he is not-there yet exists as *having-been*. This *placelessness* of the dead is crucial. The ritual will always be a care for *something* in the place of *someone* who has been, as a shaping and articulation of this being with the dead. This is its temporal and historical reality.

To say this does not amount to affirming a superstitious interpretation of what is natural and evident. On the contrary, it seeks to remain true to the phenomena. If we are to follow the theoretical dictates of both

Durkheim and Husserl, to remain with the things themselves and not lose ourselves in constructions and fictions, we need to remain within the space of such an experience as the epicenter of what we in other contexts and under other circumstances take for granted: the existence of transindividual, cross-temporal cultural formations, whether they are called societies, communities, peoples, or traditions. What is important is that they are united not simply as objective entities but through the continuously reenacted experiential category of being-with that comprises both the currently living and the dead, as well as those projected to come. We can then begin to sense how the phenomenon of such entities cannot simply be "explained" by facts of biology or by the material and technological devices that secure the connections between and across generations, from tools, to cultural artifacts, and to written archives. But this is only possible through the unstable bond of a *with* that finds an original articulation in the act of caring for the dead other in and beyond death.

3

Ancestrality

GHOSTS, FOREFATHERS, AND OTHER DEAD

> What do the dead make of us
> that we'd flay ourselves trying
> to hear them though they may
> sigh at such close loneliness.
> —Denise Riley, "Under the Answering Sky"

Introduction

There are no known human communities that have not developed some ways of being with their dead, of relating to, communicating with, and even struggling with their dead. In the course of exploring how this predicament was thematized in the human sciences, we repeatedly come across a hermeneutical limit, where they display the ambiguity of their own ethos in regard to the dead. In their attempts to understand death, to map and contain death in its physical and social reality within an economy of life, these disciplines created a hierarchical-evolutionary value scale, where the different forms of mortuary culture and communication with the dead were situated on a lower (religious-superstitious) level of spirituality in relation to which the secular-theoretical comportment and its commitment to life and to the living was seen as a sign of progress and cultural distinction. When confronting not only the death of members of the scientific community but also the ways in which a secular culture of spirit both continues and deepens the commitment and devotion to the dead in its own practices, this ethos reveals its inner ethical and conceptual tensions and contradictions. By bringing out this inherent structural differentiation in response to death and to the dead, it is possible to move the discussion and theoretical interpretation to another level, where the exploration of the existential predicament of being with the dead can make use not only of the anthropological-sociological evidence these disciplines gathered but also of the interpretive schemes they proposed to reach further in our analysis and understanding of the phenomenon in question.

This ambiguity becomes particularly relevant in response to so-called ancestor worship, ancestral piety, or simply cult of the dead (the name varies). In an exploration of the different ways in which human life is constituted by being with the dead, this phenomenon holds a special place. If burial customs and mortuary culture in general primarily involve the *bodily* remains of kin, ancestor worship is not necessarily connected to corporeal remains or to an actual burial ground (even if this is also often the case). Instead, it functions as a collective term for various ways in which the living interact, stay in contact, and communicate with their dead.

The very concept of this cultural practice occupies a unique and contested position within the modern human sciences, with its own history and legacy that we revisit here. When it was first introduced as a descriptive generic term in the anthropological literature during the first half of the nineteenth century, "ancestor worship" was codified both as an expression of *primitiveness* and as an *original* position within the evolution of human spirituality. Or as it was expressed at the outset of the book-length exposition of this phenomenon in the 1908 edition of the *Encyclopedia of Religion*, "It reflects the usual feeling of savage and barbaric man toward his kinsfolk who have passed into the other world."[1] Ancestral piety was temporalized as a form of sociality that belongs to a *past* humanity, or to the past of humanity as such (and then as living on in what is seen as anachronistic communities). But throughout the philosophical and anthropological interpretations of how the living relate to and honor the dead, a scission can also be traced between a supposedly superstitious and primitive form of ancestral piety and one that perceives ancestral lineage and devotion precisely as an expression of higher forms of spirituality, leading up to religion and ultimately to historical consciousness. Whereas the historical human sciences identified, defined, and thus to a certain extent created ancestor worship as its superstitious-religious *other*, the questions that this phenomenon poses also return the historical desire and imagination to its own affective and existential roots. In short, enlightened historical consciousness produces, exteriorizes, and folds into itself the figure of "ancestor worship" as its own secret and rejected source and double.

Just as in the case of burial customs, ancestor worship is a vast topic in itself. The historical-anthropological documentation of its different forms and manifestations is extensive, even though it stems mostly from earlier phases of anthropology of religion. During the second half of the twentieth century the previous preoccupation with ancestor cults among anthropologists was largely replaced by the study of the related topic of *kinship*. In recent years, however, there are indications of a growing interest in the restored potential of this phenomenon.[2] The political, economic, and sociological implications of ancestor worship are extensive. It has been designated as the origin of all religions, but also the origin of political and social organization. References to *ancestry* are constantly reactualized in the context of claims to legitimacy, property, and power, not least in the contested areas of cultural heritage, political and religious orthodoxy, and nationalism, where the latter is sometimes interpreted as rooted directly in ancient practices of ancestor worship.[3] A difficulty that one encounters when trying to theorize this phenomenon from a presumably more neutral perspective is also its seemingly inherent connection to different forms of cultural *conservatism* and *authoritarianism*, a connection to which we return later.

Following the discovery of the human genome and the ability to extract genetic information from ancient human remains, the preoccupation with ancestry and origins has reached new heights in recent decades and has metamorphosed in new theoretical-political configurations. The quest for *biologically* secured ancestry, within families, cultures, nations, and humankind, is now sought and enacted in laboratories in ways that build on—while also concealing—the original existential-ontological meaning of this phenomenon. To this general trend also belongs the worldwide growing preoccupation with family genealogy, the single largest domain of historical research carried out today, mostly by amateur historians who are now aided by the growing availability of commercial online resources such as the website ancestry.org. Within the frame of a single chapter it is possible to touch on only a limited number of examples of this extraordinarily multifaceted phenomenon. We aim to identify a core meaning of the phenomenon of ancestor worship through an analysis that also historicizes its previous conceptualizations. For this purpose, the phenomenon itself needs to be moved from the conventionally understood domain of religion, where it has usually been situated, and relocated to the more general necropolitical and social ontological domain of being with the dead and thus to an expanded sense of historical existence and belonging.

Notes on Terminology

A few words need to be said about the term "ancestor worship" itself. The Latin *ante-cessor* just refers to one coming or going *before*.[4] According to the *Oxford English Dictionary* the English term is first documented as an import from the French *ancestre* and first spelled *auncetres*. The Greek equivalent is *progonos*, the one born before, the "progenitor," which is also a synonym in English for "ancestor." The name "ancestor" usually designates someone from a temporal "before" who at the same time in a certain sense prevails in the present. An ancestor is a forerunner who still remains operative through a relation of belonging and reciprocity, as is marked by the present tense. An ancestor is someone who one *has*, not someone who one has *had*. Thus, its peculiar temporality also signals the presence of *grounds* and *foundations* in an ambiguous combination of cause and reason, through lineage and inheritance. Even in its earlier uses it is not necessarily restricted to biological lineage but can also designate source and origin in a more indirect sense. The combined term "ancestor worship," *culte des ancêtres*, or *Ahnenkultus* in German, is a modern invention, emanating from the comparative study of cultures and first documented in European languages from around the mid-nineteenth century, and then often with an explicit reference to China and Chinese religion, where it was taken to mark the dominant trait of its spiritual life.[5] The term is thus a central conceptual component in the framework developed for cross-cultural interpretation of religions, through which the human-historical sciences established themselves as a universal discourse within the parallel sociocultural context of globalization and colonialism.

In a survey article from 1987 Helen Hardacre defines "ancestor worship" as "rites and beliefs concerning deceased kinsmen" that include "personal devotions, domestic rites, the ancestral rites of a kinship group such as a lineage, periodic rites on the death day of the deceased, and annual rites for collectivity of ancestors."[6] The earlier colonial rhetoric of "savages" is now obviously absent, yet there is still no attempt to connect these practices to anything on the European continent or within Christianity. In a more recent survey volume on the anthropology of religion published in 2013 there is no longer any article on the subject of ancestor worship. It is as if the whole topic, which once so deeply captivated the anthropological imagination, more so perhaps than any other phenomenon in the anthropology of religion, just disappeared, presumably as a result of its deep and by now embarrassing colonial-political legacy. When the phenomena associated with this term are analyzed in the present, it is instead in the context of an article on the ontologies and values of contemporary hunter-gatherer societies by the Canadian anthropologist Sylvie Poirier. She describes how these societies maintain and transmit themselves with the help of what she now refers to as "ancestrality," which she defines as "worlds where ancestors and spirits of deceased relatives are existentially coeval with the living and communicate with them in various ways."[7] In calling forth an image of how life in communication with ancestors has to do with the maintenance of culture and tradition, she points toward the question of the constitution of historical culture at large, but without trying to explore the underlying ontological framework. Her text can thus be seen as an end point of two centuries of attempts to conceptualize this phenomenon within the human-historical sciences, where it was first situated at the center of their concerns and posited as the negative other of historical consciousness itself, to finally appear as the positive traditionality of the other. It is this trajectory that we must understand if we are to reach beyond the value-laden explanatory schemata of the human sciences and into their socio-ontological foundations.

Ancestor Worship and the Birth
of the Human-Historical Sciences

On the first of the eight pages that Hegel devotes to Africa in his lecture series *The Philosophy of History*, he introduces it as "the land of childhood, which lying beyond the day of self-conscious history, is enveloped in the dark mantle of Night."[8] After having summarized the geographical, spiritual, and political destiny of the entire continent, he finishes with a note on slavery. While being essentially unjust—since humanity has a shared essence and freedom is an unconditional value—slavery still needs to be dismantled slowly to permit enslaved humanity first to "mature." The last lines of this infamous passage read: "The gradual abolition of slavery is therefore wiser and more equitable than its sudden removal. At this point we leave Africa, not to mention it again."[9] From the viewpoint of our question it is significant to note that Hegel's depiction of Africa as the "dark" and unconscious continent specifically involves his understanding of ancestor worship. The key to the "African character" is said to be the lack of a sense of that universality that first presents itself in religion as the consciousness of a "higher power." Instead of being committed to an independent higher principle, its peoples are described as "sorcerers," believing in their own "magical" power over nature, concentrated in an artifact endowed with spiritual power, a so-called fetish. From Hegel's viewpoint, this type of spirituality has not even reached the level of elementary religion. The latter requires the belief in a spiritual force located outside the space of the self and its subjectivity. There is, he writes, no sense of "dependence" (*Abhängigkeit*) in this religion.[10] There is, however, one feature that does point to something "beyond," the worship of the dead (*Totendienst*), "in which their deceased forefathers and ancestors are regarded by them as a power influencing the living."[11] Yet after having recognized this inkling of a higher-order spirituality, Hegel retracts and notes instead that the dead in the African context are mainly a source of "vengeance" and "injuries," perceived primarily as a threat "like witches in the Middle Ages."[12]

In the sharply contrasted spiritual economy that Hegel elaborates here, the core matter concerns the question of death and the survival of the spirit. More specifically, it concerns the mode in which the living engage with their dead. For the African, he writes, death is not a "universal law" but is looked on instead as the unfortunate effect of sorcery. And in what is perhaps the most remarkable statement in this entire discourse Hegel notes that Africans "have no knowledge of the immortality of the soul [*Seele*], although specters [*Gespenster*] are supposed to appear."[13] This statement is followed by a series of derogatory generalizations of how Africa is predisposed for tyranny, cannibalism, slavery, and violations of justice and morality. In short, it is precisely around *the different ways in which the living understand and relate to their dead* that the defining characteristics of the two cultural spheres are hierarchically established and through which the cultural-colonial discourse here secures its legitimacy.

According to Hegel's account, it is the African way of relating to the spirits or ghosts of their dead that distinguishes them as primitive. At the same time, the Europeans' belief—indeed their "knowledge" (*Wissen*)–of the continued life of the souls of *their* dead is a prerequisite for these societies, which are seen as based on the universal values of justice and morality. Whereas Westerners receive their superior spiritual and moral position precisely through the way they care for the survival of their ancestors, the Africans are doomed to degradation precisely for the way that they handle theirs. In the end, it all comes down to the quality and nature of the dead. While the African land of the dead is occupied only by *ghosts* (*Gespenste*), the land of the dead in the West contains both *souls* and *spirits* (*Seele* and *Geiste*). In an extraordinary and at least on the surface blatantly contradictory tour de force, European superiority is thus articulated explicitly as a question of how to view, care for, and relate to the dead, and ultimately on the basis of the proper knowledge of the ontological distinctions concerning the modes of their afterlife. *Geist* or *Gespenst*—the juridical and political verdict falls along this fault line, separating freedom from servitude.

Hegel's analyses of this "worship of the dead" (*Totendienst*)—he does not yet use the term "ancestor cult" (*Ahnenkultus*)—is sweeping in its analysis and deeply disturbing in its conclusions. Yet it establishes certain basic traits of a discourse that will continue to guide the conceptualizations of these phenomena for a century to come. It is true in particular of the way that a supposedly primitive, superstitious, and authoritarian comportment with regard to the dead ancestors is contrasted with a more beneficial and culturally formative reverence for the souls of the departed and their legacy. As we try to explore the general predicament of what it means to *be* with the dead, these normative cultural patterns need to be taken into account, as dimensions of a larger territory with far-reaching moral and political ramifications.

In relation to Hegel's explicitly Eurocentric perspective on the worship of ancestors, Denis Fustel de Coulanges's minor classic *La cité antique* from 1864 marks a new step in the conceptualization of this phenomenon.[14] The book is a study of how religious practices among Romans in regard to their ancestors contributed to shaping the Roman city. Beliefs in the afterlife of the soul in the underworld, the necessity of providing a correct burial, and continued ritual services for the dead are here seen as rituals through which Rome secured the proper continuation of the lives of its citizens. For Fustel de Coulanges the worship of the dead is the original form of religious consciousness, a transcultural fact that is found not just in Africa and China but also among Hindus and—as is the topic of his book—in European antiquity.[15] He traces the formation of the state to the moment when two families or tribes unite with each other and establish a unity on the condition that everyone's devotion should be respected, symbolized by the lighting of a sacred fire.[16] Fustel de Coulanges writes in a sweeping and speculative style with limited archaeological evidence to support his claims. Yet his basic observations remain valid: the Romans often buried their dead on their own land, and the families often kept a private sanctuary for their ancestors. Thus, the Romans continued a tradition of city dwellers—who have later been documented in very much older Neolithic archaeological sites—living close to the remains of the dead, sometimes literally inhabiting the graves of deceased ancestors.[17]

When Hegel refers to a "cult of the dead" in his lectures from around 1820, the term "ancestor worship," or the equivalent *culte des ancêtres* or *Ahnenkult*, had not yet been established. And Fustel de Coulanges speaks intermittently of a "cult of the dead" or of "offerings to ancestors." But when Herbert Spencer publishes *The Principles of Sociology* twenty years later, "ancestor worship" is presented as "the root of every religion."[18] In his attempt to trace the various forms of spiritual life across different cultures and to bring them together in an evolutionary schema, Spencer devotes an entire chapter to ancestor worship in general. From the Dolores mission in San Francisco in the 1770s he quotes reports of tribes who apparently had "no word for god, angel, or devil; they held no theory of origin or destiny." Yet through their burial rites they appeared to have some conceptions of the presence of a spiritual other. From this Spencer concludes that "we may hold it as settled that the first traceable conception of a supernatural being is the conception of a ghost." And furthermore, "almost as widely spread as the belief in ghosts, may be looked for a more or less developed ancestor-worship."[19]

After having settled the question of the transcultural nature and prevalence of ancestor worship, Spencer turns explicitly to the question of European exceptionalism: "I have seen implied, I have heard in conversation, and I have now before me in print, the statement that 'no Indo-European or Semitic nation, so far as we know, seems to have made a religion of worship of the dead,'" in other words, that "superior races were never ancestor worshippers."[20] With the support of much evidence he then goes on to state, continuing the argument of Fustel de Coulanges, that the Aryans did indeed practice ancestor worship, as did the Semitic peoples.[21] The point is now that this follows a general evolutionary scale, where "all superior people have passed through this lower cult." On this scale, however, there are definitive and even defining differences that again institute and secure the European cultural superiority. Whereas "Negroes who, when suffering, go to the woods and cry for help to the spirits of dead relatives" by these acts demonstrate the "groveling nature of their race," the offerings made by the Romans to their *Lares* were "merely marks of proper respect to forefathers."[22]

To the earlier and founding generations of anthropology, ancestral worship thus represents an elemental form of spiritual and religious life, projected along an evolutionary scale. Traces of it are still said to be present in contemporary European society, with its depictions of forefathers and cult of graves. "Even Protestants," Spencer writes, yield "undeniable traces of the aboriginal ideas and sentiments and acts," a tendency that he partly attributes to a "revived Catholicism." For it is, he continues, "among Catholic people that this primitive religion most distinctly shows itself." From the original "ghost, once uniformly conceived, have arisen the variously-conceived supernatural beings."[23] In this way, he concludes, we should understand the root of all religiosity. In this treatment of the topic a similar cultural logic as in Hegel is thus at work. The cult of the dead is interpreted as the first mark of a sense of transcendence of the human spirit. It is a general anthropological trait, on the basis of which higher forms of spiritual culture are seen to arise. From African superstition to modern-day Northern European religion there is a ladder of gradual sophistication, where Catholicism, especially in its Southern European form, occupies an intermediate position. Yet in the image of the Roman nobleman paying tributes to his elders we have an early image of a superior form of culture, manifested in and through the proper cult of ancestors.

In one of the greatest achievements of late nineteenth-century philological scholarship, Erwin Rohde's *Psyche* (1890), the line of argument from Fustel de Coulanges and Spencer was taken up and developed further in relation specifically to the Greeks in Homeric and pre-Homeric times. The topic of his book was the extent to which the Greeks also practiced a cult of the souls of the dead.[24] Arguing against the standard interpretation that a cult of ancestors is absent in Homer and that this form of superstition appeared only later in Greek life, Rohde traces the vestiges of an earlier Greek conception of the soul as not only surviving death but also in need of sacrifices and rites of burial in order not to return and trouble the living. What he is looking for and what he finds are thus traces of a more "primitive" and "irrational" Greek spirituality beyond and behind the presumably "rational" world of Homer as professed by the earlier representatives of classical philology, in a critical intervention that recalls his and Nietzsche's shared interest in the Dionysian core of Greek Apollonian culture. This world can still be glimpsed through the textual sources, including the Homeric epic itself, and most notably its depiction of the sacrificial rites performed by Odysseus at the entrance of Hades. The underlying idea is that such cultic practices bear witness to an original *fear* of the dead, who must be appeased by means of sacrificial rituals. In the most rudimentary forms it is also said to bear witness to a lack of historical awareness and of history as such that is common among "savages."[25]

When James Frazer explores the topic of an original cult of ancestors and the dead in his Trinity College lectures in 1932, published as *The Fear of the Dead in Primitive Religion*, the emphasis has been slightly altered, yet the same Hegelian teleological-spiritual framework remains operative. Frazer stresses that he himself is an agnostic in regard to the question of the survival of the spirit after death. The superior position here is no longer that of reformed Christianity, as in Hegel and Spencer, but of *science*, even though this science remains colored by a distinctively reformed Christian ethos. Using the metaphor of warfare, Frazer anticipates that in due time the "battery of science" will reach into "the frowning bastions of faith," a faith so "flattering to human vanity and so comforting to human sorrow." The belief in the immortality of the spirit and the consecutive cult of the dead is described not only as a core conception in all advanced religions but also as a general conception in all primitive religions, a cultural constellation he defines as "the religion of the backward or uncivilized races, in other words savages and barbarians."[26] Frazer recognizes that there are exceptions to the general rule "that primitive folk regard the spirits of the dead with more fear than affection," and he exemplifies it by a series of reports on how the living relate to their dead with affection, through house burials; ritual caretaking of skeletal remains, in particular of children; and through different ways of bringing back the souls of the dead. Yet the basic scheme of the book, supported by a wealth of anthropological data, is that "fear and scrupulous avoidance" are what most often characterize how "primitive man" relates to the souls of the departed.[27]

Frazer's Gifford lectures establish a fundamental ethical and political distinction based on differences in relating to dead kin and ancestors. And in the final passage of the preface to the published lectures, directly after having professed his hope that "the battery of science" will finally overcome the bastions of faith, his discourse turns into eulogy and honorific praise. He thanks Trinity College for having "bestowed on him an honor" by associating the lectures to his "honoured friend," William Wyse, who by his "noble foundation" has created a "monument to a life unswervingly devoted to the pursuit of truth and to all that is good and beautiful in humanity." And he ends with the wish that his "contribution to the monument were less unworthy of it and of him." This ritual confession of praise, gratitude, and commitment to long-lasting ideals connected to the memory of this dead predecessor constitutes a genre of speaking and acting that is appropriate for the occasion. Yet in this particular context, and in relation to the overall theme of the book and its cultural-political agenda, it also illustrates how the anthropologist locates his pursuits and concerns in a space constituted by and thus also occupied by the continued presence of dead forebearers to whom he thus ritually offers his praise in a self-humbling gesture. Recalling Spencer's analysis, Frazer performs what any good Roman (i.e., British) man should do on the occasion: pay his respects to the dead. Following the nineteenth-century philosophical-anthropological matrix, paying one's respects to forefathers, biological as well as spiritual-social, can both be an expression of the most despicable backwardness and a sign of the most dignified spirituality. It all hinges on *how* the living are with their dead.

Freud and the Inner Savage

To modern anthropology, following its self-critical and postcolonial turn from the 1970s onward, Frazer and his legacy are an embarrassment. Today he is rarely even recognized as belonging to the history of the discipline, which prefers to date its origins to the work of Durkheim, Mauss, and Mead. Yet for a long time, and certainly during his own lifetime, Frazer was one of its key proponents, very much respected and with a far-reaching impact, not least on psychoanalysis.[28] In *Totem and Taboo* (1913), Freud cites extensively from *The Golden Bough*, as the notion of an original fear of the dead and the taboos surrounding the physical contact with the dead occupy the center of his argument. To Frazer's teleological-developmental model of a gradual liberation from the fear of the dead, Freud adds an *inner* genealogy concerning the relation to the dead. The neurotics are said to fear the dead in a similar way as the "savages." Freud subscribes to the comparative and reciprocal ethnological model according to which the psychology of "primitive peoples" as taught by social anthropology can teach us something about the psychology of "neurotics." Inversely, the psychology of contemporary "savages or half-savages" can give us access to the earlier stages of human development.[29] Referring to the example of the Australian Aborigines, one of the "most backward and miserable of savages," he writes that they do not show any sign of "religion in the shape of worship of higher beings"; instead, the place of religion is occupied by "totemism" as the material representation of the common "ancestor of the clan," who also functions as a "guardian spirit and helper."[30]

The most interesting part of Freud's analysis from our present point of view concerns the specific taboos surrounding the dead. Echoing Frazer, he refers to it as a historical fact that the basic attitude toward the dead is fear.[31] This is exemplified not just in the precaution and even refusal to touch the body of the deceased and his or her relatives but also in the refusal to even use the name of the dead. In conjunction with this discussion Freud also notes that peoples who are most meticulous in their precautions in dealing with their dead, to the point of refusing to mention their names, consequently "possess no tradition and no historical memory." Thus, we see again how the connection is explicitly established between the cult of the dead and historical consciousness. Freud does not say so explicitly, but the underlying conclusion, just as in Hegel, is that where there is too much anxiety in relation to the individual dead, where the dead are *too* close, humans become incapable of relating to them in a *spiritually* adequate way, which is what history and historical memory is essentially all about.[32]

After having recalled a number of Frazer's examples of this presumably original fear of the dead, Freud turns to the question of how to explain this anthropological constant. He directs his attention to the conception that the dead may "return," perhaps in the form of a "ghost."[33] He explains the fantasy of the dead threatening the living as issuing from an unconscious death wish toward the deceased, a socially unacceptable affect that is *projected* onto the image of the departed and that therefore transforms him or her into a malicious spirit.[34] Thus, the basic feelings toward the dead—pity and fear—are taken to mirror the two elementary responses to death, mourning and desire. According to Freud's genetic-psychological schema, the comportment of "primitive" peoples mirrors not only the workings of the deranged psyche of contemporary humans but also an elemental level of all humankind. From Freud's letters and the preface to the second edition of *The Interpretation of Dreams*, we know that this sober conclusion concerning the response to dead kin had a more tormented personal background in his own case, in regard to the death of his father, Jacob Freud, in 1896. In the 1908 preface he recalls that the book grew essentially directly out of his own self-analysis following the death of his father, as "the most significant event, the most decisive loss, of a man's life." It is directly following the attempts to come to terms with his contradictory reactions to his father's death that he develops his ideas of "survivor's guilt" as well as the theory of the Oedipus complex, the combined desire and shame of having "surpassed" the father. Psychoanalysis partly emanates from the necessity of having to come to terms with a dead father and with the anxieties resulting from this present absence, as both spirit or ghost, indeed from the aspiration to spiritualize the potentially harmful ghost of the father.[35]

Freud's approach to the topic of the response to and culture of the dead inserts itself along a linear and hierarchical trajectory from its first articulation in Hegel and developed by sociology, philology, anthropology, and the comparative study of religion. According to this model, human spiritual culture takes its point of departure in the response to the death of kin, first in the form of superstitious and "magical" conceptions of the survival of the dead in the form of often malicious ghosts, and then gradually through more refined and abstracted conceptions of the soul and spirit. Ultimately, these conceptions are abandoned altogether in favor of a rational-psychological explanation in which they are seen as misguided affective responses to personal and collective loss in and among the survivors. Whereas the African is initially positioned as primitive in virtue of how he worships his dead in the cult of ancestors, the European triumphs precisely through how he cultivates his dead: through his belief in the immortality of the *soul,* and his ability to remain faithful to the *spiritual* inheritance of the dead, as a vital force that he takes upon himself to keep, honor, and cultivate through a historical culture of learning. The development of historical and comparative anthropology from the time of Hegel to Freud thus establishes a linear progression of refinement in terms of relating to the dead, where the supposedly rational cultivation of the dead in historical awareness emerges as a supreme spiritual task in itself. In the course of this development its rejected other—the superstitious, the primitive, and the savage—becomes the target of a patronizing and at times even violently hierarchical discourse. It is as if historical consciousness needs this confinement of the death cult of the other in order to produce and maintain itself.

Ancestors, Elders, and New Regimes

Since the beginning of the postwar era the discourse of the cultural-historical disciplines in general, and of anthropology in particular, has sought to distance itself from the openly hierarchical, colonial-political, and culturally biased models of interpretation that previously guided them. Today we are in a different position than at the time of Frazer and Freud. The preoccupation with the fear of the dead that so much captured the imagination of the older generations of anthropologists is scientifically a nonissue. Expressions of animism and totemism are today explored within very different contexts, for example, through a new interest in pan-psychism that is now also linked to ecological issues and critiques of overly rationalized civilization.[36] Yet throughout these transformations of the interpretive orientation, there has been no real attempt to *rethink* the conceptual foundations of the previous understanding of the culture of death. Instead, the topic has been toned down and gradually abandoned. At this point it is therefore necessary to return to and explore the earlier practices of exclusion and denigration within historical consciousness in regard to relating to the dead, in order to visualize its underlying ontological predicament but also to engage critically with the consequences of its reversed legacy.

For this purpose the various comportments summarized under the often misleading term "ancestor worship" should be interpreted within the more general matrix of being with the dead, which in turn combines various affects, as well as various levels, of more or less "authentic" responses to dead kin. The earlier discourse of the human-historical sciences understood and explained ancestor worship in terms of superstition, fantasies, and "projections," originally generated from within a misguided process or "work" of mourning. According to this schema, whoever learns to mourn in a rationally efficient way need not preoccupy himself with the dead, since they are gone and whatever effects they may have on the living are purely phantasmatic. But at the same time this rational system of thought is also characterized from the start precisely by its ability to deepen and expand its own engagement with the dead, incessantly at work on the project of keeping the dead "alive" through historical knowledge, textual hermeneutics, and reenactments, and of securing access to ancestral lines with the help of the most advanced methods of natural science:

unearthing graves and archives, drilling through bones, and probing the minuscule traces of human lineages. This pursuit of *knowledge of the past* remains a supreme mode of spirituality of Western global culture, through which it triumphs and reaches for transcendence. However, it too constitutes a mode of ancestrality, for which epistemic access and existential reciprocity to predecessors continue to orient its aspirations.

What we think of as "historical culture" marks a disciplined mode of being with the dead. It preserves and cultivates long lineages of ancestors in the arts, sciences, and politics. It is a culture that emphasizes inheritance and its preservation through ritual enactment of and critical struggles with legacies. On a more personal-family level it is manifested in the maintenance of family lineage, of remembering and paying respect to elders and keeping their legacy alive as an ethical imperative. Seen from this perspective, the way in which the classical anthropological literature was preoccupied with rejecting the culture of death and ancestor worship as signs of primitiveness obtains a new and more complex meaning. Throughout this domain or territory, we can sense a broader concern that has to do with creating new forms and modes of life where the dead and the living can exist together, and of which historical culture marks a disciplined manifestation. The violent expulsion of the primitive then becomes partly explicable as a step in the construction of such a rational historical awareness and culture. By organizing the history of human cultures in both a diachronic and a synchronic hierarchy, in terms of its modes of dealing with the dead, it established itself as that system and technology of knowledge that we know as "cultural history." Its target, as demonstrated by quotations from Spencer, Frazer, and Freud, was not just the primitive cultures beyond Europe but also a primitiveness within itself: the church as the institution claiming the privilege of handling mortuary rituals and having the knowledge or the *techne* concerning life after death and the nature of the souls of the departed. Once the very notion of life after death and the idea of a continued communication with the souls of the dead was placed in a historical-anthropological comparative perspective, the uniqueness of the Christian interpretation was ultimately reduced to a version of a more general phenomenon.

Once this work was completed, it was no longer necessary to pay as much attention to ancestor rituals and to their moral and psychological deficiencies as did earlier generations of researchers. Instead, the anthropological interest could move to the study of *kinship* as a key to unraveling social, economic, and political structures, where the specific rites concerned with ancestors could also be framed within a structuralist matrix reflecting power relations rather than as an actual way of communicating with the dead. This is true of what is often mentioned as the major work on ancestor worship within the postwar scholarship on this topic, Jack Goody's *Death, Property and the Ancestors* (1962).[37] It meticulously analyzes and compares burial rites and ancestor worship in two tribal cultures, the LoDagaa and the LoWiili in Ghana, in relation to how property is inherited over generations, from a neo-Marxist and structuralist perspective. Here any meaning ascribed to the survival of ancestral spirits is framed and situated in the context of economic relations among the living.

In 1971 Igor Kopytoff took a different and critical approach in a short but significant contribution to the more conceptual discussion on ancestor worship in Africa, which anticipates subsequent postcolonial critiques.[38] Most of Kopytoff's examples were taken from the Sukus in southwestern Congo, but in Weberian fashion he claimed to have grasped an ideal type that he took to be true for most African tribal societies. Kopytoff's basic point was that the very term "ancestor worship" is misleading if we are to understand the specific nature of African social organization. He stresses that there is no specific word for "ancestor" in these communities; instead, they are referred to as *bambutata*, meaning "the old ones" or "the big ones," as a general designation for the elderly. He proposes that we refer to this entire phenomenon instead as "eldership complex." Authority in these communities is practiced in a hierarchical-linear way, in which people obey upward. Supplication for support, advice, and blessing is directed upward toward the eldest, which means that the living elder will turn to the even older ones, that is, to the dead. "If there be a 'cult' here," Kopytoff writes, "it is a cult of *bambutata*, of elders living and dead," to which respect, *buzitu*, is paid.[39] He notes critically that anthropologists have been misled to designate phenomena as "worship" and "sacrifice," where it is instead often a question of paying respect and tribute.

With this analysis it was as if the discourse of cultural anthropology had come, inadvertently, full circle to its point of departure. According to Spencer's argument, it was precisely this dignified way of paying respect to the elders that so completely distanced the Romans from their African counterparts. But for Koptytoff the idea of separating ancestors from living elders is deemed a "Western ethnocentric conviction" that conditions how cultural interpreters approach and theorize about African data. He concludes his article with a sharp judgment: "The selection by anthropologists of the phrases 'ancestor cult' and 'ancestor worship,' in dealing with African culture, is semantically inappropriate, analytically misleading, and theoretically unproductive."[40] But in the course of articulating this important critique, he is thus led to affirm a cultural relativism that from around this time will gradually become increasingly influential in anthropological research. He does not see or recognize that it was precisely the idea of a more and a less dignified way of relating to ancestors that structured the anthropological imagination in the first place and that the behavior that he now ascribes to a presumably African mode of relating to ancestors replicates the imagery through which it was initially excluded from a proper and authentic relation to the past.

We, however, can now look at his conclusions and the entire debate from a different perspective. The evidence in this case does not testify to a specific African or indigenous people but rather to a modality of the larger phenomenon of being with the dead as itself a fundamental human predicament, of which the "historical culture" practiced in historical anthropology constitutes one expression. When interpreting his evidence, Kopytoff does not leave the space of a Western, European intellectual context, but he spontaneously activates a more general framework for understanding what it means to exist as a historical being in order to make this observed evidence understandable. With his critical assessment of previous anthropological models, he set the pattern for a mode of thinking that would gradually gain currency, where the prejudices of earlier anthropologists was challenged. But at the same time the possibility of exploring the more general existential-ontological platform for understanding expressions of ancestrality was thus also obscured.

Thinking Ancestrality Anew

Against this background we can now return to the article by Sylvie Poirier where she describes how surviving current hunter-gatherer societies in North America maintain and transmit themselves with the help of what she calls "ancestrality," which she defines as "worlds where ancestors and spirits of deceased relatives are existentially coeval with the living and communicate with them in various ways."[41] She connects this phenomenon to the larger theme "relational ontologies," which she here characterizes as an "acknowledgement of those who were here before."[42] The article is written from a similar critical perspective as Kopytoff's, but instead of just disparaging the presumably outdated concept of ancestor worship, Poirier proposes the term "ancestrality" to capture the peculiar mode of maintaining a sense of *tradition* in these specific societies. Yet in recalling this connection to a *culture of the past* and *tradition*, she too inscribes phenomena previously connected to ancestral worship within a conceptual matrix elicited from historical culture and historical aware- ness. And just as in Kopytoff's analysis this is done only implicitly and under the pretext of describing something unique and *other* to a Western conceptual and cultural schema, while inadvertently reproducing its core values. Compelled for good reasons to question the ethical and political consequences of a previously construed evolutionary-hierarchical cultural taxonomy, contemporary anthropology repeatedly finds itself in this same position. In its overly cautious urge not to classify or objectify the other by means of universalizing concepts, it misses the possibility of thinking a deeper and shared and common predicament.

Within an expanded social ontology we can work with the concept of "ancestrality," but understood instead as a basic existential-ontological predicament and as a root phenomenon of human historicity. Following the analysis in Chapter 1, this condition would be understood as a condi- tion for what we think of as historical culture and the experience of the past. The different types and modes of relating to and being with the dead can then be seen as existential variations and as different ways of living and comporting oneself vis-à-vis those having-been. Within this existential-ontological space the historical-genealogical trajectory that we have traced can instead work as empirical support for affirming a gen- eral ontological schema of being with the dead. But it can also serve as an illustration of how within this space it is always possible to question the mode and extent to which the living communicate with the dead. There is always a question to be asked concerning the "authenticity" of this relation, such as, "What are the dead saying to us?," "What are they asking from us?," or "What do we owe them?"

"Cult of ancestors" was a name coined in the context of nineteenth-century socioanthropological study of religion to designate a variety of isomorphic practices first observed in the colonies as characteristic of the other. They were then gradually brought homeward, first as characterizing the idealized Roman and Greek predecessors and eventually the primitive heart of human subjectivity in general as in the cultural psychology of Freud. By identifying ancestor worship as the "root of all religion," the human sciences were able to situate their own Christian culture within a larger comparative domain and thus create a space for it under its new spiritual dome of *historical awareness* and *historical knowledge*. Under this larger sky the past in its totality could ideally be gathered, classified, and cataloged and thus controlled chronologically, morphologically, and geographically. But in relying on the creation of history and historical awareness as simply the rational antidote to the superstitious engagement with ancestors, it receded from fully thinking and conceptualizing the existential-ontological predicament of being with the dead as itself a condition of historicity.

As anthropology in its postcolonial and critical phase explicitly sought to distance itself from the necropolitics of its predecessors, its modern critical representatives nevertheless tended to reproduce earlier hierarchies but under inverted labels, where the other's traditionality or ancestrality would be essentialized as a more genuine ethico-political relation between the living and the dead. But if we are to understand both ourselves and the presumably other, we need to reach beyond the relativization of cultural practices having to do with ancestrality. Following a similar argument as in Johannes Fabian's criticism of how the contemporary and culturally other is made into a temporal-historical other, we need to visualize how the social ontology of being with the dead constitutes a transcultural domain.[43] All societies live with their dead. All societies develop practices for being with ancestors. The ethos of historical consciousness conceptualizes the past as *spirit*, in the name of which it could claim to have disparaged the *ghosts*, as the past of the other as well as the ghost itself. But if we think the predicament of ancestrality instead as a general condition and dimension of human historicity, it should be possible to reclaim this domain from a new angle. Then it will appear not just as a relative, regional, and archaic life world but as a transcultural predicament where there is no given and obvious guidance. The living will always have to find a way to respond to the dead, and in their daily practices they will have to come to terms with the nature of their mode of being and what they owe to them.

Only if the human sciences can see themselves not just as the liberated descendants of earlier ancient and primitive cults of the dead but also as practices that in increasingly sophisticated ways continue to cultivate modes of living with the dead, only then perhaps can they also move beyond the violence and the fear inherent in the earlier conceptualizations of this domain. And only then can they claim more authentically to engage in the critical and potentially violent battles with those who claim to know once and for all how to live, think, and act by complying with tradition, inheritance, and ancestral demands.

The question can always be posed: How do you remain in contact with the ancestors, and to whom do you listen, and to whom do you not listen? Historical research is the most advanced epistemic practice available for determining *how it really was with the dead others,* but ultimately it is not located outside the ethical-political space of ancestrality. In its attempts to study and understand the different forms of this socio-ontological predicament, the human-historical sciences themselves became participants in a battle of ancestral power and legitimacy, for a time relying on the *logos* of a single *spirit* to control and sometimes silence the multiplicity of all regional *ghosts.* Today the global spiritual-parliamentary situation demands a more subtle ear.

Necropolitics

Contested Communities and Remains of the Dead

> King, father, royal Dane. O, answer me! Let me not burst in ignorance; but tell why thy canoniz'd bones, hearsed in death, have burst their cerements; why the sepulchre wherein we saw thee quietly inurn'd hath op'd his ponderous and marble jaws to cast thee up again.
>
> —Shakespeare, *Hamlet*

Introduction

In the fall of 1918, as the German Empire was collapsing and the First World War was coming to an end, Max Weber addressed the students of the University of Munich with what would become his most famous lecture, "Science as Vocation." He presented the idea that would eventually obtain an emblematic status, not only for his own work but for the self-understanding of enlightened intellectual postwar existence: that we are living in a "disenchanted" world, an *entzauberte Welt*.[1] What characterizes this condition according to his famous definition is that "there are no mysterious incalculable forces that come into play, but rather that one can in principle, master all things by calculation." At the heart of this diagnosis is also the question of the meaning of *death*, which Weber introduces through Tolstoy, whom he presents as an exemplary witness. Tolstoy had seen and explored how within a world characterized by the progressiveness of human spirit and culture an individual human being can no longer imagine itself to die a meaningful death after having lived a fulfilled existence, unlike "Abraham, or some peasant of the past" who could die "satiated with life." Death for civilized man will be only "a meaningless occurrence" through which he is deprived of taking part in the continued adventure of humanity.[2] For the same reason, there is no longer any room for the sublime and monumental in the public political and intellectual sphere, just as there is little room for prophecy, spirituality, and religion, especially not in the academy. Weber's somber advice to the students of his time, professed just a year before his own premature death, was instead courageously to confront this condition and meet the "demands of the day" in personal as well as in academic affairs.[3]

Two years later in the fall of 1920 a new type of public monument and ritual was introduced, first in London and then in Paris, and followed by similar monuments in several other countries: the Tomb of the Unknown Soldier. This public memorial, created around what could be seen as the most meaningless death possible, an anonymous disappearance in the trenches of the Great War, was thereby made into a symbol and place of reverence for the citizens of the modern (increasingly) democratic nation-states. As these states reconstituted themselves following the disaster of nationalist-imperial politics, they coalesced around the ritual piety and respect before the anonymous bones of someone who precisely in virtue of his anonymity could symbolize the collective loss and sacrifice of the nation. At this very disenchanting historical moment in European history, it was around the sacralization of an unidentified corpse (or in some cases an empty grave, representing such a corpse) that a political community gave itself a new spiritual-political focus.

The exceptional symbolic-political importance of these new monuments was highlighted by Benedict Anderson at the outset of his celebrated study of nationalism, *Imagined Communities* (1983), where he refers to them as the most "arresting emblems of the modern culture of nationalism." For Anderson this proves that nationalism is ultimately connected to "religious" fantasies and the desire to give sense to the cruel passage of time by connecting the dead with the not-yet-born, making the graves ripe with "ghostly national imaginings." He even ridicules the idea that there would be a monument to a dead Marxist or liberal, since "neither Marxism nor liberalism is much concerned with death and immortality."[4]

If Anderson had recalled the strange fate of the body of Marx in London, not to speak of the mummified body of Lenin on display in Moscow, he would not have expressed himself so frivolously on the matter.[5] The ease with which he at this point thought that he could handle the connection between politics, burials, and the dead, both among Marxists and their liberal rivals, would soon look different. When Reinhart Koselleck and his colleagues brought together a large volume on modern war memorials and the cult of death ten years later, the tone was more serious. In their preface they spoke of the political cult of the dead as an anthropological given "without which history would be unthinkable."[6] They too took a particular interest in "monuments to the common soldier," of which they traced the first efforts back to the years immediately following the French Revolution.[7] With their analysis and interest in this topic they anticipated what would become an increasingly relevant issue following the political developments that transpired in the meantime. With the events of 1989, postwar Europe fundamentally changed its face, and with the political upheavals the question of the politics of the dead obtained a new urgency. One event from those tumultuous years has come to stand out as emblematic for this new constellation: the unearthing and reburial of Imre Nagy's corpse in Budapest in the summer of 1989, a public ritual in which the battle between totalitarian Marxism and liberal democratic opposition took the form of a struggle over a dead body and its representation in death. The communist reformer who led the revolt in 1956, but who was overthrown and then later hanged in 1958, had been buried facedown with his compatriots without coffins in unmarked graves. But on June 16, 1989, a quarter of a million Hungarians followed his remains being unearthed, placed faceup in a coffin, and then reburied with full honors, an event that is generally recognized as one of the catalysts for the ensuing revolution.

The complex sociopolitical symbolism of this particular event and how it fueled the final collapse of the Iron Curtain has been analyzed by several writers, notably Katherine Verdery in *The Political Lives of Dead Bodies* (1999).[8] Among her examples are how the violent and bitter breakup of former Yugoslavia involved complicated negotiations concerning access to the graves of the dead and, in some cases, unearthing of graves so deterritorialized populations could bring the remains of their dead with them.[9] In response to this and similar parallel events, Verdery develops an interpretation that tries to bring these phenomena under a more general sociological-anthropological matrix in which older theories of kinship and ancestor worship are actualized again to interpret the role of the dead in the constitution and maintenance of political communities.

This revival in recent times of necropolitical phenomena and their interpretation was often exemplified with events in Eastern Europe, where it was connected with the liberal-conservative nationalist upheavals of former communist regimes, but also with waves of collective mourning over previously silenced crimes of the past. However, the significance of necropolitics and the question of the connection between the constitution of political communities and the remains of the dead have many dimensions. Important in this context has been the role of bodily remains in postcolonial and indigenous struggles for recognition and political representation, notably among Native Americans and Australian Aborigines from the 1970s onward, which have also inspired similar movements worldwide.

In Thomas Laqueur's study of mortuary culture in Europe beginning with the Enlightenment, *The Work of the Dead*, the focus is also on the "agency" of the dead. His basic message is that whatever people in different epochs may have done to the bodies of the dead, the dead continuously prove their significance by actually doing *work* for, with, and on the living, indeed, that they "are active agents in history" and "make civilization."[10] Through a wealth of material on changing burial practices in modern times from the French Revolution onward, Laqueur circles around the fundamental questions. How can we understand the nature of this postmortem agency, or this *work* that the dead are said to perform in the world of the living? In thus framing his argument, he also returns to Weber's distinction, but in order to question its reach precisely in regard to the remains of the dead. His book is an open contestation of what he sees as a long line of *disenchanted* views of the dead body that he traces back to the earliest Greek enlightenment, Heraclitus and Diogenes in particular, for whom the dead body was seen as waste to be thrown to birds and dogs. In its place, he seeks to encircle the *enchanted* body, to understand the remains of the dead as a form of *enchantment* manifested in what he describes as a "universally shared feeling that there is something deeply wrong about not caring for the dead body."[11] He does not posit a linear-teleological story of disenchantment but sees it as an ongoing struggle between disenchantment and reenchantment in regard to the remains of the dead that is enacted throughout history, in which the twentieth century is seen as marked by an unusually disenchanted ethos.

The recounted examples all point toward the need of coming philosophically to terms with the complex set of phenomena that historians, archaeologists, and anthropologists are currently trying to encircle and capture as the "work," "agency," "intentionality," or simply "power" of the dead. In ascribing such terms to those who cannot, by the very definition of their condition, *act*, current humanities are challenging a Weberian paradigm, implicitly or explicitly. But simply positing *agency* or *work* as a possibility for the dead, and thereby extending these concepts from the animate to inanimate, as is done particularly within various forms of posthumanism and neomaterialism, is a too easy solution. Instead, we need to reflect more carefully on the existential, ethical-political predicament in which we find ourselves compelled to respond to, care for, and act in relation to the dead and their bodily remains. More specifically, we need to consider how this category is linked to the historical, what it means to be historical and to have a history as outlined in the preceding chapters.[12] For this purpose, we need to explore *sociality* as an ontological domain that comprises both the living and the dead and to do so in a critical engagement of social and socioanthropological thinking on this topic.

Whereas traditional custodians of social sciences will still recoil before the idea of granting agency to the dead, the new attempts recalled here of a neo-animistic discourse often tend to replicate the basic dualism of the original scheme. The dilemma can be formulated as follows: How can we think and understand the *effect* of the dead in and on the lives and actions of the living without giving way to the magic and superstition that modern science in its supposedly disenchanted phase has left behind? And how can we interpret the full meaning and impact of necropolitical phenomena without just abandoning this conceptual schema by reinstalling *agency* or *work* as concepts applicable to what by its very definition would seem to exclude it: the dead? My answer to this challenge is that instead of simply reversing a previously established framework and its metaphysical vocabulary, we need to explore the domain of being with the dead as a social-ontological and existential-hermeneutic category in its own right, without committing ourselves to a strategy of reenchantment that ultimately only confirms an inherited dichotomous conceptual framework and its binary space. With this goal in mind, the chapter explores some of the more difficult distinctions that emerge in current attempts to reach beyond a Weberian matrix, as well as the theoretical shortcomings of traditional sociology in regard to thinking and conceptualizing a society that comprises the living and the dead. It then presents the work of Alfred Schütz as one possible bridge between phenomenology and Weberian sociology in this respect, in particular his analysis of "the world of predecessors" that links the social relation to the dead with the problem of history. But ultimately it also points beyond Schütz's epistemological framework in an attempt to outline how the questions of legacy, inheritance, and justice draw the dead and living even closer to each other in a shared necropolitical domain.

Living on the Remains of the Dead:
Some Difficult Distinctions

When Benedict Anderson sought to capture the meaning and significance of the monument for the unknown soldier, he turned to the common conceptual strategy of pointing out that this proves the religious core of modern nationalist politics. As previously discussed, this way of turning to "religion" as an explanatory category when confronting phenomena that involve ritual, expressions of piety, and in particular the concerns and care for the dead is intellectually unsatisfying and often counterproductive. It appears to provide additional information and background to a phenomenon, while in the end it just subsumes it under a concept—*religion*—whose reach is already so broad that the gesture contributes only to further diluting it. To say that something is "religious" often amounts to signaling that it belongs to the other side of the Weberian distinction, to the space of enchantment and sacrality, thus making it seem either as atavistic or sentimental and therefore at least ideally possible to explain in terms of psychological needs, inclinations or distortions, or alternatively as an unconscious function of a larger sociopolitical constellation of forces.

But in the case of the relation between political communities and the bodies of the dead, this strategy accomplishes little. If the political "use" of the bones of dead citizens displays a religious core of politics, then we may just as well also ask if indeed religion did not originally arise from exactly the strategies involved in preserving the dead members of the group—in other words, if religion is really at heart itself a form of necropolitics?

A premise for our analysis is that the living do not just use or need the dead for this or that purpose. Nor do they create their different monuments over the dead only to represent them in this or that fashion or for this or that purpose, as the argument goes in the standard sociological-anthropological literature on mortuary practices. The deeper and more complex task is to see how the fact that a society consists of both its living and its dead implies that the remains of the dead are *involved* in the constitution of these communities in the form of an irreducible reciprocity. It is tempting to think of this primarily in terms of *desire* and as a work of mourning, in short, in terms of the *unconscious* as understood and explored by psychoanalysis. But when seen primarily as a *psychic* phenomenon, the full constellation will not come into view. The limited reach of psychoanalysis when confronting these matters is illustrated in Paul-Laurent Assoun's recent book *Tuer le mort* (2015), which retells and analyzes the remarkable story of the second "killing" of the already-dead kings of France in 1793.[13] With sanction from the revolutionary government, the bodies of kings from earlier centuries buried in the Saint-Denis basilica in Paris were unearthed and vandalized, providing a powerful illustration to Walter Benjamin's ominous remark in the *Theses on the Philosophy of History* that "not even the dead will be safe from the enemy if he wins."[14] As his explanatory matrix Assoun actualizes Freud's analysis from *Totem and Taboo* of the death wish toward the original father as a model for understanding this revolutionary violence against the remains of the past. But in thus framing this event within a psychoanalytical model of an archaic psyche, he not only aligns himself inadvertently with the cultural-colonial legacy of this model but also bypasses the larger historical-philosophical context that involved not just the destruction but also the construction of new bodies of the dead as part of shaping a new political space. The way in which the dead form part of a larger sociality challenges us to seek an expanded definition of the social as such, which is then understood not just as the imaginary superstructure on the basis of individual mortality but precisely as the space of the *historical*, understood as rooted in ancestrality and being with the dead.

The story told by Assoun demonstrates how the revolutionary violence also came to be directed against the dead. But as a parallel to this destruction of the bodies of the former kings in the revolutionary transformation, we can also recall the postrevolutionary initiative of transforming the recently refurnished dome of St. Geneviève, which contained the remains of the patron saint of the city of Paris into a "Pantheon of France" in the style of the Greeks and Romans to hold the remains of its "great men." In 1791 the ashes of Voltaire were brought to the Pantheon by the revolutionary government, replacing the Christian saint with the worldly philosopher. Three years later he was joined by Rousseau. But with Napoleon's reestablishment of the Catholic Church in 1806, the structure was returned to the church and obtained the dual purpose of a church in the upper parts and secular-national shrine in the crypt. With the return of the Bourbon dynasty in 1815 the entire building was again designated as the church of St. Geneviève, re-creating the reliquary of the saint that had been displaced and partly destroyed in 1793 and moving the philosophers' ashes to a separate and sealed compartment of the building. Throughout the turbulent political history of nineteenth-century France, the control and designation of the building and the contents of its graves were moved between different parties, claiming its legacy and its remains for the current political power, from "temple of humanity" to national basilica, from secular to religious ancestry. During the Third Republic in 1879 it was suggested that the Pantheon should again resume its revolutionary inheritance, and following the death of Victor Hugo in May 1885, its current role as Pantheon for the great men of the nation was established with the return of Voltaire's and Rousseau's ashes to the center of the crypt.[15] These necropolitical transactions anticipate and overlap August Comte's Rousseau-inspired program for a "civil religion," at the core of which were also detailed directives for how to care for and pay respect to the remains of the dead.[16] The fact that many enlightened revolutionaries from the last two centuries sought to usurp the place of religion in public life, and that this was concretized precisely in acts directed to the remains of the dead, provokes the question of how to understand if in doing so, were they intentionally, and perhaps even cynically, repeating the gestures of the same Christian religion that they sought to overcome? Or were they in fact through these very acts complying with a more fundamental condition of the formation of human societies that always involves situating its notable dead? Again, simply referring the matter to the sphere of "religion" pays off poorly. We need to think the issue further.[17]

The question of revolutionary and republican necropolitics brings to the surface a further problem concerning the ideological dimensions of politicized corpses. Anderson's judgment that liberals and Marxists have no particular interest in the bodies of their dead was obviously premature. Yet there is a further argument to be made that the very fascination and attraction of the bodies of the dead as political orientation points constitute a retrograde atavism, despite and perhaps even by virtue of its also being used by the inheritors of the secular revolution(s). This could also be made as a Weberian argument in the face of these continued practices of necropolitical mobilizations when they are carried out—as was often the case in recent decades—by groups representing suppressed minorities seeking justice. Perhaps the whole language and affective register of necropolitics are somehow at heart and in essence a testimony of a *conservative* political inclination. When raising the question in this way, we see how the issue points toward the limits of a political vocabulary that continues to vacillate between the two concepts of conservative and radical, between those on the right and those on the left in the Chamber of Deputies in revolutionary France. In the debates on how to handle the fate of the monarchy, those on the left came to the conclusion that both the living and dead kings needed to be decapitated, just as the Soviet-backed communist regime in Hungary decided to punish the corpse of Nagy and the liberal opposition restored its posthumous honors. Where on this scale should we locate the necropolitical imagination? Does it have a place on a scale of left and right, of radical and conservative? Or is the fate of its location in an ideological landscape to be sought elsewhere, beyond or even across the lines and lineages of these modern revolutionary distinctions?

The difficulty of properly situating the politicization of the remains of the dead does not only collide with the standardized repertoire of the sociological and political-ideological vocabulary; it also provokes the core ethos of a philosophical rationality. Weber's somber analysis of death in the modern disenchanted era as just a meaningless termination of an individual life gives no particular place and rationale for a sacralization of the bodies of the dead, even less for making them into political foundations. In his commitment to a life of learning and spiritual and moral perseverance, Weber was more of a modern Diogenes, for whom the body and the bodily remains were not important, the same Diogenes that Laqueur chooses as his main adversary in his attempt to restore the significance of the bodies of the dead. The position of Diogenes, however, is not just as an extremist among the ancient wisdom teachers. It also carries a resonance from the teaching of Socrates and the core doctrine of Athenian enlightenment. In Plato's description of his teacher's last hours in life in *Phaedo*, Socrates is depicted as himself performing the proclaimed ritual care for the body of the dead in the company of his friends. Through this radical gesture, he seeks to comfort them but also to relieve them from making a ritualized monument of his corpse. The reason for this, as is made clear in the last conversation, is that the corpse is not what is important. This had been a central element of his teaching all along, and he makes it very clear that in the moment of death we should be cautious not to mistake the body for the soul, and the corpse for the spiritual afterlife. The genuinely *rational* man is the one who is able to tell the difference, who does not mistake a useless piece of decaying tissue with what is truly significant. The ability to look upon the passionate preoccupation with remains of departed kin from a position of restrained elevation would then mark the true and authentic ethos of a person of science and learning, in short, of a *philosopher*. When seen from this perspective, the very preoccupation with and hermeneutic benevolence vis-à-vis necropolitical phenomena become even more problematic. Why should a real philosopher even care about the bodies of the dead, except maybe as an illustration of a common incapacity to make elementary distinctions and to permit personal and collective grief to develop into politicized necrophilia?

When expressed in such sharp terms, the basic distinction concerning necropolitics would not be between radical and conservative, but again between superstitious irrationality and philosophical rationality. Yet the question of the final philosophical verdict on the meaning and role of the bodies of the dead continues to elude even this polarized distinction. Behind the Socratic disdain for the exaggerated rites devoted to the bodies of the dead there is also a disdain for the bodily as such. Behind the Socratic and Cynic rejection of the cult of corpses we find not just a self-transparent rationality but also an ascetic idealism that looks on both the body and the earthly temporal life itself as secondary in relation to the real and eternal life of the spirit. This is not the proper occasion to explore the details of Socrates's doctrine of the soul. I recall this rough depiction only as a reminder of the other and inverse side of this legacy, the one that Nietzsche—a philosopher whom Weber also admired and whom he even highlights alongside Tolstoy in his final lecture—identified as the root of modern *nihilism*: the rejection of the value of finite corporeal life. According to this critique, Socratic-Platonic rationalism rejects not just the bodies of the once living but also the bodies of the living, and ultimately of life itself. This was at least how Nietzsche saw and analyzed it in his own attempt to restore to finite life a sense of its own irreducible value. For this reason, he also declared in *Thus Spoke Zarathustra* in a section titled "On Free Death," which can also be read as an explicit reversal of Socrates's message: "Thus would I myself die, that you friends might love the earth more for my sake; and into the earth will I turn again, that I might rest in her who bore me."[18]

Nietzsche's verdict anticipates what became a recurrent point in the postwar anthropological-historical literature on death and mortuary culture, that modern society had gone so far in its technical-medical conception of death that it resulted in a rejection and suppression of death itself and consequently of the whole domain of caring for the dead. This is captured in Zygmunt Bauman's verdict that modernity "banished death and the dying out of sight and thus hopefully, out of mind."[19] The disenchanted, technical, anonymous conception of death would then appear not just as a sign of superior philosophical understanding but also as a symptom of a society that refuses to recognize the fundamental and inescapable condition of human bodily finitude.

Together with the atrocious history of the millions of anonymous and unburied corpses produced in the name of progress by Enlightenment and post-Enlightenment political utopias in the twentieth century, this argument obtains an even more ominous ring. The disenchanted view of human existence as just a finite stretch in the progressive movement of the human spirit, as expressed by Weber in his speech a year after the Russian

Revolution, can then also be heard as a terrible anticipation of disasters to follow. Recent attempts to resacralize and reenchant the bodies of the dead in the interpretive literature should partly be seen in this light too, as a deep echo from a century of extraordinarily lethal politics, where a manifest disdain for individual human life—and often in the name of enlightened progress—was brought to new historical levels. The way and extent to which posttotalitarian societies are able to incorporate and host their dead, in particular the dead that fell victims to their own politics, are today a question of great ethical and political importance.[20] Through the analyses by Etkin and others of the contorted dynamics of posttotalitarian memory politics, we are led back to a problem with which we started: understanding and situating philosophically and phenomenologically the nature, presence, and impact of the dead as part of the larger problem of how we live with those who are no longer "with us." And as our discussion has shown, necropolitical phenomena and their imaginary domain cut across not only the political spectrum but also the spectrum of rationality itself.

In the contemporary discussion around necropolitical phenomena the real challenge has to do with how to properly *situate* them within a historical-anthropological framework, while not repeating the inclination of earlier generations of cultural historians to archaicize, primitivize, or just psychologize the present. Contemporary preoccupation with the bodies of political deaths and with politicization of anonymous bodies invites a gaze that locates them as echoes of a past, alternatively an inclination to restore to modernity the enchantment that it presumably left behind. But as we have seen, the Weberian dichotomy comes to an impasse as we confront these issues, and at the same time the self-historicization—or archaicization—of the present risks producing an artificial distance to something that is actually taking place in the present.

However, there is also a tendency in the contemporary understanding of necropolitics, especially where the examples are taken from indigenous and marginalized communities, to idealize these bonds by positioning them within a different, non-Western, and presumably more organic sense of community and society that combines the dead and the living in a larger whole. This alternative sociological conception is then highlighted as a possible corrective to the individualized, and again disenchanted, view of life seen as characteristic of the societies of Western modernity. In many of these examples the very interpretation of necropolitical phenomena inevitably becomes politicized, as the question of legitimacy, lineage, inheritance, and thus of *power* over the present comes to the fore. But instead of falling into the trap of politicized cultural dichotomies, we must expand our understanding of the existential-ontological foundations of the necropolitical domain itself while heeding its inner tensions and differences.

Instead of taking Weber's distinction for granted as a historical-philosophical category and as a way of organizing time, we can look at it as itself a production of an anthropological-philosophical difference that recalls the Hegelian distinction between cults of death and rational spirit discussed in the previous chapter. If we follow that argument, we can see how the modern human sciences constituted themselves and their discourse precisely around the distinction in relating to the dead, where fear and ritual interaction with the dead were located hierarchically below the reflexive and symbolic reverence for the dead. There we also saw how the articulation of the latter and presumably superior comportment also coalesced with the invention of "history" and "historical consciousness" as domains in which the dead are contained, as both preserved and pacified. Seen from this perspective, historical culture—with its epistemic, material, and institutional structures—does not mark the end of an interaction with the dead but its transformation. When modern critical anthropological and historical interpreters of mortuary culture challenge the distinction between a supposedly enchanted past and a disenchanted present, charting the different ways in which the dead continue to operate, work, and influence the lives of the living, even in supposedly modern societies, they also inadvertently cross their own paths and the conditions of their own epistemic matrix. To put it differently, the dichotomous space between enchantment-disenchantment is not only a figure proposed by the human-social sciences but an element in the constitution of their own ethos, as they invent themselves through the rejection of more "primitive" forms of interacting with the dead. From this it follows that a simple reversal of its foundational taxonomy, which reintroduces enchantment and material agency as legitimate scientific topics, will not automatically bring us closer to the phenomena that we seek to understand.

Ultimately the heart of the problem does not lie with the distinction enchantment/disenchantment but with how to think what it means that a society consists not only of the living but also of the no-longer living and the not-yet-born. To understand any political entity, whether a community, society, or nation, we must think of it as existing over and along a temporal stretch, where it is held together along lines of kinship, ancestry, and inheritance. Standard sociological handbooks usually neglect to theorize this fundamental fact, but in the more philosophically oriented literature it nevertheless resurfaces as a legacy from Durkheim, and going back to Hegel. Verdery expresses it well in her analysis: "Any human community consists not only of those now living in it but also, potentially, of both ancestors and anticipated descendants."[21]

At the same time, her analysis bears witness to how difficult it is to approach and capture this condition from within standard sociological vocabulary. The phenomenological and deconstructive way of thinking the constitution of history as spectrality and as being with the dead will remain inaccessible to the conventional sociological matrix. A standard textbook in sociological theory, for example, George Ritzer's *Sociological Theory* (2008), does not mention anything about the culture of death.[22] A reason is that these phenomena are considered to belong to the sphere of religion and therefore covered by the particular discipline of history of religion or cultural anthropology. It is as if the very nature of the social structure of the living and the dead cannot be part of sociology because it presumably exists only in the imagination of and interaction between the living. What sociology takes itself to study is the structure of the social world, often defined as a constructed space of social meaning and communication. Yet a social world, when looked at from a diachronic perspective, is by definition precisely a world consisting both of the living *and* of the dead (and the anticipated not-yet-born).

From the viewpoint of conventional sociological thinking it does not matter if an individual is dead or alive, since specific individuals are not at stake. It is the *function* of the individual in the totality of the social world that counts, and this function does not cease with death; it is simply occupied by a new living being who enters the space to fulfill a role in the

workings of the whole. But since a society by definition exists diachronic-
ally over time, the fact that there are members that it *has* had (as well as
members that it *will* have) is not an incidental but a necessary condition
for its subsistence. When seen from this perspective, the relation between
the living and the dead within and for a society cannot be reduced to the
possibility of replacement within a function, but it constitutes something
essential for its experience of itself precisely as a *society*, as well as for its
ability to function and operate as such. What it does as a society, it does
partly in order to maintain, care for, and respond to what *has been* done
in the name of the same society, to exist in a sense of shared responsibility
with the members who are no longer there, with *the dead*. From this we
can conclude that to understand what a society is, we need to understand
how there can be coexistence and cooperation between the living and the
dead. In short, we need a social ontology of being with the dead.

Weber was attentive to the inner tension in the objective sociological
approach, and he was open to seeing the interplay between individual and
structure in accounting for social meaning. Yet the question of the social
meaning of being with the dead never seemed to have caught his interest,
even though he was preoccupied throughout his career with the impact
of religion on the nature and development of societies. If we are looking
for a Weberian answer to the question of how to conceptualize the social
significance of the relation between the living and dead, we have to look
elsewhere. At this point the phenomenological work of Alfred Schütz on
social ontology opens itself to a new and expanded reading. Schütz, more
than any other of the followers of Weber, tried to bring out the underlying philosophical-phenomenological presuppositions of his thinking. But
Schütz is also someone who thinks *in the wake of* Weber, who literally
speaks in response to him across the border that separates him from the
living. It is this double role and its implications that interest us here, as a
way also to articulate the more complex hermeneutic-historical terrain of
necropolitics as the social ontology of being with the dead.

Weber, Schütz, and the Ontology of Predecessors

Schütz's mission in life was to provide a more solid theoretical-
philosophical foundation for Weber's sociology by grafting it onto

Husserlian phenomenology. By basing it on Edmund Husserl's analysis of subjective life as ultimately constituted by internal time consciousness, he sought to lay the theoretical bridge between social and subjective meaning. For Schütz, the very concept of an objective mind or consciousness—be it Hegelian or Durkheimian—was an illegitimate anthropomorphism. In its place, he wanted to follow the direction of Weber and translate the social and intersubjective meanings of life and action back to individual acts of intentional consciousness, as they obtain meaning within different types and levels of life worlds, where the act is understood in an "ideal" or "eidetic" sense, fusing the terminology of Weber and Husserl.[23]

A central part of his book is the description of different social "worlds," the three main categories of which are "consociates," "contemporaries," and "predecessors."[24] According to Schütz, we occupy a social world, a *soziale Mitwelt*, which comprises the people in relation to which we live spontaneously in a shared world within a common horizon. This world is then divided between those whom we feel more immediately close to, our "consociates" (*Mitmenschen*); and those whom we perceive as our "contemporaries," those living *alongside* us in this same world (*Nebenmenschen*), located on various levels of cultural and geographical distance. In addition to these two worlds, we can also "be cognizant of a social world that existed *before* I myself did and which at no point overlaps with any part of my own life." This is the social world of "predecessors" (*Vorwelt*), another name for which is simply *history*. In relation to this social world, he adds, "I can only be an observer and not an actor." To this structure he also adds a fourth dimension, the *future*, "another world, one also inhabited by others, that will exist when I am no more, a social world of successors [*Folgewelt*]. These are people of whom we cannot know anything as individuals." It is a world, he writes, which "I can only vaguely grasp but never directly experience."[25]

For Schütz, "social action" or "social behavior" is grounded in the more basic phenomenon of "intentional conscious experience directed toward another self."[26] It is a subjective conscious comportment essentially directed toward a *living* other, not as a body but as a "field of expressions for his subjective experiences" that posits the other as existing (*Daseinssetzung*), or as he writes, "that a thou lives."[27] To act socially toward an other in this way thus also implies the subjective experiences of this other in a future, in an anticipated reciprocity. The "thou" that is part of this space of action ultimately rests on a presumed shared horizon of a "we." For "I can live," he writes, "in your subjective meaning-context only to the extent that I directly experience you within an actualized content-filled 'we-relationship.'"[28] Within the horizon of this shared intersubjective world there are levels of reciprocity, as we move from friends and relatives, to associates, colleagues, functionaries, and so on, in a gradual weakening of personal commitment until we reach the last of the eight enumerated steps in this hierarchy, which consists only of the "artifacts of any kind which bear witness to the subjective meaning-context of some unknown person." The conclusion then reads: "The farther out we get into the world of contemporaries, the more anonymous its inhabitants become, starting with the innermost region, where they can almost be seen, and ending with the region where they are by definition forever inaccessible to experience."[29]

It is only after thus having secured the central part of his argument and toward the very end of the book that Schütz turns to "The World of Predecessors [*Vorwelt*] and the Problem of History," or as the subtitle reads: "The Past as a Dimension of the Social World."[30] It is a short section, fewer than ten pages, and Schütz himself is quick to point out that it "does not present undue complications, and it can be dealt with briefly."[31] Still, the questions raised here have implications that ultimately point beyond the confines of his own thinking and conclusions.

The past is here depicted as a kind of mirror-image world in relation to the living present, a world in which all the relations in the present are mediated only through "memory" (*Erinnerung*) and sharply distinguished by time itself. A "predecessor" is defined as a "person in the past no one of whose experiences overlaps in time with one of mine." The world of predecessors is thus essentially what is "over and done with." It has "no open horizon toward the future," and there is no longer anything undecided, uncertain, or awaiting fulfillment. For this reason, Schütz writes, I cannot *await* the behavior of predecessors, for their behavior is "essentially without any dimension of freedom." Thus, there is nothing I can do to "influence them" (there is no *Fremdwirken*), even though, he adds, they can still "influence me." What at first glance may seem to constitute a social *relationship* between myself and a predecessor is therefore ultimately a "one-sided Other-orientation on my part." At this point he explicitly mentions "the cult of ancestor worship" (*Ahnenkult*) as an example of such a social interaction, which, despite appearances, is said to be essentially one-sided.[32]

Immediately after this remark he adds, however, that there is indeed one case where we can speak meaningfully of "reciprocal interaction," when someone has "bequeathed some property to me." Together with a subsequent remark on how we "come to know" our predecessors through "records and monuments . . . that have the status of signs," he thereby again breaches the limits of this interaction, since the way that "historical research" approaches these sources "is at this point the same as that used in interpreting the words of someone who is speaking to me."[33] On the one hand, he seems to be making it quite clear that a social relation of reciprocity with the dead will always remain a one-sided orientation. On the other hand, the dead can exert some influence on us through the inheritance that they have left (intentionally or not), to which clearly belongs the potentially meaningful material remains through which they manifest themselves in the first place.

How should this potentially dynamic relation between the present and the past be conceived? Toward the very end of the section, Schütz vacillates between different images. On the one hand, history is precisely something "over and done with," something that occurs in "objective time," where we can retroactively look for the causes of individual actions and events. On the other hand, history can be understood as "one continuous we-relationship," where consociates become predecessors, and successors become consociates in a single flow of "ever changing partners."[34] This image of history as a potential encompassing horizon of we-ness with the past opens a new window in Schütz's account, while also bringing out its inner tensions in regard to how we should view the social reality of the dead. It repeatedly stresses that history is what has already happened, that it therefore has no remaining freedom, agency, or future horizon of its own, while being open to the inspection, interpretation, and explanation from the viewpoint of the present. Following the standard sociological approach, only in relations between the living is social meaning generated and enacted. Whatever meaning is experienced in relation to the past and to the dead can therefore be only indirect and hypothetical. From such a perspective, the cult of ancestors, as well as political interaction with the remains of the dead, could be understood and supposedly accounted for as ultimately misguided actions and responses within the social world of predecessors. Following Schütz's analysis, there is a world *shared* with the dead. But this is the world of the past or of history as something preserved in memory and through tradition and ultimately accessible only through the interpretive-epistemic techniques of the historical disciplines.

Difficult Predecessors

We could stop at this point and conclude with Schütz and his carefully crafted phenomenological sociology that through this analysis of the structure of the social world of predecessors, we have retrieved the most reasonable way of *situating* the phenomenon of interactions with the dead, not as expressions of religious superstition or culturally primitive inclinations but as more or less naïve expressions of the more general human predicament of inhabiting a transtemporal shared world between contemporaries and predecessors, which we also call *history*. History, in the sense of the past, would then be a social space where we in some sense *are* with the dead and where we continue to communicate with and permit ourselves to be acted on by them through their legacy. To recognize this context does not imply that we legitimize or support superstitious beliefs concerning the ontological status of the souls of departed kin, nor does it require the introduction of categories that speak of the *force, work*, or *agency* of the dead, but it can help us see from whence they arise within a larger social-ontological framework. When read in this way, Schütz's phenomenological extension of Weber's sociology into the world of the dead seems to give us no apparent reason to abandon the latter's basic matrix and understanding of what it means to inhabit a disenchanted world. But before closing the argument, I want to take a few more steps, using Schütz's own reflections on the nature of his project in order to complicate and move beyond his own stated position and conclusion in regard to how to finally conceptualize our interactions with the world of predecessors and how to understand what it means to be *with* the dead.

On the manifest level of the text, Schütz is clear in establishing the limit between the living and the dead. It is only within the domain of the living, and first of all in its most intimate sphere of the we-horizon of reciprocal face-to-face interaction, that *genuine* social meaning emerges and is made possible in the first place. In a gradual and declining curve we still have social meaning and reciprocity, and thus the experience of an intentionality of the other, all the way down to the confrontation with artifacts that still carry and communicate a subjective meaning through the very fact that they *have* been conceived and made by someone. In this sense we all inhabit a world of ultimately inexhaustible semantic density. Still, unlike the drawing-board version of such a strict hierarchy, ranging from close personal interaction to lifeless artifacts, this space is diverse and unstable, where some present and living relations can mean almost nothing but certain lifeless objects can have an overwhelming significance. This is especially true of those objects that carry and transmit relations to the dead, all the "signs" that Schütz refers to as a general name for the records and monuments through which the dead remain accessible.

To these examples we could also add personal details, such as images of dead kin, precious objects that have been in their possession, and, most important, bodily remains, such as locks of hair or bones kept in a sanctuary. In fact, the act of caring for the dead in burial stands out as a case where Schutz's idealized model of the constitution of social meaning is pushed toward its limits. When defining social behavior generally in terms of "intentional conscious experience directed toward the other self," he explicitly excludes acts that are directed only to the other person's "physical body, rather than as a field of expression for his subjective experiences."[35] Yet the body in burial is precisely what provokes and destabilizes this ontological structure. When caring for the remains of the dead, there is no longer anyone who can have experiences. Still the acts of a mortuary practice are not acts directed solely toward the body as a physical object, since they essentially issue from a sense of reciprocity toward that very person in his or her absence.

The example of the body in burial could be brushed aside as a marginal and limited case in relation to the larger argument that Schütz is developing. But from our present vantage point we have become especially attentive to the deeper semantic and social ambiguity of the remains of the dead also as indicators of a larger context of a social reciprocity toward a life that has been and the demands that come with it. In burial, throughout the multitude of practical, emotional, and ritual responses documented in the anthropological and archaeological archives, there is always a question not just of handling a body but of responding to a relation to an other that does not end with death. It is not for the corpse as corpse that the cares, concerns, demands, and responses are elicited but toward the person who in virtue of no longer being there is both absent and present, but now as someone having-been.

This sense of *responsibility* toward the dead can issue from bodily remains but also from the artifacts and institutions and legacies through which those who once lived sought to communicate over the threshold of life. We saw that Schütz recognized a possible influence of the dead on the living through inheritances and testaments. At the same time, he made it clear that the living cannot influence or work on the dead. But when the living start to interact with the remains of the dead, these borders also tend to become blurred. The only way for the dead to exert their effect on us is for us choose to relate to them, to transform them through our own activity, permitting them to take place in our own bodies, lending our life to their potential, to make their force as it were come to *happen*. This is at least one way of describing what takes place when someone reads, not just in the literal sense of deciphering characters from a printed page but also in making sense of a created artifact. For Schütz, reading and interpreting written signs would be a marginal social phenomenon, eight times removed from the primordial form of social meaning of reciprocal oral communication. But if we see it only in this way, we fail to see the full potential of its impact, especially in regard to the relation to the world of predecessors. What it permits us to see is that this world not only has the capacity to act on us but also that it involves us in acting on it, usurping, digesting, transforming, and letting ourselves be guided by it to make its potential appear and happen.

As we begin to interact with our predecessors and their work through the most sophisticated means at our disposal, the art of writing and reading, we are led to recognize that in this endeavor it is never just a case of letting them influence us but also one of influencing them and their legacy through a work that we do on them. This can be exemplified through Schütz's own relation to Weber. When Schütz published his book in 1932, Weber had already been dead twelve years and thus belonged to the realm of "predecessors." In his preface, Schütz recognizes that his own work is entirely "dependent" on that of Weber. It is Weber, he writes, who has "determined conclusively the proper starting point of the philosophy of the social sciences."[36] But already in the very next sentence he declares that "his analyses did not go deeply enough to lay the foundations on which alone many important problems of the human sciences could be solved," especially what concerns the notion of "subjective meaning." In other words, what Weber left behind as his legacy was not enough to carry the full potential of this legacy. It was not enough for the work that Weber himself had already completed. To truly become his own work, it was in need of another work to make it, retrospectively, the work it deserved and supposedly wanted to be. Only in this way could it really become something that Weber could leave behind as his true legacy. From the viewpoint of Schütz and his own work, there is still something that Weber can *do* for the present on the condition that his legacy is given a *foundation* that he was not able to provide himself. It is as such a reworking of the meaning of an already transmitted legacy that Schütz sets to work on the already completed work of Weber, who thus comes forth as someone who is not just confined to the past. Instead, he appears to be semipresent, still belonging to a larger world of contemporaries, perhaps as one of the "souls of deceased" of whom Schütz in another essay says that in "primitive societies the dead are deemed to be contemporaries."[37]

This way of paying respect to, while working with a predecessor across the threshold of death to bring a legacy to its full potential in and for the present, could seem to exemplify only a very specialized academic-hermeneutic enterprise. But my point here is that this is not necessarily the case. There is a more general lesson to be learned from this example. Through his remarks on the legacy of Weber and on how he wants to situate his own work in relation to it, Schütz has in fact invited us—*his* posthumous readers—to move beyond the confines of his own attempt to expand the Weberian analysis to include the world of the dead, of predecessors and ancestors. Through his own hermeneutic-scientific practice, he has given an example of how the living *share* a world with the dead in which they are compelled not only to carry on but also to care for, elaborate, criticize, and enact their inheritance. In Schütz's program for a phenomenological sociology this does not in any way involve the bodily remains of Weber, which lie undisturbed and safely interred in

Bergfriedhof in Heidelberg. But the way that he articulates his own work in relation to that of Weber can still serve as a clue to how the remains of the dead can *compel* the living to act on them as a way to transform what they have left behind.

When describing such a situation, we usually speak of it as a work of *memory*. It is by keeping the dead in our personal or shared collective memory that we do for them a work that they are no longer able to do themselves: holding and carrying the name, shadow, or impression of them forward. And on one level we are talking here about a work of memory. Yet ultimately the concept of memory itself fails to capture the full sense and impact of how the living share a world with the dead. Memory subjectivizes this relation, making it into an only internal affair, of an *interiority*, be it construed psychologically or sociologically. What we are looking for is a way of understanding how the dead reach into the world of the living and, reciprocally, how the living reach into the world of the dead. Here the formulations of Schütz concerning the purpose of his own sociological-philosophical endeavor in relation to his dead predecessor provide further clues. It illustrates how the living can make it their task not just to remember the dead but to give them a legacy that they for different reasons were not able to give themselves. In doing so, they also become part of and coworkers in the only work that the dead, still according to Schütz, can still accomplish: to influence the living through their legacy. For this activity we have another familiar phrase, *to give someone a place in history*. But what does this really mean? Have we fully fathomed the nature and implications of this gesture? To give someone a place in history. What kind of gift is this? And what is the domain in which the giving of this gift takes place? What is the ontological nature of the relationship in which this kind of giving is enacted?

Giving the Dead a Place in History

Alfred Schütz's analysis of the world of predecessors provides a link between Weberian sociology and a phenomenological understanding of historicity. In a situation where necropolitical phenomena, struggles, and challenges call for a deeper understanding of the socio-ontological domain of being with the dead, his careful attempt to trace the lines of the inner intentionality of the interaction between the living and dead complements the framework of spectral historicity outlined in Chapter 1. Schütz never engaged explicitly with Heidegger's work, and there is no sign that Heidegger ever read or commented on the *Aufbau*. The question here, however, is not one of concrete influence but of the problem itself and what the inner similarities and differences can teach us. Schütz did not take a great interest in the problem of history. As gathered from the previous discussion, he seems to have seen the domain of the historical world as something that a phenomenology of the social could handle fairly easily through its analysis of predecessors. The separate issue of the constitution of the historical as such, in the sense of a presumably objective space of the past, was not addressed in his social-phenomenological analysis.

For Heidegger the situation was of course the inverse. The historicity of existence permeates all understanding and the question of being as such. It is when he seeks to ground the phenomenon of pastness and of history that he turns to the category of *Dasein* as *having-been*, as another name for the dead, as its existential foundation. Schütz was never looking for a phenomenology of the historical in the first place. But as he tries to build a comprehensive account of the social world through a detailed analysis of the various forms of reciprocity that constitute it, he too comes across the interaction with predecessors as a peculiar domain that then leads him toward history and the historical. In his own attempt to account for the inner movement of what it means to have and assume a legacy, he plunges, almost inadvertently, into the more complex logic of being with the dead. Together these trajectories delineate a socio-ontological space where the necropolitical phenomena with which we began need not be simply historicized along an evolutionary scale of gradual disenchantment. Instead, they point toward a fundamental existential condition. From this perspective, the recent rise of interest in the work, agency, and impact of the dead among anthropologists, archaeologists, and historians can be understood in the larger context of an expanded theory of history as a space of *life with the dead*, as a life with those *having-been*.

Ethically and politically this is an inherently contested space, where piety and desecration can compete around one and the same body and one legacy. The bodies of the dead will become sites of contestation because they are placeholders and concretizations of time, as a shared social space of the past. To speak of them as "agents," however, is dubious, since it bypasses too easily the critical genealogy of this ascription. In the older anthropological discourse, the ascription of agency to the dead—often taken to be a malicious agency—was used as a way to disregard the "primitive" or "savage" mind that manifested itself precisely through this kind of superstition. The educated and historically minded person is one who is guided by the knowledge *that the dead have no agency*. But in the wake of the self-critical and postprimitivistic paradigm in anthropology, and also in the wake of posthumanism and new materialism, "agency" is again becoming possible to ascribe to nonliving artifacts, as well as to the dead. But this recent use of the term only risks adding new confusions. It risks limiting the discussion to the tiresome question of whether or not this is *really* agency in a literal sense, which ultimately distances us from the basic existential-historical condition of the whole problem in the first place. Because this is where the questions lead us once we follow them through: to the irreducible condition of inhabiting history and of being historical as grounded in the existential-ontological predicament of being with the dead. To inhabit this space with prudence, we should not deny it or brush it aside as illegitimate beliefs and concerns. On the contrary, it is it a space onto which one must learn to tread with care and good judgment, especially since dogmatic, rash, and opportunistic actions will abound.

To illustrate how necropolitical activism can not only serve "ghostly national imaginings" (to quote Anderson again) but also work for deepened social reciprocity and confront historical traumas, I end with two contemporary examples. They are also interesting in how they illustrate that the remains of the dead and their memorials co-constitute a sociohistorical space. The first example is a project organized by the young historian and entrepreneur Witold Wrzosiński, called the Foundation for Documentation of Jewish Cemeteries in Poland, which has been producing a field guide of all Jewish burial sites throughout the countryside, now often neglected, overgrown, and partly dismantled, with the stones used in construction works. The images from this project display tilted moss-overgrown gravestones, located in various semideserted forest or agricultural landscapes, or as desolate spaces within an urban fabric. The project has documented fourteen hundred grave sites, approximately four hundred of which still have visible gravestones. For local Polish residents, these sites often became sources of anxiety and avoidance after the war. But with the slow, tormented, and still contested recognition of the profound importance of the Jewish presence in Poland, of which the POLIN Museum in Warsaw is the foremost example, their meaning changes too.[38] It is captured in Pawel Pawlikowski's movie *Ida* from 2013 about a Catholic nun who discovers that she is in fact the daughter of a murdered Jewish family, whose unmarked graves she then tries to locate in order to give them a final and proper burial.

In the present historical situation, the neglected sites can be redefined as possible sites of "heritage," not just for visitors from outside but, more important, as integrated in a shared social space where this heritage is not just that of the *other* but also of oneself. With the third postwar generation of Eastern Europe, among people born in the 1980s onward in Poland and the Baltic countries, there are several initiatives of discovering and responding to the history of the persecution and destruction of the Jewish communities throughout Eastern Europe. What is especially important about the planned field guide is that it is primarily directed toward the local population, with advice on how to handle these sites. For the young director of this project, the stated idea is to preserve them by inviting the local communities to contribute to their preservation. The underlying idea is that this will be possible only if they "become meaningful as sites that commemorate an important part of their own history," where a teacher can inspire children to try to read the names and "to tell the stories of the people buried there."[39]

The project is one among many initiatives in multifaceted European memory politics in response to the Holocaust that has emerged over the last forty years, first in the western and then, after the fall of the Iron Curtain, in the eastern parts of Europe, where the Jewish victims of the crimes of National Socialism are recognized through public memorials not just as generic victims of fascism but as victims of politically organized anti-Semitism. In this context the cemeteries hold a particular significance. Through taking responsibility for the graves, the many graveless dead are also memorialized but through their ancestors and families, whose generational lines were interrupted and destroyed. Through this initiative the once living are reinvited to have a share in a public space, where they until then marked only an eerie absent presence. The project could therefore be described as giving a legacy to those who were never permitted to have one. It is notable that the director speaks of this precisely in terms of making them part of "our history." History is then the spontaneously pronounced name for a world of predecessors as a space shared between the dead and the living. To encourage the living to care for the graves of these unknown dead also means expanding the shared space of this community.

The second example comes from the United States. In 2014, Sandra J. Arnold, who is a descendant of African American slaves, initiated the National Burial Database of Enslaved Americans (NBDEA) in collaboration with Fordham University and partly sponsored by the National Endowment for the Humanities. The idea is to document the often anonymous, hidden, neglected, and sometimes destroyed and covered-over burial grounds of enslaved African Americans. Occasionally such graveyards show up when construction work is being done. The slaves had their own burial grounds, sometimes in the vicinity of but separated from the local official church. Often the descendants could not afford to have engraved stones, so the graves would be marked by naturally shaped stones. Just like the project of documenting the neglected Jewish cemeteries in Poland, the project initiated by Arnold is an act of memory politics. This is also how she describes it in an article in the *New York Times* in March 2016, where she speaks of "memorialization" as a way of keeping us "connected to what is most significant about those who are no longer with us." She speaks of how the memory of slavery in the public eye often "becomes abstract," whereas graveyards are "visual reminders" that exist because "we desire to memorialize those buried there."[40] The database under construction is thus both an ambitious historical archive, explicitly in the service of both research, visitors, and of living memory, and a way of actively paying respect to the dead.

The activities taking place around this initiative contain some remarkable examples of practical history, as in the case of a Tennessee plantation, where one of the descendants of slaves who had gathered information of hundreds of graves of former slaves erected a monument on the plantation property for the no-longer-existing cemetery, thus a cemetery for a cemetery, that was paid for by the current descendants of the pre-vious plantation owner. In a commentary on this event, the initiator, John Baker, says that "he was honored to see so many descendants of the enslaved and the plantation owner come together to honor our ancestors." Arnold sees such community initiatives as possibly contributing to "heal-ing, understanding and potentially even reconciliation," since preserving their memory is said to contribute to "our humanity." She speaks of these "overlooked lives" as an inextricable part of the historical narrative of "our country."

In a condensed way, the project displays *history* as the name of the ontological domain of being with the dead, or rather as the always con-tested site of this sharing. It shows that the constitution of a community involves not only the living but also the dead. For a nation that is still struggling to come to terms with the legacy of three centuries of slavery and to forge a shared understanding of its past with which to continue together, the necropolitical initiative touches the existential-ontological core of the work that is simultaneously being done by both professional historians and popular dramatizations of the history of slavery. It directs attention toward the remains of dead as the reality of a history of repres-sion and neglect, in this case with the purpose of inviting them back into a shared past by securing a minimal legacy of a nameless memorial.

The politics of the dead is not over: It is not a thing of the past in the sense of what is behind us. Instead, it is a mark and a symptom of how the past itself continues to be constituted in and through the involvement of the living with the dead and of how the dead shape the space of the living. It is our situation.

Ossuary Hermeneutics

THE NECROPOLITICAL SITES
OF ARCHAEOLOGY

> You may bury my body in Sussex grass,
> You may bury my tongue at Champmedy.
> I shall not be there. I shall rise and pass.
> Bury my heart at Wounded Knee.
>
> —Stephen Benét, "American Names"

Introduction

The grave is a metaphysical site. It is situated in space and in time,
yet it destabilizes this matrix, warping the linearity of time and the spati-
ality of space. In this chapter, we approach the phenomenon of the grave
through the discipline that probed this question deeper and more persistently than any other, *archaeology*. Through its intimate relationship to
the grave, as its source, its topic, but also as its own hidden ethos—as the
self-proclaimed custodian of human material remains—*archaeology* could
also be described as a *taphology*, a discourse on the grave, perhaps even a
discourse *from* the grave. For the archaeological imagination, the grave
is an archive and the world is one large cemetery that holds the traces of
those having-been. Thus, the grave is also a principal route of access to
its own terrain, "the past." For an exploration of the inner bond between
being with the dead, mortuary culture, and historical consciousness,

archaeology and its self-interpretation are a decisive test. Because here the dead and their material remains are the source and focus of an intellectual-spiritual enterprise that gathers and concentrates the ethos of historicist culture and its internal tensions to the present day.

Archaeology has sought to access and say the ontological *truth* of the grave—what the grave *is*—but also to read and interpret the grave to learn and to know what the graves *say*. For this reason, it is also understandable that the question of the grave and its proper interpretation has generated some of the discipline's most turbulent modern internal theoretical debates over the last half century. The fact that humans have cared for their dead over vast stretches of historical time is for archaeology an enabling condition for its own practice, but it is also its supreme epistemic-ethical challenge and defining situation. For the archaeologist, the grave is a metonym for the earth as an essentially historical space. And the ethos of the discipline is to occupy this site as its responsibility and calling. But when everything is a grave, there are no graves, and the gravelike shape of the earth will tend to disappear from sight, until archaeology is jolted back into an awareness of where it was standing in the first place, at the contested heart of a culture that for time immemorial has buried and cared for its dead.

Throughout history graves were opened by strangers who were not inhibited by any ethical commitments to the dead but who simply approached them as possible deposits of valuable goods. With archaeology and the emergence of modern historical consciousness and its institutions—its departments, archives, and museums—a new ethical and conceptual framework for approaching graves was made possible, actualizing the idea of a purely "historical interest in the past" that also motivates breaking their seal as a *rational* pursuit or as a *pursuit of reason*. The transformation of graves and the remains of buried corpses into *objects of knowledge* from the second half of the eighteenth century reflects an emerging speculative interest in the temporal movement of the human spirit and the urge to grasp and secure its chronological and cultural-evolutionary narrative. For two centuries, this ethos and its ethical and political implications remained mostly unthematized, concealed under what was taken to be precisely a neutral scientific-historical interest. During this time archaeology built a vast archive of burials and of their different types and structures across the earth. But after having opened and excavated tombs for two centuries in the search for historical goods and for knowledge of the past, it suddenly found itself questioned at the heart of its desire from the descendants of some of the people whose graves it had disturbed, forcing it to confront the deeper nature and implications of what it means to engage with the remains of the dead. From the 1970s onward archaeology found itself immersed in necropolitical struggles and debates, having to respond to questions of legitimacy and responsibility, which in turn has generated codes of conduct and professional ethics, as illustrated by numerous publications that seek to determine its role in a new globalized postcolonial epistemic and political situation.

No discipline has exposed the ontological-ethical tensions of the human-historical sciences in relation to the dead more than archaeology. On the one hand, it is oriented by a commitment to the dead, enacted through the careful attempt to re-create—both conceptually and through material montage—the life and meaning of the past others through their cultural artifacts, refuse, and bodily remains. On the other hand, this desire for the *truth* of the dead other has also led to a *reification* of the dead other as an object of scientific curiosity. In this sense, it exemplifies the inner conflict of the historical as such, stretched between the hermeneutic sensibility of being a link in the chain of historical life and the aspiration to be the objective *science of the past* as the ideal sum of true statements of events and actions that have been. Of course, these two approaches were never as distinct as some of their respective defendants would have wanted, but in the field of archaeology they came into a sharper, more critical and controversial focus than in any other of the historical disciplines.

The necropolitical *site* refers both to a site on which archaeology operates and where it today finds itself challenged and more deeply engaged than ever and to its condition of possibility. The subject matter of archaeology has the ontological and epistemological structure of a *tomb.* To archaeology, the world, and nature as a whole, is a vast grave field that holds the remains and traces of the dead. Its method can therefore be schematized as the "interpretation of bones," in other words, as an *ossuary hermeneutics.*

Archaeology and the Ancient Dead

The modern academic discipline of archaeology emerges from antiquarianism and the search for antiquities during the second half of the eighteenth century.[1] Thus, it also marks a new technical-spiritual mode of relating to burial sites and to the remains of the dead. Whereas graves that contain goods are created for the keeping, protection, and more generally caring for the dead—and are in that elementary sense *sacred* places, in the sense of what is set apart and protected—they will always, from their very inception, also be vulnerable to plundering and thus to being *de-secrated*. Whereas a living community will care for and protect its dead and their remains, its rivals and enemies will often show as little care for the dead as for the living. This basic necropolitical condition means that in the ongoing struggle between groups and peoples throughout history—for territory, wealth, and influence—the dead and their remains were often drawn into the rivalries of the living. For someone seeking treasures, graves of foreign peoples would not be something to be respected. On the contrary, they are a potential source of wealth and adventure and a possible instrument for effectively displacing and possibly destroying that group's sense of and claim to belonging to a particular temporal-geographical domain, ultimately as a way to make them not even having existed.

Plundering graves to retrieve precious artifacts and metals not only for their use value but also for "historical," "cultural," or "antiquarian" interest is documented already in Roman times. But it is only with the rise of classicism in Europe that the real competition for Roman and Greek artifacts truly begins, and with it the search for treasures in the ground, especially from graves.[2] The sought return of the ancient world in an aesthetic, intellectual, and spiritual sense thus also implied a new and intensified interaction with graves and the remains of the dead. Even though the term "archaeology" was coined earlier in the modern European languages, it is only around this time that it also begins to designate a distinct discipline and a branch of the historical sciences, with the task of transforming randomly preserved "buried" remains of human life and activity into sources for evidence-based narratives of the past.

Archaeology's core skills had to do with the systematic unearthing, documenting, and especially the dating of human cultural-material remains. In its overall theoretical approach it moved from the classificatory and chronological approach of traditional art history to a general explanatory framework of anthropology and sociology and, in later decades, incorporated approaches from phenomenology, hermeneutics, and memory studies, as well as neomaterialist and actor-network theories, cognitive science, and molecular biology.[3] But throughout these different avenues and approaches, it continued to circle around the deposited remains of the dead as its principal source and task. Kant, in a footnote to the *Critique of Judgement* from 1790 (§82), first mentions the idea of an "archaeology of nature" (*archaeologica naturae*) to refer to an earlier and different state of nature, the reality of which is indicated only by fossils of creatures that no longer exist. To seek such a knowledge, he writes, will not just amount to "imaginings," but it will require an investigation "to which nature herself invites and even demands of us." His formulation is noteworthy, as it points toward the most distant past as something both inaccessible and compelling through its material traces, in particular its traces of petrified life, of *life having-been*. As archaeology eventually comes into its own as a name for a branch of the historical sciences, it is precisely with the aspiration to be a *logos* of the *arche*, a discourse on origins and beginnings of human culture, as a "science of the past." For those who henceforth seek *knowledge* of the most ancient past, the earth with its artifacts and remains is the archive and the archaeologist is the "primary custodian and the most authoritative interpreter of the material remains of past cultures."[4]

Archaeology deals with objects to the extent that they bear witness to *what has been*. The historicity of its materials has its meaning within this horizon, which actualizes precisely the predicament of being with the dead. The archaeological artifact can be *an artifact of the past*—and thus have the mark of *pastness*; that is, it can convey pastness—only for a present that is open to being touched and addressed by no-longer present others, the dead. The necropolitical role, situation, or *site* of archaeology is unique through this relation to the graves of the ancient dead. It is only through the patient efforts of archaeologists that we have today such a vast archive of burial sites, dating back to the earliest phases of the human species on earth and beyond humanity, and from which the commonly stated dictum that "humans bury their dead" has achieved the status of a historical truth.

The rise of historical consciousness during the second half of the eighteenth century could be described as the rise of the dead from their tombs. In a literal sense, the end of the eighteenth century marks the beginning of an epoch of reopening graves throughout Europe. From this point onward, pre-Christian burial mounds throughout Europe emerge as potential sources of knowledge of the past.[5] Hegel does not seem to have taken a particular interest in the new discipline of archaeology, whose revolutionary impact on the very image and understanding of the long prehistorical past of humanity was taking place during his active years as a philosopher. One such decisive event occurred in 1823 when the British scholar and priest William Buckland found the skeletal remains of a body in a cave on the Gower Peninsula in southern Wales. The bones had been painted with red ochre and were surrounded by artifacts that were interpreted as burial gifts. Buckley first believed he had found the remains of a female person from Roman times. But as the analysis of the remains progressed, it gradually became clear that it was very much older. Eventually it turned out to be one of the first known samples of a burial on the British Isles, the body of a young man placed in the ground around twenty-eight thousand years earlier, a timescale of human culture inconceivable for Buckley, who still relied on the biblical chronological framework.[6] In the following year, the Danish archaeologist-antiquarian and museum director Christian Jürgensen Thomsen first suggested a periodization of the earliest phases of human history in terms of stone, bronze, and iron, based on the available findings of ancient tools, and responding to a need to somehow sort and organize them chronologically. Forty years later, the so-called Stone Age—that comprised by far the largest time span—would again be divided by the English archaeologist John Lubbock into old, middle and new, or Paleo- Meso-, and Neo*lithic* (from Greek *lithos*). Through these classificatory inventions—accomplished within in the course of only two generations—the chronology of the most ancient phases of human culture obtained the basic conceptual shape in which they are still organized today.

In 1856 a group of skeletons was found in the Neander Valley (*Neandertal*) in Germany, eventually dated as approximately forty thousand years old, which appeared to have been intentionally interred. This finding not only pushed back the limit of funerary practices on the European continent, but it also opened a debate that is still going on concerning the cultural level and spiritual beliefs of the hitherto unknown "Neanderthal" hominids that lived alongside and interbred with *Homo sapiens* for long stretches of time.[7] In excavations during the 1920s in what is today Mount Carmel, Israel, a number of bodies of *Homo sapiens* were found in caves, some of which were surrounded by shells, and dated as between 100,000 and 130,000 years old. Today they are recognized as the oldest example of *Homo sapiens* burial. Finally, in connection with a railway construction in Burgos in northern Spain a system of caves was discovered in the 1960s, the most famous of which was a deep crevice that contained twenty-eight skeletons that seemed to have been deposited over time in an intentional way, which became known as the "Sima de los Huesos" (Pit of bones). The remains were identified as ancestors to the Neanderthals, so-called *Homo heidelbergensis*, and dated as approximately 500,000 years old.[8]

It was through the excavations of graves, and in particular through the excavations of the most ancient Paleolithic graves, that the idea of burial as a transcultural and transtemporal human/humanoid character- istic obtained its deeper meaning and relevance for the whole humanist- historical project. For the *archaeo-logist*, as the one aspiring to the *logos* of the *arche*, no other trace of humanity holds a deeper promise than the origin of this practice itself. In the act of caring for the dead, the human animal emerges for the first time as not only a technically capable being but also as a being who is able to *symbolize*. But what does it mean to symbolize? What is the relation between the symbol and death? And how can we know that a symbolization of death has really taken place? In the following section, the first of our three *sites*, we look at how the search for an origin of burial is inextricably intertwined with the interpretive tools by means of which it is explored. As archaeology approaches burial through language, it also confronts how language itself always already seems to have begun to bury and how the presumably objective study of burial finds itself situated at the extension of this evasive practice as itself a mode of being with the dead.

Site I: Symbolic Origins and the
Grief of the Chimpanzee

The question may seem straightforward at first: What is the origin of burial? But it directly splits into two. The first is historical-chronological: At what point in time do humans begin to bury their dead? This question is intertwined with a philosophical and conceptual concern: What *is* burial, and what *is* a grave? There has to be an answer to the second question to respond to the first. There can be no chronology without determining the nature and essence of what is to be chronologically organized. However, the historical beginning itself is indeterminate in ways that make the philosophical question uncertain. Somewhere along the trajectory of humanoid life on earth something reminiscent of what we today tentatively understand and designate as "burial" begins, but in such a way as to leave it uncertain if indeed it has begun, and if so what precisely it is that really has begun. The dilemma is illustrated and analyzed in an exemplary fashion in the British archaeologist Paul Pettitt's *Palaeolithic Origins of Human Burial* (2011). The book is particularly interesting from our present viewpoint, both for its comprehensive survey of all known Paleolithic burials and for its attempt to provide a genealogical explanation of this phenomenon.

Pettitt repeats the standard anthropological truth "that among humans, organized and cultural responses to death are universal." And like most authors in this field, he takes his point of departure in the early analyses of Hertz and van Gennep and the idea of mortuary culture as a technology for social healing. The basic meaning of burial rituals is seen as "transitions, marking the journey of the deceased into new worlds, and providing a structure for mourning and the renegotiation of society after the removal of a social agent."[9] Pettitt's ambition is to contribute to the archaeological record of how humanity has created such "meaningful" and "expressive" responses to the elementary impact of death. But whereas the traditional Durkheimian approach understands burial as an always already established social-ritual *representation* of death, Pettitt uses the historical-archaeological archive to reach for a *genealogical-evolutionary* account of the very emergence of the *meaning* of mortuary culture as such, in other words, of the giving of a meaning to death. In the course of this project, he also mobilizes accounts of nonhuman expressions and acts in regard to death. Whereas Hertz sought to capture the basic meaning of burial rites by studying them in their human social context with examples from a specific population during a distinct period in time, Pettitt activates the entire known record of Paleolithic burial sites from the earliest toolmaking hominids two million years ago to the emergence of advanced agricultural societies some ten thousand years ago, building his compilation on work from recent decades on mortuary behavior by anthropologists and archaeologists.

On the basis of this extensive material, he seeks to respond to the same question that was first articulated philosophically by Hegel, and then explored repeatedly in comparative anthropology, to determine *the (social) origin and meaning of burial.* For Hertz the original phenomenon was accessible through a rational reconstruction of the principal *needs* of society in general. For Pettitt, who comes from evolutionary anthropology, the question of the origin is first approached not through a comparison with contemporary "primitive" societies but with even more elementary forms of behavior observed among nonhuman primates. For him, the idea of *emergence* and *origin* are understood and explained in terms of the transformation and movement from a less developed to a more developed biological comportment. This leads him to posit a series of behavioral and conceptual thresholds as a way to grasp the stepwise genealogy of burial practices. Along this lineage of "mortuary activities," he isolates ten different idealized stages or steps (all of which are documented among different species and populations): "curation" (carrying around corpses or parts of corpses), "morbidity" (an inquiring concern for the injured, diseased, or dead body), "cronos compulsion" (the urge to dismember, injure, or consume parts of corpses), "abandonment" (leaving helpless individuals to die), "structured abandonment" (deliberate placing of the corpse for protection, e.g., under bushes), "funerary caching" (structured deposition in a chosen place, such as a cave), "cairn covering" (piling of stones over the corpse), "formal burial" (creating an artificial place for containing the corpse), "place of multiple burial" and "cemetery" (larger than formal burial and often separated from the dwelling ground).[10]

If and when any of these stages has first been actualized will be a question of interpreting often disputable archaeological evidence. Pettitt argues for at least the possibility that a site comprising the well-preserved remains of seventeen individuals of the species *Australophithecus afarensis* in Hadar, Ethiopia, excavated and published in the early 1980s and dated to around 3.2 million years ago, *could* have been brought to the site with the intention of "funerary caching" to hide them from predators.[11] But as an illustration of how disputed this early evidence is, among the hundred or so sites that have been presented as *possible* Paleolithic burial sites, a majority of trained observers agree that only about a third are indeed samples of some sort of burials.[12] It is only from around 120,000 to 100,000 BP that there is a general agreement around a few cases of human burial culture, including the burial of children and traces of ochre on the site. The first cremation is documented around 75,000 BP. From around 29,000 BP there are multiple findings that point indisputably to the existence of a more general culture of burial, with gifts and secondary processing and ritual uses of bones. Finally, organized grave sites or "cemeteries" appear from around 15,000 to 12,000 BP. From that time onward, human societies across the earth (partly) independently of one another gradually enter the so-called Neolithic and agricultural mode of life, from which there is a continuous burial tradition—eventually including monumental burial architecture in various and culturally distinct parts of the world—that lead directly up to the present. From then on, if not earlier, the archaeological record supports beyond all doubt the general statement that "humans bury their dead."

Today, most accounts that address the question of the historical origin of burial take for granted that this is a cultural activity somehow rooted in more elementary layers of animal behavior. And for Pettitt, the definitive limit is not one between humans and nonhumans, or even nonhumanoids, since the first levels of his hierarchy of morbidity behavior have also been observed among primates. Using observations of the behavior of chimpanzees, he proposes that certain "basic parameters for the physical responses of behavioral acts toward death and the dead body" can "provide clues to what our 'core' responses to death may have been in the dim evolutionary past."[13] In Pettitt's words, they give us an "essential blueprint for the earliest manifestation of such behavior among the earliest members of the Hominidae."[14] What takes place in a group of primates is then interpreted along a temporal-historical axis, where these apes are seen as contemporary witnesses across time, uniting present humans with humans of the most ancient past, of whom only a few scattered skeletons remain. To assess and critically analyze this approach and draw out its implication for our larger argument, we should first look more closely at the example used by Pettitt, which stems from the work of a group of researchers led by the Japanese primatologist Tetsuro Matsuzawa.

In 1992 Matsuzawa's team observed a scene among a group of Bossou chimpanzees in Guinea, involving the death of a two-year-old infant from disease. The large apes were observed and filmed for two weeks before the death and then for another month following it. Instead of abandoning the dead body of its child, the mother carried it with her for a full month, through its physical decay and mummification, until finally abandoning it. During this period, other members of the flock would display curiosity toward the decaying body and occasionally take it and toss it around, as if it were a toy.[15] During a later visit to the same community, Matsuzawa's team observed the same phenomenon, but this time with two mothers carrying their dead children, one for as long as sixty-eight days, showing affection and care for the decaying bodies, scratching and poking them, and preserving them from harm by grooming and chasing away flies.

In the article that summarizes their observations, Matsuzawa and his colleagues conclude that the repeated instances of this same phenomenon suggest that this is not a rare event in a singular community but a more general form of behavior. In the article, they do not speculate on the *meaning* of the behavior. On one level the scene would seem to speak for itself. The image of the mother who refuses to let go of her dead child, holding on to its decaying corpse, conveys a compelling species-transcendent predicament of grief. But what would it mean really to understand this behavior in the sense of providing an explanation for it? How can it be made sense of from a scientific, biological perspective? Is there a logic of life—a *bio-logic*—that can make this continued caring for the dead child comprehensible beyond the simple unwillingness to let go? Does this creature demonstrate only a misguided reflex of maternal instincts, or does the scene signify something else and something more that would point instead to subsequent and evolutionary more "superior" responses to death? In the original article, the authors pose what they call the "obvious and fascinating question" concerning the extent to which the two mothers "'understood' that their offspring were dead." To this they reply that "they treated the corpses as live infants, particularly in the initial phase following death. Nevertheless, they may well have been aware that the bodies were inanimate, consequently adopting carrying techniques never normally employed with healthy young (although mothers of handicapped young have also been known to respond appropriately)." The article concludes with the hope that new data will emerge from this "threatened community."[16]

But what is it that really occurs in this scene? Does it display a creature whose maternal instincts have misled it to continue to carry out an ultimately useless behavior? Or does it present a being grieving for her dead child, which she refuses to let go? There are other examples of advanced mammals that display continued concern for bodies of dead kin, notably among dolphins and elephants.[17] But the mother carrying her dead child over two months displays a "mortuary behavior" of a different kind. The primatologists' question "does she *know* that it is dead?" captures the core of the problem. From her behavior, they conclude that she behaves *as if* the child were still alive, yet other aspects of her behavior indicate that she is clearly aware that it is not. The meaning of this question—"does she *know*"—focuses the inner paradoxes of the situation. For what does knowledge amount to here? What does it mean to know that the child is dead? Does the animal that leaves its kin behind the very moment when it ceases to move and breathe really know that it is dead? Does it know this fact better than the chimpanzee mother who refuses to let go? In other words, What is knowledge in response to death? And when is it fully realized?

To put it differently: What would a *rational* response to death amount to? Would it be to simply leave the body of the dead child behind in the bushes to be taken care of by an efficient ecological system, as is the common practice among most living beings, including many primates? Or is it to hold on to the decaying corpse and to somehow care for it and protect it? The reason that the description of the chimpanzee is so moving is not that the mother is farther away from the *truth* of the death of her child than the animal that simply leaves it on the ground but rather that there is something in her way of responding to this fact that brings her closer to what we would recognize as a care for the dead. When we look at her and contemplate her behavior, it is as if she, in a glimpse, permits us to see something that is not just the hypothetical objectifying matrix that *explains* why humanoids in a distant past presumably began to care for their dead. Instead, it exposes us to the possibility of a cross-species shared sadness of finitude and powerlessness before the death of kin. But again, we do not know what it is we are seeing.

In his own summary of the research on the mortuary behavior of the chimpanzee, Pettitt lists a wide table of behaviors in relation to their offspring, ranging from aggressive to caring, from infanticide and cannibalism, to cases of caring for the body of the dead long after death. Alongside the results from Matsuzawa, he also mentions earlier reports by Jane Goodall on the varying reactions among chimpanzee children to the death of parents, of how they display distress, consternation, and depression. All these behaviors exemplify what he classifies as "detachment." To these elementary responses belong curiosity, caring, aggressiveness, and remaining around the body for different periods of times, in sum, enacting a kind of "social theatre" around the dead. In one case recorded by Goodall the body of a dead infant was deposited in thick bushes, motivating the question if this should perhaps be seen as a case of "structured abandonment," as an elementary form of burial behavior.

Reflecting on this evidence, Pettitt summarizes four "original" responses to death of kin: caring for the corpse, displaying signs of mourning, enacting a "social theatre," and cannibalizing the body. He concludes that the different reports from primate behavior point toward an "important evolutionary link between these basic realms of morbidity and mortuary activity and their importance to the Hominidae."[18] This is also what leads him to conclude that the basic set of behaviors toward the dead observed among these beings gives us a blueprint for human burial behavior. Elsewhere he even speaks of an "inevitability among hominids at some point in their evolutionary history to invest certain locales with meaning about the disposal of the dead." Ultimately these ways of showing interest in and compassion for the corpse are credited with a metaphysical impact of unprecedented scope. When seen as original and elementary ways of responding to the question of what happens beyond death, they point to "the root of all cosmology and religious belief."[19]

This extraordinary statement motivates us to reconsider the premises for the discussion of which they form a part. At the sight of a chimpanzee mother in Guinea, dragging the mummified corpse of her child through the woods, we are invited to contemplate the "root of religion and cosmology" as well as "historical necessities" and "essential" truths. What kind of hermeneutics is deployed and operative in such a statement? What does the vocabulary of metaphysics—of *essences* and *origins*—mean here, in the context of a theoretical account that on another level is so eager to stay close to an empirical observable domain?

To begin with, it displays the immense stakes involved in the interpretation of mortuary behavior and practice. It displays how the discipline of archaeology, in its most technical form and with the support of comparative anthropology, primatology, paleontology, and genetics, competes with the entire legacy of speculative philosophy of history to access the origin of human culture. But just as in the case of the socioanthropological models, we need to be attentive to the inner conceptual structure and limits of this approach. Part of the problem hinges on the question posed by the primatologists themselves—does she know?—as well as to the further implication of this question: What does knowledge here mean? What does it mean to know death, to know that the other is really dead, in such a way that we can imagine and represent her as no longer there, and thus as someone who *has been*?

When phrased in this way, the riddle posed by the mummified chimpanzee child can be traced throughout the trajectory of Pettitt's summary of the Paleolithic archive. Surrounding the discussion of almost all cases of the earliest retrieved samples of burial is precisely: is this *really* a burial, or does it just *appear* to be one? In other words, has someone *really* been interred here, or has this corpse simply ended up in this place? And what this question ultimately points to is the phenomenon of *symbol* and *symbolization*. "Symbol" is the term most frequently applied to capture the fundamentally evanescent capacity to represent absence and that cultural and evolutionary anthropology from early on designated as the defining trait of (cultivated) human life. After having established the genealogical-evolutionary hierarchy of morbidity or mortuary practices, and after having reached for the affective blueprint for burial through the meditation on the grieving chimpanzee, Pettitt's search for the origin ends up precisely here: in the question of the symbol, in the possibility and emergence of the symbol and its offspring: the *concept*. Or as he writes in a concluding and more explicitly speculative-theoretical chapter of the book, the development of burial practices "must be suggestive of deliberate concepts." And furthermore, "the archeological record pertaining to human mortuary activity should allow us to evaluate exactly when and how the dead came to be embodied in symbolic systems."[20] In order to know if someone has been buried, we need to know if these remains have become a symbol, or if they have entered a symbolic space. The ability to create a tool for a particular purpose does not require symbolization in this sense. Symbolization has to do precisely with the ability to represent what is absent. Ultimately the origin of burial is transformed into a question of the emergence of symbolization and conceptualization as such.

In a concluding sequence of steps the previous ladder of different mortuary comportments is thus mapped onto a ladder of symbolization, from the earliest supposedly nonsymbolic behavior of consternation and socially codified curiosity before the dead, to the fully developed symbolic grammar of deposition of the dead in designated spaces according to social rank.[21] This elementary ability to symbolize is said to be manifested already in the documented Neanderthal practice of cleansing soft tissue from the heads of the dead. In the shaping of a naked skull we are invited to see the making of a *sign* through which the dead is *represented*. Pettitt's conclusion, with which he also ends the book, reads as follows: "From this [data] it can certainly be said that mortuary activity was fully symbolically structured after 30,000 BP, possibly beforehand; and that a degree of symbolic underpinning is evident in Middle Palaeolithic burial back to ~100,000 BP."[22]

What is the philosophical significance and wider implications of this statement? Two centuries of extensive practical and theoretical efforts in the human-historical sciences separate his account from Hegel's reflections on burial as a sign of spiritual freedom in the face of finitude and biological necessity. At first glance, it bears little resemblance to Hegel's analysis. But if we look at the organizing framework of the whole theoretical pursuit, the differences begin to fade. As the human sciences reach for the origin of burial, they inevitably find themselves facing their own cultural-semantic foundation and thus the condition of possibility for their own practice. The question of *when* the human being becomes recognizable before and to itself is somehow inextricably connected to *when it sees itself as able to represent the other in and beyond death.*

So when do humans really bury? In the attempt to capture the origin and genealogical emergence of this core cultural practice, the human sciences are seeking the historical truth of something that we presumably already know *what it is.* And while repeatedly stressing the variety and genealogical-evolutionary obscurity of these practices, they nevertheless refer to it with one and the same term—"burial"—as if it really did have one basic and fundamental meaning. And still the question "has burial really taken place?" is one that does not have a definitive answer. We can never be quite sure if what has been done was really a burial or even if there is anything like a natural and clear-cut burial, because we do not know what a real and genuine response to the death of kin is. To be sure, rituals and technologies have emerged within every known culture to respond to the event of death, permitting humans within specific temporal-cultural frameworks to feel that they have done what should be done. But the urge to respond and to care for the dead remains an open-ended challenge, with no definitive limits, as a need that we *share.*

Through the intensified preoccupation with the remains of the ancient dead, and in the attempt to understand the confused grief of the chimpanzee, the archaeologist is reaching into this inheritance, both from an outside, from which the other is the enigma to be solved, and from an inside, where he is drawn closer and closer to himself and his own pursuit. In seeking to grasp the meaning of caring for the dead, he is led back to that very conceptual adventure in and through which the care for these bones was actualized to begin with, to what we could perhaps call *the vertiginous passion of the grave.* As the archaeologist leans over the petrified bones in a pit one hundred thousand years old in the attempt to grasp their meaning, he finds himself also looking back into his own historical consciousness and its enigmatic desire to hold and represent the other who has been.

Site II: Visualizing the Past through
the Lens of a Grave

During the last half century, *the grave* rose to a new level of theoretical concern in and for archaeology. It was conceptualized as a window into the social reality of the past, before which the archaeological community mobilized its most advanced interpretive resources and fought its hardest intradisciplinary battles. In the previous section the analysis centered on a contemporary attempt to use the models of evolutionary anthropology to interpret the earliest traces of human burial. Here I take a somewhat broader perspective and show how it was precisely the question of the interpretation of burials and mortuary culture that released in an exemplary way the inherent tension in archaeology between its social-scientific and its humanist-hermeneutic ethos from the 1970s onward, leading it to confront its own position in regard to that very human past for which it saw itself as the proper caretaker.

In 1971 James Brown edited a volume of the *Memoirs of the Society for American Archaeology* devoted to approaches to the social dimensions of mortuary practices. The title essay was written by Lewis Binford, a towering figure in the modern history of the discipline who a few years earlier had coedited an influential collection of articles, *New Perspectives in Archaeology*. The *Memoir* volume is a landmark for how modern archaeology approached and deepened its practical-conceptual interaction with graves and the remains of the dead.[23] Binford's basic premise was that while burials constituted "one of the most frequently encountered classes of cultural features observed by archaeology," up until then archaeologists had generally failed to deal with them as a "distinct class of variable phenomena."[24] For this purpose, he too returned to the sociological-comparative model of Durkheim and Hertz and the idea that mortuary rites could be seen as collective social efforts to handle and integrate the destructive impact of death. But he sought to expand this approach by focusing on varieties and differences within given societies to draw conclusions from how bodies were "disposed" of to the inner social organization of a specific society or community.

The core act of burial was described precisely as a matter of "disposal," the simple moving of useless and possibly obtrusive matter from one position or state to another. But the different ways in which this elementary act was performed and this material core was charged with meaning enabled him to posit the grave as a readable sign, a "representation" of the underlying social condition and the status of the individual around which it was created. An important impetus was an observation from Hertz's essay concerning the different kinds of burials awarded to individuals of different social status. But whereas Hertz based his theory of eyewitness reports of living (or recently living) communities, the idea behind Binford's "New Archaeology" (or "processual archaeology," as it was also known) was to use ethnographic comparison between living observed communities and the archaeological evidence to form hypotheses of the type of social structure that it represented. Together with system theory and ecology it grew into a social-scientific research program through which the inner structure of entire societies of the past could ideally be re-created using the preserved evidence from graves as a magnifying lens. Explicitly distancing themselves from earlier "idealistic" and "cultural theoretical" interpretations, these "new" archaeologists saw culture as structures and systems of adaptation, within which differences in symbolic expressions should in principle be interpreted in terms of the inner organization and evolution of the society under investigation. The same functionalist idea was developed further around the same time by the young anthropologist Arthur Saxe, who set up a long list of such correlations between burial practices and social structure, and in particular one that posited the strict correlation between the location of burial grounds and land claims under conditions of limited or restricted resources.[25] Through these new approaches, and what would henceforth be referred to as the "Saxe-Binford hypothesis," the dead in their graves were mobilized and reconceptualized as frozen images of the societies to which they once belonged. Their graves were no longer traces of unknown superstitious religious "beliefs" but functions and reflections in death of their social positions in life and of their worlds as a whole.[26]

The overall effect was an extraordinary rise of interest in graves and the remains of the dead as means of reaching into social reality of the past. With this also came an increased interest in other and complementary sources of information, mostly biological data concerning diet and health and more refined osteological analyses that were later complemented with genetic analysis. With the focus moving from structures and artifacts to include the bodies and biological context and conditions of the dead, archaeology from this moment rose to the pretension of constituting a "social science of the past" with the excavation of graves as its principal source of information.

Ten years after the publication of the Brown *Memoir*, the British archaeologist Ian Hodder published the study *Symbols in Action— Ethnoarchaeological Studies of Material Culture*, a book generally recognized as the catalyst for archaeology's version of the *Positivismusstreit*, a theoretical rivalry between a social-scientific and a humanist-hermeneutic approach that within the discipline became known as "processual" versus "post-processual" theory. Seen from a distance, Hodder's intervention amounted to a fairly moderate hermeneutical observation that we cannot always take for granted a "straightforward link between behavior and artifacts" or the "purely functional, adaptive viewpoint."[27] But among the founding generation of "processual archaeologists" there was little interest in critically reflecting on the theoretical premises of their own interpretive enterprise. The shape and structure of burial were simply posited as a readable text or as a frozen image of the society that once produced it, which could then be re-created as archaeological knowledge of the past. In its place, Hodder proposed what he called a "contextualized archaeology" that should also take seriously the significance of "norms and beliefs."

At the heart of these remarks was again the notion of *symbol* and the question of the body in death. Human action takes place through symbols that can have different meanings depending on ideological and political context, in the past as well as in the present. To engage in interpretations of such symbols is therefore also to enter a *contextual* space. As an example of his principal point Hodder referred to excavations of Neolithic graves on the Orkney islands, where bones appeared to have been gathered and redistributed in consecutive steps, indicating that they were not only determinate representatives of sociogeographical realities at a certain moment but also that they also somehow reflected the "special importance" attached to the "life/death boundary."[28] In a subsequent book he expressed himself more sharply on the core issue of what we can read from bones of the dead. Explicitly addressing Binford's seminal 1971 paper, he wrote, "The generalizations which are used concerning the relevant links between burial and other aspects of life must be concerned with meaning and ideology, not only with adaptive functional utility." Thereby he disparaged the idea that "there should be a strong relationship between the complexity of the status structure in a socio-cultural system and the complexity of differential treatment of persons in mortuary ceremonialism."[29]

In visualizing the dead as pure materiality on which a society imbues meaning, the processual approach failed to see how burial also operates at the sociosemantic intersection of the dead and the living, where the dead are not disposed of but remain among the living and where the living continue to *be* with the dead in and through these acts and their material remains. Following death, the society of the living does not simply reproduce itself without loss; it also carries and maintains a relation to the dead as a continued responsive relation to their absence. To occupy this space of the symbol of the dead—or of the dead as symbol—is to continue to live in the indeterminacy of its meaning and impact. In the positivist processual approach, all meaning is seen as at least potentially available, as it is projected onto the blank bodily matter of the material support. Or in the words of Christopher Tilly, "The traditional way of viewing material culture, and more widely the archaeological record, is that it is in some way a self-sufficient repository of meaning."[30]

When confronting remains of the dead in burial, the interpretive pursuit displays a deeper circularity than in the case of other material cultural remains. Here the interpreter is not only confronting a section of the past, whose inner meaning marks the hermeneutic challenge from the viewpoint of the present. When confronting the remains of a burial, the interpreter is also confronting *the inner pastness of that past itself,* because this is what the dead are, once their remains are made into the concern of the living. The bone in burial is not just the material basis of meaning projections among the living. It is a *sign* of a past as the having-been of an other, to which the act of burial responds. Burial remains are not just remains from a specific present of a past but from the past of that past, as both legacy and an anticipated future: as *the historical* in history. In its very ambition to recover the past for the present, the historical interest will often display a temptation to bypass precisely the historical in the sense of the inner temporality of time, or the symbolism of the symbol. More precisely, the desire to reach into the other in his or her pastness will tend to bypass the inner distance that constitutes the past other in his or her being with the dead. This general hermeneutic predicament is concentrated in the interpretation of burial, which more than any other cultural activity is concerned with the constitution of a culture's inner temporality.

The critical debate in archaeology on how to interpret burial remains that was first triggered by the social-scientific attempts to use graves as lenses through which to objectively observe the past, thus led to a new and deepened attention to the ontological specificity of these sites. This was the case in particular with the megalithic monuments, which from the 1990s began to be conceptualized in terms of *ways of relating to the dead* and described in terms of ancestry, time, and memory. An important publication in the English-speaking world was Richard Bradley's *The Significance of Monuments* (1997).[31] At different points in historical time, from 10,000 to 2000 BC, depending on geography and climate, humans across the earth begin to create monuments around the remains of the dead, of a kind for which there is no evidence in earlier periods. Understanding the conditions of the emergence of these monuments was always a central topic of archaeology. Bradley questions the received view that the construction of large monuments, especially on the British Isles, was dependent on the initial emergence of an agricultural society and the freeing of labor.[32] Instead, he argues that the rise of an agricultural society was dependent on the previous development of a new sense of *time* as manifested in these stone structures, which ultimately seem to go back to the construction of houses for the dead and funerary architecture.[33] And the central evidence for this interpretation is precisely the monuments themselves and how they partake in the shaping of a new kind of sociotemporal space.

Bradley showed how recent findings and analyses made the previous material-agricultural interpretation increasingly problematic, both because these monuments originate in preagricultural settings, with little signs of a subsistence economy, and because of later interpretations of their actual use.[34] The earliest excavated forms of the stone structures indicate that they were the site of rituals with audiences concerned with how "the living approached the dead."[35] Through an analysis of different architectural solutions, he shows how this transaction could be articulated in various ways through entrances leading into spaces where remains were kept and defleshed and the bones disconnected. Often only some parts of a specific person seem to have been kept in one "burial" place, and other parts may have been kept by and circulated among the descendants. In view of this, he even comes to the conclusion that "it hardly seems appropriate to maintain the conventional description of all these monuments as 'tombs.' At best, we can suggest a close association with the rites of passage of the dead. A more neutral term is to describe these constructions as 'mortuary monuments.'"[36]

What exactly took place in these structures we will never know. But by stressing that in both previous and later ages humans were more "cut off" from the dead, Bradley's reading of them emphasizes the uniqueness of the Neolithic revolution and its position as a historical origin of the historical as such in the shape of a living *relation* to the dead. He even writes that "only those structures which allowed access to the ancestral remains expressed a clear continuity between the past and the present."[37] Mike Parker Pearson's survey of burial archaeology from around the same time brings out this correlation even more explicitly. Like most writers in the field he simply sees modern Western secular societies as no longer really caring for the bodies of the dead, since they no longer perceive these bodies as vehicles for the interaction between the living and the dead. He makes the point that for a society that does not believe in an afterlife and that seeks only "secular salvation" through its humanism, the body becomes something "disposable," which is also the reason that it comes in conflict with cultures that still care for the remains of the dead.[38]

Today, most commentators of these debates that raged within the archaeological community seem inclined to call off the theoretical rivalries and recognize their complementary value for the common purpose of accessing the lives of the dead. In a volume from 2005 on burial archaeology, which explicitly aligns itself with the original Brown collection from 1971, the editors Gordon Rakita, Jane Buikstra, Lane Beck, and Sloan Williams come out in defense of the embattled Saxe-Binford idea of "correlating mortuary practices with sociocultural systems" to "monitor social complexity," while also claiming to have reached beyond the "constraining critiques" of the 1980s.[39] But as examples of new development in interpretive strategies, they too point to how burial practices and use of landscape are concerned with "meaning" and reflect different ways of relating to "ancestors" and of shaping the relation between the "living and the dead."[40] In their own jointly authored contribution to the volume, Rakita and Buikstra seek to expand Hertz's original schema of secondary burial by bringing in the case of both mummification and cremation as significant "exceptions to the rule." In reference to the early Andean practice of mummification, the oldest traces of which go back to 5000 BC, and how the bodies of Inca royalty were part of recurring public rituals in which they were brought out, fed, and cared for in different ways, they draw the conclusion that "rather than serving as preparation for their future life in the afterworld, mummification made permanent their place in the world of the living."[41]

In this reading, the mummies are seen as reflecting a different conception of death, not just a "final" event but one in which the dead remain as "powerful social and ritual forces" that also connect them to "ancestor cults." According to this interpretation the ancestors "never entirely *leave* this world but are nevertheless not quite *of* this world," what the authors also refer to as an "extended or permanent liminality." In virtue of being preserved as mummies, the dead can occupy a liminal state from which they can "bridge" the worlds of the afterlife and the living and thus "continue to structure the lives of their descendants."[42] While declaring their principal loyalty to Binford's original way of approaching burial practices—and thus presenting themselves as the inheritors of his legacy—the authors nevertheless challenge one of its fundamental premises that burial is really a case of "disposal" in and through which the previous social position of the dead is represented. Instead, they point to the question of an inner pastness of the past and how burial can be a way for the dead not simply to be disposed of and represented but also to prevail in an indeterminate liminal phase as continued "forces" among the living.

This survey of the interpretive itinerary of burial archaeology in the last half century has shown that the graves and sites of mortuary practices from the agricultural Neolithic period onward reemerged not only as localized events in time but also as sites of the experience and production of time and pastness itself. In the course of this transformation they motivated, challenged, and interacted with the archaeological-anthropological imagination as itself a cultivation of historical awareness and a communication with the dead. When the archaeologist "reopens" the ancient burial mound that had been covered over by later inhabitants and by the anonymous processes of sedimentation, he or she becomes an actor in the space of the production of this pastness. Through the archaeological activity, the bones begin to circulate again with the explicit purpose of entering into a relation with the ancient dead. It is in the course of this process that the site itself emerges as a hermeneutic site in its own right, housing the transaction between the living and the dead.

As archaeology moves closer and closer to the ontological reality of these spaces, it is also exposed to a vertigo of the hermeneutic imagination, where the graves that first appear as readable signs of a distant past begin to activate the full speculative resources of the historical imagination in its own historical predicament and self-understanding, as itself a culture of time, history, memory, and communication with the dead. In the final section, we look at how this hermeneutic realization within archaeology has run parallel to a more concrete experience of its own necropolitical entanglement.

Site III: Necropolitical Awakenings

The year 1971, when the Brown volume on burial archaeology was published, with its interpretation of burials as symbolically significant "disposals" of bodies and empirical material mostly taken from Native American burial sites, is also the year that marks the beginning of what we here refer to as archaeology's "necropolitical awakening." A group of archaeologists in Iowa were excavating a burial site that had been discovered during highway construction. The site contained mostly remains of white settlers but also a body identified as a Native American woman.[43] Whereas the remains of the settlers were reburied after the excavation, the bones of the Native American were collected for transportation to a museum for storage, according to what up until then had become standard practice for almost a century. But at this moment the handling of the remains was challenged by a group of Native American activists, led by Maria Pearson, who protested against what they recognized as a racially biased treatment of the dead. Further protest actions followed over the course of the next decade, when the political activity of the American Indian Movement (AIM), especially the separate group American Indians Against Desecration (founded in 1974), made handling remains of the dead into one of its political causes, eventually calling for repatriation and reburial. Around the same time similar actions were initiated in Australia, where the collection of Aboriginal bones in archives and museums also became a decisive battleground for Aboriginal rights and social status, followed by similar actions among Inuit on Greenland and Sami in Scandinavia.

Through these events, the disciplines of archaeology and anthropology were challenged and exposed as complicit collaborators in the history of colonial-political violence. During the following decades this question would lead to inflammatory debates between representatives of the disciplines and activists and political-juridical institutions. But it also rocked these disciplines themselves from within, in a way that would transform their self-understanding and practice and generate an entirely new body of critical and self-critical literature exploring the ethics and politics of burial.[44] In one of the earlier studies on this topic, Tamara Bray describes it as the dawn within archaeology of a "new, more humanistic orientation toward the past," propelled by new theoretical orientations in the human sciences, but in particular through the repatriation issue and legislation.[45] In retrospect, it can be seen as a rift within the humanist-historicist ethos, which also tells us something important about its original situation. In and through these controversies, it was forced to confront a legacy of an inner violence of history and the historical sciences as also necropolitical enterprises, where certain dead were *us* and certain dead were *others*, and where the presumably neutral organization of knowledge of the past also reflected a sociopolitical structure in the present. Whereas the previous unearthing and mapping of the dead in their graves had seen archaeology concerned only with a *knowledge* of the past, it was compelled to recognize that its own interaction with the dead also reflected power relations that were still operative in the present. The way that archaeology has largely sought to redefine itself in the aftermath of these battles has brought the relation to the dead and their bodies to the forefront of the historicist ethos in a way that also actualizes the broader context of the existential necropolitical predicament of being with the dead.

Archaeologists and anthropologists began to collect the remains of dead Native Americans beginning in the mid-nineteenth century. During the Indian Wars, the bodies and craniums of the dead were sometimes even taken directly from the battlefield and transported for storage. The American anthropological museum burial archives grew until eventually the remains of approximately 150,000 bodies had been collected nationwide.[46] The inner logic of this practice is complex. By the end of the nineteenth century, the native populations had begun to be viewed as doomed to extinction as an effect of modernization. Thus, they were conceptualized as the responsibility of the historical institutions, according to a logic of "manifest destiny" that also served the colonial enterprise.[47] The collecting anthropologists and archaeologists saw themselves as caretakers of an inheritance that was otherwise fated to be destroyed or simply to perish. With the 1906 Antiquities Act, skeletons of Native Americans came under cultural heritage legislation, literally making them into "historical artifacts." With the rise of biological anthropology and racial biology, special institutions were also created in the early twentieth century that gave a new impetus to collecting bones, in particular such bones that were considered valuable for the (mostly) pseudoscientific reconstruction of racial hierarchies and historical lineages. This was particularly the case with Australian Aborigines, whose skeletons were also exported and sold to European institutions.

Even though the 1971 protest action would eventually be recognized as the starting point of the critical self-reflection within the anthropological and archaeological disciplines, protests had been voiced earlier. When, for example, in the early 1930s, the Czech American anthropologist Aleš Hrdlička, then head of the section of physical anthropology at the Smithsonian and founder of the *Journal of Physical Anthropology*, unearthed the remains of approximately one thousand individuals in Larsen Bay, Alaska, and brought them to Washington, the excavations were sharply contested by the local inhabitants, but to no avail. Only fifty years later in 1987, following the transformation in public perception of the issue, the Larsen Bay Tribal Council of the Kodiak Island demanded the repatriation of the remains for reburial, which resulted in an extended series of hearings and debates concerning the legitimacy of the claim that involved questioning their right to this inheritance and during which anthropologists served as witnesses on both sides. In the end, the secretary of the Smithsonian agreed to a broad interpretation of the issue of legitimate inheritance, and the entire collection was returned for reburial.[48]

At first the reaction toward such claims within the archaeological-anthropological community was dismissive. When the leaders of AIM addressed the Society for American Archaeology in 1982 on the issue of repatriation and reburial, the response was largely negative. But over the following decade, the general sentiment changed rapidly, from refusing to even address the issue to accepting that it moved to the center of archaeology's own disciplinary ethos. When the World Archaeological Congress arranged its first meeting in 1989 in Vermillion, South Dakota, the topic was "Archaeological Ethics and the Treatment of the Dead," and among the invited were also representatives from indigenous groups. During this meeting the so-called Vermillion Accord on archaeological ethics was adopted. By that time, the issue had already passed beyond the scope and responsibility of the archaeological community and its internal ethical debates and found its way to federal legislation, where only one year later a new law was adopted, the Native American Graves Protection and Repatriation Act (NAGPRA), which then took on a dynamic of its own.[49] Here I focus on some of the formulations in the Vermillion Accord, which is especially interesting within the context of our discussion, since it is the first document that speaks of universal "rights of the dead" as a unique necropolitical legacy of archaeology.[50]

The accord consists of six short paragraphs that all circle around one word, "respect," which was precisely what the Native American communities had demanded and what they had previously not received, as manifested in the desecration of their graves and the institutionalization of their dead. The third paragraph speaks of the respect that should be granted "the wishes of the local community or guardians," in other words, for the living that care for the dead. But in the first two paragraphs there is yet no mention of the descendants or of the living. Here the recipients of the respect are *the dead themselves*. The first article of this document reads: "Respect for the mortal remains of the dead shall be accorded to *all* irrespective of origin, race, religion, nationality, custom and tradition." The "all" in this sentence designates not the bodies or the bodily remains but the dead themselves, who are here thereby recognized as subjects with rights. And the second article states: "Respect for the wishes of the dead concerning disposition shall be accorded whenever possible, reasonable and lawful, when they are known or can be reasonably inferred."

While thus recognizing—for the first time in human history—*a general right of the dead*, the overriding purpose of this extraordinary declaration is to establish an ethical consensus that makes it acceptable for archaeology to continue to do research on bodies of the dead—that these bodies can also be legitimate sources of knowledge. For this purpose, the text, in a somewhat odd twist, uses the same language of "respect" when speaking of the practice of historical research and science. Its fourth paragraph speaks of how a "respect for the scientific research value of skeletal, mummified and other human remains (including hominid fossils) shall be accorded when such value is demonstrated to exist." In the following section it speaks also of reaching "agreement" between communities and science in regard to the "disposition of ancestors." Finally, in the sixth paragraph the desire to reach such "acceptable agreements" is said to rely on a mutual respect for the respective "concerns" of "various ethnic groups, as well as those of science."

As a first formalized response to the inflammatory situation that had developed between the necropolitical activists and archaeologists, the formulations seem straightforward. They reflect a desire on the part of the scientific community to be able to solve conflicts between two distinct *types of interests* through rational dialogue. But in using the liberal-theoretical language of "rights" and "respect," it also conceals the shared underlying existential-ontological structure of the dispute and how it actualizes the deeper interconnectedness between history, historical consciousness, and the dead. By positing the *interest* of the other as a cultural difference to be *respected*, the other is respected, but precisely as *other*. While seeking to solve an issue that was indeed in need of formalized negotiations and agreements, it also reproduces a stereotypical image of the different parties that has continued to color the discussions even today. Just as in the case of the debates on "ancestral piety" discussed in Chapter 3, these disputes are conceptualized as clashes between fundamentally different worldviews, where the indigenous is re-anthropologized as distinctly *other*, even by the people who are truly committed to the political cause of disenfranchised communities. In a recent essay, Larry Zimmermann, one of the earliest and most influential critics of previous archaeological practices, writes that whereas "archaeologists and bioarchaeologists tend to call skeletons 'human remains,' many indigenous people tend to think of skeletons as people who are still alive but living on a different plane, people to whom those living in this world have obligations."[51] But this way of thinking about human remains, as something toward which there is a responsibility that corresponds to some sense of afterlife (if only understood as in the memory of the descendants and/or as represented by a grave) of the person is not peculiar to so-called indigenous people but is a shared sentiment among all humans in relation to *their* dead, including bioarchaeologists. Humans are with their dead, even if the way this basic predicament is concretely articulated varies from community to community. More important, the appropriate way of enacting this responsibility is never fixed once and for all but is instead a question of continued renegotiation, including the concrete physical handling of bodily remains.

Following the formulations of the Vermillion Accord there have also been philosophical attempts to give a more precise meaning to the idea of "rights" of the dead, using the vocabulary of normative ethics. Those who have engaged themselves in this discussion have sought to frame it in the conceptuality of Enlightenment political philosophy and human rights discourse from which the accord also originally draws its rhetoric. Notable among them is the philosopher Geoffrey Scarre. In his article "Archaeologists and the Dead" he asks if it is possible to "harm the dead." He also presents the background of the problem through what he takes to be a fundamental difference between a "scientific worldview," according to which "death is extinction," and various "indigenous conceptions" of how the living "stand in a symbiotic relationship to their ancestors" on the condition that "their bodies are not disturbed," something he too, strangely, describes as an attitude "unfamiliar in Western culture."[52] In an attempt to try to provide a rational-philosophical foundation for this conception, he then turns to Kantian ethics, exploring to what extent we can still speak of harm to the dead and if the dead can also be seen as "ends in themselves." He finds a rationale for this if there were a "wish" for a particular "posthumous future." When this wish is not respected, we can say that the person has been harmed. In principle he activates the kind of ethical-juridical framework that would be applicable to the construction and implementation of a will or testament. His conclusion reads: "Before proceeding with an investigation, an archaeologist should think about the interests of the dead as well as of the living."[53]

On one level, the analysis is motivated by a perfectly clear rationale seeking to give philosophical credibility to the idea of the rights of the dead, and its normative-ethical and legalistic conclusion captures a practice that is already being encoded in legislation. Still, it does not seek to fathom the underlying predicament that generated the dispute in the first place. As long as the commitment to ancestors and remains of the dead is designated as primarily a non-Western belief deserving respect and recognition, we not only fail to understand the underlying ontological predicament, but we are also likely to fail to respond appropriately to its demand. As long as the other is anthropologized as a representative of a different worldview, there can be no real understanding of the other or of the self. What clashes in this dispute is not two different worldviews where one cares about the bones of the dead and the other does not care, but the fact that both care about these bones as different ways of continuing to be with the dead and thus of inhabiting the space of the past. For archaeology the remains of the dead other, not just the bones, but everything preserved that could open a window toward the world of the past other, was always *valuable* as also a key to a history understood as *our* past.

The eight hundred–page *Oxford Handbook of the Archaeology of Death and Burial* (2013) gathers the state of the art of the knowledge of burial practices and the interpretive techniques used to gain information from human remains. It is also a testimony to the significance of these debates for the discipline. A main section of the book is devoted to the ethics and politics of burial, and the volume itself is partly motivated by the increasing need to think through the implications of this new sensibility. In their preface, the editors describe how the rising criticism of the use of human remains and claims for repatriation of bones has "reshaped the discipline considerably," to a point where archaeologists are prepared to "surrender the scientific privilege that previous generations of archaeologists and anthropologists had often assumed."[54] The editors' approach is first to accommodate the criticism and to recognize the need for stricter ethical and juridical regulations. But in the end the legitimacy of burial archaeology itself is defended as also a means to come "face to face with the past," to enter into a knowing relationship with individual human beings and to "rewrite a person back into history, to lend them a voice, and to tell a story about their life by drawing on a wide variety of approaches, methods, and perspectives."[55] Thus, the scientific excavation and epistemic engagement with the remains of the dead would ultimately amount to a way of coming into deeper contact with the dead themselves, not just the generic dead but also the individual *person*.

The purpose of the editors' remarks and reflections is to argue for the continued relevance of burial archaeology in the face of current contestations and to uphold the scientific privilege (or right). But it also becomes evident that the discipline does not simply contrast with a presumably "non-Western" piety toward the dead and ancestral worship, since it is oriented by a shared desire. If archaeologists of earlier generations worked on the premise that their purely theoretical interest in the past automatically gave them the right to excavate grave sites for information, the contemporary politicized situation has led to an awareness that the notion of a responsibility toward the past is at least twofold. It can have the form of seeking knowledge of what took place on the basis of discovered remains, which can include both artifacts and human remains. But it can also have the form of respect toward the dead, which implies not disturbing these remains. The volume editor, Liv Nilsson Stutz, carefully tries to navigate this new and more controversial territory of burial archaeology by stating that "archaeology cannot back off" completely from engaging with burials only because they are emotionally and politically charged. When placed in conflict, she writes, "we must defend the principle that our perspective remains a valuable contribution to understanding the past even when it is contested."[56]

From the perspective of our overarching question this statement is significant. It bears witness again to an inner recursivity in regard to the problem of the dead. Once the implicit ethical dimension of burial archaeology is made explicit, it forces the discipline itself to reconsider not just its theoretical self-understanding but also its actual practice. From the viewpoint of the practicing archaeologist this can take the form of handling a more complex juridical space, where the very act of opening graves and of handling the remains of historically and culturally distant people is drawn into a legal framework that is more reminiscent of how the archaeologist's own culture handles its burial sites, where the sanctity of graves is taken for granted and juridically secured. But from our overall theoretical perspective this new situation permits us to see how archaeology was always also situated as a unique practice within the existential predicament of being with the dead. Through the lens of historical consciousness and its "purely historical interest" it became possible to enter the spaces of the dead with a new task: to secure knowledge about them, both as individuals and as generic historical humans, and to build accounts of their existence on the basis of their cultural practices and temporal and geographical position.

This is manifested not just in archaeology's necromantic language of "bringing back" the dead to life but also in often repeated hopes that the representatives from the indigenous communities themselves will channel their commitment to their dead through archaeological-anthropological education and research in order to see that their traditional ways of connecting to their ancestral past can in fact be fulfilled in this way too. But in this gradual merging of perspectives, in a symmetrical respect between recognized differences, something is still lacking. As different ways of relating to the past through the dead other, the idealized poles of *knowledge* and *piety* must both respond to the inner difference and uncertainty of this relation. There are always the questions: How do we, as inheritors, respond to the obligation of the dead other? How do we inhabit this space as legacy? How do we do justice to the dead, and how do we as a culture carry them forward?

As archaeology was jolted into an awareness of its necropolitical transgressions by the claims from some of the descendants of those whose bones it had collected, it sought to reinvent itself with the help of the rational-philosophical discourse of rights for the dead. And as a manifestation of this new "respect" thousands of skeletal remains have been returned for reburial within and across national borders over the last three decades. But contrary to popular belief the storage rooms for the dead once inaugurated by the institutions of historical consciousness are not being evacuated. In fact, every year the amount of bodies and bodily remains in museums and research institutes grows, following the standard legal framework of archaeological research according to which human bones of a certain age are defined as historically protected material. Indeed, with the constantly expanding ability of genetic analysis to elicit knowledge from the remains of the dead, even the tiniest piece of ancient human tissue has increased in value as a potential means to come closer to the dead themselves. These "second burial" spaces are meant to serve the interests of both the living and the unborn. Because in keeping the remains of the long dead in storage for future generations, archaeologists see themselves as enabling the not-yet-born to perhaps know more of those having-been than we are able to know of them in the present. Thus, it amounts to a vast and expanding institutionalized care for their afterlife under the aegis of historical culture.

Burying the Archaeological Eye

The questions raised so far can be exemplified by an extraordinary event in the modern history of archaeology, a burial ceremony that took place in Vermillion in 1989 during the meeting of the World Archaeological Congress. During the same meeting that also led to the adoption of the new accord and that was meant to heal the fractured relation between archaeology and indigenous populations, the convener of the conference, Larry Zimmermann, orchestrated a ritual outside the town of Vermillion in memory of the Wounded Knee massacre nearby.[57] On this occasion the skeletal remains of a Native American who had been in local museum storage were "reburied." From this occasion, there is a black-and-white photograph that depicts archaeologists standing in a deep pit into which they are carefully placing a package.[58] Around this "grave" are archaeologists and various representatives of indigenous populations from all over the world. The event triggered great interest and reached the front page of the *New York Times*. Organizing an archaeological reburial of Indian bones was done to amend the colonial legacy of archaeology's disrespectful treatment of the remains. Through this ritual the fractured relation between victims and perpetrators in a cultural conflict could thereby presumably be "healed." From this perspective, the ritual would amount to a symbolic concretization of the formulation of the adopted accord, which had declared its "respect" for the remains of all dead, not just the dead of the white European majority. In performing a gesture of reburial, this new attitude of respect could be seen as not just words but also deeds.

But what was it that really took place during this extraordinary necropolitical event?[59] To begin with, we can ask *who* was really buried here. The bones belonged to a nameless individual whose remains in this case were given a generic, symbolic meaning.[60] In this particular situation, the body signified a generic Native American, who as an unknown soldier was honored as the representative of a larger community and its sufferings. But whereas the affective-necropolitical sense of the grave for the unknown soldier was to manifest the loyalty and gratitude of the community for whom this individual had sacrificed his life, the inner logic of this burial was much more complex. Here the burial was enacted not by the descendants and peers of the dead but by the intellectual descendants of those who at an earlier point in time had killed and then desecrated this human being in death as an explicit recognition of their historical guilt.

In this ritual, descendants of both perpetrators and victims of colonial violence stood together in an attempt to share a past that had pitted the forerunners against each other, not just politically but also chronologically-historically, where the latter had been made into a temporal-historical *other* by the former. The theoretical enterprise of history had provided the framework within which this particular body could be desecrated by being refused a proper burial or an undisturbed grave. The gesture of the archaeological burial in Vermillion thus also marked a recognition of the limit of the historical-archaeological-anthropological approach to the bones as it had been understood until then. The bones that were placed in the ground had once been unearthed (or never given a grave) and kept for "historical-scientific" reasons. With the return of the bones to the earth, the historical discipline thus recognized the limit of its own gaze in an act that had a sacrificial structure. It was not only the bones of a nameless generic Native American that were placed in the ground through this ritual but also the eyes of a generic archaeologist. Standing around this generic pit, dug by archaeologists, not to excavate its content but to bury and restore a generic content that had once been taken from it, archaeology was (re)burying not only the other but also itself and its hegemonic interpretive access to the dead.

The Vermillion burial marks not just an important symbolic date in the transformation of the ethos of the archaeological discipline in recent decades. It also brought it closer to the existential root of its own ethos.

The debates on reburial and repatriation of bones are still conceptualized in terms of *different* relations to the dead, the scientific and the pious-religious-ancestral. But through this emotional and awkwardly eclectic ritual the borders between these relations were blended and crossed. While the conceptualization of the bones as anthropological-historical artifacts enabled them to become the legitimate property of historical museums and archives—as epistemic links to the past and thus as a *past in the present*—the reconceptualization of them as *someone's* bones deserving burial meant that they were redefined in temporal terms to became part of a present legacy, inheritance, and tradition and thus as a *presence of the past*. In gathering archaeologists and activists around this second burial of an unknown Native American, the participants in the ritual sought to establish a sense of common humanity and shared history. And the means for this purpose was *an act of burial*. Thus, it was not only a question of caring for an individual or a group of individuals but for history itself, which through this act should also be able to take a new course.

But did a burial really take place here? Was this act a *genuine* act of burial, and in that case in what sense? Who or what was really buried in this grave? Who or what was cared for and remembered? If indeed it was a burial, did it also involve the self-burial of the burier and perhaps of history itself or at least a certain phase or sense of the historicity of history? Who can know, and who will ever be able to fully interpret it? Will archaeology be able to understand this grave in which it also buried a part of itself and where the bones of an anonymous Native American were also meant to seal a new social contract of universal respect for the dead—for all the dead?

No theoretical discipline has come closer to the grave than archaeology. It emerged from out of the grave, gradually transforming itself from looter of antiquities to professional historian seeking *the truth of the dead*. It was through its efforts that humans learned to think of themselves as *we who bury our dead*. The critical rehearsal of the history of burial archaeology has shown us how its attempt to use the buried dead to know the buried dead also displays the circular temporal and existential structure of the grave. In seeking to find the truth about the grave and what the grave can tell us about the past, the archaeological gaze found itself drawn toward the grave. In seeking to name the origin of burial, it found itself before the origin of its own ability to speak and name, to *symbolize* and to *conceptualize*. In searching for the historical meaning of the grave, it found itself confronting the question of the meaning and possible origin of historical culture itself, precisely through the desire to hold on to the dead and to serve as their true custodian. While seeking to posit itself securely *outside* the grave looking down into it, archaeology was gradually compelled to realize that it had already from the outset been situated *inside* the grave, in that enigmatic space of caring for those having-been, indeed as their most careful caretakers. In building its rational archives of bones, it believed itself to master the truth of death and its cultural responses, only to be forced to recognize that in making itself responsible for all the dead of history, it desecrated the graves of the other. Through this extraordinary trajectory, archaeology was led back to its original existential-ontological and necropolitical predicament: a qualified mode of being with the dead.

What *was* the burial of the dead? Where did it begin? Where will it end? What shape and form will the care for the dead take in the future? As members of the human species we never stopped burying. Perhaps we only just started. Perhaps we are still looking for the right and proper way to bury. Perhaps we are only now slowly beginning to learn to live more authentically with the dead, not just with our own but with all the dead of the earth, through our historical culture and memory.

Visiting the Land of the Dead

HISTORY AS NECROMANCY

> The mirror of history has melted, and beneath it, a patient, hybrid organism grows in his cruciform shadow.
>
> —Derek Walcott, *Omeros* LIX

Introduction

When Odysseus, after his long captivity on the island of Calypso, is washed ashore in the land of the Phaeacians, he is treated with a feast by King Alcinous. Initially the king does not know who his guest is, because Odysseus has refused to say his name. At the height of the feast Alcinous asks the blind bard Demodocus to sing the stories from the great Trojan War as though they had already become folk mythology and oral epic during Odysseus's long years of delayed homecoming. In the presence of one of the protagonists who actually experienced it, the story of the dramatic events is thus recounted within the framework of the epic itself. In this remarkable early instance of metaliterature, the author of the epic poem inscribes the oral performer of the epic into the text, situating the social and technical origin of his own endeavor as a writer within the narrative. When Odysseus hears the stories of his own adventures and is reminded of his lost companions, he is deeply moved. He tries to conceal his tears, but Alcinous sees them and compels him to reveal his identity and to explain why he is so saddened by the narrative. It is at this point that Odysseus first says his name and that he begins to tell his story, not only of who he is and where he comes from but also what he has experienced. Throughout the night of the feast he takes over the story from the bard and tells the story of his adventures after Troy, leading up to the shipwreck and his encounter with Calypso.[1]

In her essay "The Concept of History" from the collection *Between Past and Future*, Hannah Arendt pointed to the particular scene where Odysseus listens to Demodocus as marking the "beginning of history."[2] As the living hero is confronted with his own deeds through a collectively shared narrative, he and his life have become objectified "history" in precisely the sense that Herodotus would later give to this term. For Herodotus, as Arendt points out, the basic and explicit motive was to secure that the "great deeds" of both Greeks and barbarians were not forgotten, but preserved in memory, and that their glory and reputation—their *kleos*—would not perish. Humans are mortal, surrounded by immortal gods and nature, but through works of greatness preserved in oral and eventually written narrative, they can aspire to take place in, as Arendt writes, "the world of everlastingness."[3]

Arendt's suggestion was taken up by François Hartog in a more recent article on the origin of the concept of history, where he explicitly discusses the relation between Homer and Herodotus.[4] Hartog argues that whereas Herodotus first simply sought to rival Homer and the Trojan epic through his depiction of the Persian Wars, it turned out that he had created a new and unique form of narrative and literary voice, *history*. Hartog recalls Arendt's remark on the scene at the Phaeacian court, but just as in her analysis, his comparison does not engage with the details of the Homeric text. The main point is simply to place Homer and Herodotus alongside each other as two types of narrators of past deeds and words. In this chapter I return to this long night of storytelling at the court of Alcinous as a means to address and reflect on the relation between Homer and Herodotus and the early Greek concept of history, as well as to deepen our understanding of the relation between history and interaction and communication with the dead. Among the many adventures that Odysseus shares with his hosts, one stands out as more spectacular and more compelling than any of the others, his journey to the land of the dead as described in Book XI, which in the literature on

Homer is commonly referred to as the *Nekya*. Rather than in the confrontation between Odysseus and the bard, it is in the report from the land of the dead that we are brought closest to the genuine pathos of history and of historical awareness in early Greek literature as emanating from a desire to share and hear from the world of the dead.

In his *Memories of Odysseus: Frontier Tales from Ancient Greece*, François Hartog also compares the mythical travels of Odysseus to those of a number of subsequent Greek writers and historians, from Hecataeus to Philostratus. There Odysseus is described as the one who made the longest journey, even to the "limits of the Underworld and the island of Sirens."[5] But since Hartog's emphasis in this context is on the role of traveling, seeing, and reporting in general, he does not pay specific attention to the significance of this journey to the underworld. Central to his argument is the faculty of *sight* and of *seeing* and of Odysseus as the one who had *seen* the most. As is familiar from all handbooks on the theory of history, the Greeks themselves did not have a specific word for what eventually became known as this particular form of knowledge. Greek *historia* means "inquiry," from the verb *historeo*, to "inquire" or "examine," but also to "report." It has been traced by philologists to the word *histor* as the agent of an archaic perfective form of having *seen*, *oida*, designating "the one who knows from having seen or learned." In the few places in the *Iliad* that mention a *histor* it designates a knowledgeable and authoritative person, often translated as "judge" or "arbiter" (e.g., XVIII.501).[6] In some cases, the *histor* can also mean a "witness."[7] If we try to create a tentative definition of the historian on the basis of these etymological sources, it could be "an inquiring witness who recounts what he or she has seen." This is more or less also how the term appears in the writings of Herodotus, in this early instance of a genre of writing that at least from that moment onward is commonly recognized as "history." For our own analysis of Odysseus's journey to the underworld, this stress on sight and of having seen across the threshold of death is important to keep in mind, because the ultimate act of seeing is performed by the person who can cross this line and who can return to bear witness from the land of the dead to the land of the living.

In his collection of essays *The Writing of History*, originally published in French in 1975, Michel de Certeau depicted history as a mode of writing operating precisely on the threshold between the living and the dead, where the dead of the past constitute the "phantasms" of historiography, which it both "honors and buries."[8] His argument has received increasing attention in the last decade among historians and theoreticians of history. Later in this chapter I present and discuss at length his interpretation of historiographical writing as a form of necromancy. Ultimately I show the limits of the structuralist framework in the face of the existential-ontological predicament of being with the dead. But what Certeau highlighted in a compelling way in his original analysis was the inner tension that characterizes the desire of the historian to be both the most skilled witness of the past and the one through whose very knowledge, notably the critique of textual sources, the hope of immediate access to the past is shattered. Later I demonstrate how this inner tension is played out in an exemplary way in the so-called Homeric question as the single most-debated issue in classical philology.

Thus, the entire chapter performs a loop: Odysseus's journey to the land of the dead is presented as an original site of the historical imagination and the historical desire. At the same time the very nature and standing of the Homeric epic as a historical source are presented as a case in point of how the historical imagination both sought to secure and eventually shattered the veracity of an original name and an original text, while still holding on to the hope of a privileged access to the past as to a ghost-like truth of the dead other.

The Nekya

In the corpus of ancient Greek literature in general, and the Homeric epic in particular, Book XI of the *Odyssey* occupies a particularly disputed position. It is located at the geometrical center of the text, as the deepest descent that also opens the way to the final homecoming. Yet in the philological critique its authenticity and its date of composition were disputed early on.[9] The whole section radiates a kind of temporal instability, as it seems to draw its imagery from the most archaic and even "primitive" historical layers, notably through the depiction of blood rites for the dead, while at the same time indicating a later date of composition and editorial addition through some of its theological imagery.[10] At once too old and too new, it seems to unhinge the spine of the epic as a whole. In relation to this particular section, the two centuries of debates on the Homeric question also obtain a particularly acute significance. Who is speaking here? From where is the voice of the text really coming? Is it from the original author or from someone else, from someone or something older or perhaps from someone more recent than Homer, from before or after this already most evanescent and ghostlike figure of ancient literature and culture? I return to these problems after first recalling the central content of the narrative with a particular view to its historiographical implications.

After Odysseus and his men have rested on the island of Circe, she advises them to visit the "rapt shade of blind Teiresias of Thebes" to find out about their future prospects (X.496). This is the first and only time that the legendary Teiresias makes his appearance in Homer and the first time that he is mentioned in the preserved corpus of Greek literature. Later, in Sophocles's *Antigone*, it is Teiresias who warns Creon not to challenge the gods of the underworld by refusing Polyneices a proper burial. But here in the *Odyssey* he already dwells in Hades as the only one among the dead who still has the power of divination, or as Circe says, "to him alone, of all the flitting ghosts, Persephone has given a mind undarkened" (X.500).

Odysseus is first appalled by the prospect of making this journey— "no man has ever sailed to the land of Death" (X.508)—yet he sets sail with his ship and crew to the limit of Oceanus, to the land of the winter people who live in constant darkness. On the spot indicated by Circe he digs a hole in the ground and performs the ordained sacrificial rites, the culmination of which is pouring of blood from slaughtered lambs into a pit. It is the blood that calls forth the demons, ghosts, or souls, the *psychai* of the dead, who when they drink it are permitted to leave their shadowy existence for a moment to see, sense, and speak to the living. As the souls of the dead, attracted by the blood, come forth in great numbers, Odysseus is first gripped by fear, and he draws his sword to keep them away from the pit and to hear them one by one (XI.43).

The scenes that follow of his encounters and conversations can be read as a catalog of different behaviors and relations in regard to the dead. First is the question of *burial.* Among the most famous moments in the narrative is Odysseus's encounter with his companion and rower Elpenor, who first arrives at the pit. Believing that he had simply left Elpenor behind on the island, Odysseus is surprised to find him there, as if he had rushed ahead of them unnoticed. But Elpenor explains that he got drunk, fell from Circe's roof, and broke his neck. Now he has only one request from Odysseus, to provide him with a burial. I pledge you, he says, "to remember me" (*mnesasthai*; XI.71) and not to leave me "unwept and unburied" (*aklauton, athapton*). He then describes how he wishes to be cremated: in his gear, with his remains buried in a small mound marked only by an oar as its sign, its *sema*, the oar that he pulled in life "with his companions." Odysseus promises to fulfill his wishes, a promise that he immediately honors after having returned from Hades, as described at the outset of the subsequent Book XII.

We can compare the story of Elpenor and his request for a proper burial with the scene in the *Iliad* (XXIII.76), where Achilles, mad and exhausted with grief after the death of Patroclus, drifts into sleep, where he is visited by the ghost (*psyche*) of his beloved friend. Patroclus also has only one request: that Achilles provide him with a proper burial to enable him to pass safely through the gates of Hades and to have Achilles's bones placed in the same urn when he has died. Compared to this death in battle of a central character of the narrative, the burial request from the miserable Elpenor marks an important ethical moment in the Homeric text. Even though Elpenor is an unimportant character in the story, and even though he has died an ignoble death, he is called forth as the first among the shadows to articulate and bear witness to the individual desire not to be left behind unmarked and unwept but to be cared for in death and preserved in the memory of the living. Odysseus's response to his request both confirms and establishes the sense of an uncompromising duty toward dead comrades through the provision of a grave.[11] The world portrayed in the narrative is a world without writing, but it is depicted in writing by Homer from the perspective of a situation in which writing has emerged. Graves in Trojan times carried no written signs, and the memory of the dead was preserved without this technical support. But it is as a *sign*, a *sema*, that the anonymous grave is defined and established in the text.[12] It is also a dimension of the literary impact of this scene that the narrative functions as part or extension of this inner movement of the story as itself a work of memory for the dead. Because through its account of the plea and its fulfillment, the text takes upon itself a work of memory in saving the commoner Elpenor's name and story for posterity, thus making itself into a memorial mound and a symbolic caretaker for the dead.

Odysseus then turns to Teiresias, for whose counsel he has come. Teiresias is a mortal but with divine gifts. To meet with and talk to him is to seek out a voice that already belongs to the past since it dwells in the underworld but still holds a key to the future. This key, however, is not a map of what is to come but a call to act wisely, to restrain their desires, and to respect the order of the gods. It is only through such a journey to the land of those having-been that the open and uncertain future can be discerned. It is concretized in his warning not to touch the cattle of Helios, an advice that they will not heed, thus sealing their fate.

Throughout the conversation with Teiresias Odysseus can see the shadow of his own mother, Anticlea, roaming around, still unaware of his presence. It is Teiresias who explains to him how it is with the dead: "I shall make it clear in a few words and simply. Any dead man whom you allow to enter where the blood is will speak to you, and speak the truth [*nemertes*, literally: to speak *flawlessly*]; but those deprived will grow remote again and fade" (XI.144–146). In other words, it is only when those no longer alive are provided blood—the very substance of life— that they will speak to the living. Unless the living perform a sacrifice (give something of themselves), the dead will remain blind and numb shadows, with no ability to communicate. In poetic form, Teiresias thus gives voice to a basic principle of historical communication and understanding: the past, in the form of the traces and legacy of the dead, depends on the living for its continued life, and the ability to *hear* the shadows of the dead is always conditional.

After having listened to Teiresias, Odysseus finally turns to the shade of his mother to let her take the sacrificial blood. When he enters the world of the dead, Odysseus does not know that his mother is already there. And as she recognizes him and begins to speak, she is upset to see that he has made the journey. He asks her in return what brought about her death, if it was an illness. She then tells him how she died of grief from never seeing him, of "my loneliness for you Odysseus, for your kind heart and counsel" (XI.196). When he desperately stretches out to hug her, she disappears into thin air, explaining to him that her body has disintegrated, for "dreamlike the soul flies, insubstantial" (XI.225).[13] Compared to the sad conversation with Elpenor, this encounter with the shadow of his mother is devastating, since there is nothing Odysseus can do in return. For Elpenor, who was the cause of his own death, Odysseus could provide for his memory and serve him in the afterlife. In relation to his mother, however, he is powerless, forced to recognize and come to terms with the fact that he himself is partly the cause of the loss of what he loves.

After Odysseus's encounter with Anticlea, a myriad of shadows emerge from the dark, first the women, the daughters, lovers, and wives of famous men, gods, and demigods, all eager to drink the blood and tell their stories. Odysseus wards them off with his sword, disciplining the dead to let them speak and bear witness one at a time. They all declare who they are, where they are from, what they have done, and how they have died. In the context of the narrative it is the dead who bear witness of themselves, but it is Odysseus who carries their voices and stories back to the living, here to the court of Alcinous, to whom the narrative is directed. Among the many stories that he recounts throughout the long night at the banquet, his visit to Hades is the one that impresses his hosts most. This is shown by the fact that after he has described his encounter with the dead women, Odysseus breaks off for the first time, saying that now it is time for sleep. The whole room is silent, as if "enchanted" or under a "spell" (*kelethmos*; XI.334). Then Queen Arete and King Alcinous begin to speak, praising him for who he is and for his ability to speak honestly and not in "lies" of "old times and places that no one knows" (literally, that no one "has seen," *ouden idoito*; XI.366). Alcinous then insists that he go on, to "recall the past deeds and strange adventures," saying there is "no time yet for sleep." In particular, he wants to hear if Odysseus met in Hades any of his peers and companions who died at the walls of Troy.

Odysseus replies that there is a time for storytelling and a time for sleep (for *mythos* and for *hypnos*), yet he agrees to go on, and he speaks through the night of his continued encounters with the heroes from the Trojan War that now all dwell in the land of the dead. As the presumed writer of the story, Homer controls this imaginary tale from start to end. At the same time, the literary narrative prepares the way for the historian to come, because it is not the bard and his songs that Alcinous wants to listen to when he wants to hear more about the heroes from Troy. Instead, it is the voices of the heroes themselves as they have spoken to the one who has traveled across the threshold into the land of the dead, bringing back not lies and fabrications but reports of how it was and what he has truly *seen*. Within the space of the mythical narrative, the text itself repeatedly insists on the necessity of speaking the *truth* and of bearing witness. As Odysseus recalls his encounters with the long line of shadows of the dead, he begins every new passage with the words: "and I saw . . . ," "and then I saw . . . ," and so on. The Greek text shifts between the words *idon*, *eisidon*, *esidon*, and *eidon*, all different grammatical forms and composites of *eido*, "to see." Thus, Odysseus emerges as an original and exemplary *histor*, as one who has *seen* and who has come back to tell what he saw and what the dead said to him, as a seeing witness for those who are no longer there.

As mentioned previously, it is common in Homeric scholarship to see the figure of the bard and singer Demodocus as a literary inscription by the poet of himself into the epic poem.[14] This comparison can be taken one step further if we note that Alcinous literally compliments Odysseus for speaking "as a poet would, a man who knows the world" (*aoidos epistamenos*; XI.364). But whereas the court poet has not experienced that of which he speaks, it is Odysseus who comes out as an image of the superior witness. In this way, too, the hero anticipates the art of *history* as a more profound and compelling mode of narrative. In Homeric times and in the language of Homer the distinction between "myth" and "true speech," or between *mythos* and *logos*, as we know it from Plato, is not yet established. Instead this distinction is enacted within the mythical narrative itself as two levels of storytelling, where Odysseus represents myth as truth, or simply a reliable and lived *mythos*. Among the few preserved fragments from Hecataeus, who is commonly recognized as the original founder of *historia* as a new form of written discourse (presumably) four generations after Homer and two generations before Herodotus, we read: "I write that which appears to me to be true" (*grapho . . . moi dokei alethea einai*).[15]

In the narrative that follows, Odysseus continues to recall his encounters with Agamemnon, Achilles, and Ajax and the different fates of the heroes from the war, who are now all dead. When placed alongside each other, the short depictions of their posthumous existence present a remarkable catalog of different modes of *living after* as also a *living with*. For Agamemnon there is only bitterness and no comfort since he has died in the most disgraceful way possible, murdered by his wife and her lover, his own brother. He asks eagerly for news of his son Orestes, but Odysseus has none to give. On meeting Achilles in Hades, Odysseus tries to comfort him, reminding him of his status as immortal in his lifetime and of his royal status in the land of the dead. But the hero brushes aside all "smooth talk of death," responding with his famous words that he would rather "serve as a simple farm hand" than as "lord of the exhausted dead" (XI.490). Immediately after this grim testimony he asks Odysseus about his son, and if he has "come after me to make a name in battle." To him Odysseus can reply with a detailed account of how his son Peleus has indeed earned himself honor and respect in battle and in council, a report that permits the hero to wander away calmly, "glorying in what I told him of his son." Ajax and Odysseus were rivals for the title of the best of the Achaeans after the death of Achilles. In the competition for his battle gear Odysseus was declared the winner by Achilles's mother, Thetis, a defeat so humiliating to Ajax that he killed himself. Odysseus now says that he regrets his victory, and blaming the suicide on Zeus, he describes how they all mourned Ajax, pleading with him to "conquer his indignation and pride" (XI.561). But Ajax just turns away and joins the other ghosts in silence. Who knows, Odysseus says, "if in that darkness he might still have spoken, and I answered." Odysseus is indirectly the source of his death simply by having lived and triumphed, but he is without moral guilt, so there is no reparation to be made, only a lingering silence as a last refusal to communicate.

In the last sections of the *Nekya*, an important shift takes place. As Odysseus enters the domain of Hades, he is first terrified, but he learns to control the shadows of the dead, tempering their desire to come forth. The conversations follow one after the other, and when a soul has spoken, it recedes into the darkness. But after this (philologically disputed) encounter with Heracles in lines 601–626, something else happens. The ghosts from the past take on a different shape. They no longer accept being controlled by the sword of the hero, but they begin to crowd "in thousands, rustling in a pandemonium of whispers," and Odysseus is overcome again by fear (*deos*) that Persephone is about to thrust toward him some "saurian death's head" (or "Gorgon's head," *Gorgeien kephalen*), and he quickly withdraws to the ship with his crew.

As discussed earlier, the relation to the dead among the Greeks is mostly one of compassion and pity. In the land of shadows even the great Achilles appears as a depressed and pitiable weakling. Yet in this concluding scene the atmosphere changes. Odysseus realizes that he is not safe among the dead and that they may engulf and draw him into their world. The sight and the sound of the dead become overwhelming. The imagery suggests that through proper sacrificial rites the living can come into contact with the underworld and hear the testimonies and stories of the dead. But if one stays too long and if one listens too closely, it is not only the living who look at the dead but also the dead who look at the living, threatening to transform them into an object of their fateful gaze.

A Note on the Sirens' Voice as the Lethal Lure of History

The scene with the terrifying appearance of the dead toward the end of the *Nekya* and the general experience of listening to the voices of the dead have a parallel and sequel in the story of the Sirens that follows immediately. Directly after having returned safely to Circe from his visit to the underworld, Odysseus is advised on how to proceed. It is Circe who then tells him of the Sirens, whose singing "enchants" (*thelgousin*) sailors and lures them to their death, and it is she who describes how he could listen to them if he lets himself be tied to the mast and his companions plug their ears. Leaving aside any attempt to address the myriad interpretations to which this emblematic adventure has given rise, I want to point out how the voices of the Sirens can also be read as depicting *history* as a voice of death and mortal danger. When interpreted in this way, the adventure with the Sirens complements the journey to the underworld as also a story of the inherent danger in seeking *too much truth of the past* as a desire to be *too close to the dead*.

The Sirens do not kill by violence or force, nor is there any mention of concrete physical contact between them and the sailors whom they lead to destruction. They are not just beautiful and deceitful women who seduce sailors to their death. Instead, it is as if they were already singing from the other side, seducing their listeners to blissful renunciation by means of promising true accounts of the past.[16] What they hold out is the promise of a complete knowledge of the past and an insight into the future. The stories that they sing are explicitly reports from the dead. As Odysseus listens to their song while tied to the mast, he hears them saying that what they offer is not just sweet words but also *knowledge* or *insight* (*eidos*; XII.188). "We know," they sing, *idmen*, all that did take place as well as all that will take place (*genetai*). And in particular, they hold out the promise of telling all that happened to the warriors at Troy, precisely the stories with which Odysseus himself has just mesmerized his audience in the halls of Alcinous. When read alongside the description of Odysseus's final moments in Hades, the scene with the Sirens can therefore be read as deepening the image of how history can be both a supreme temptation and a lethal risk for mortals. In the image of Odysseus holding out his sword to separate, organize, and discipline the dead and then forcibly restraining himself while listening to the sweet voices of the past, Homer has given an extraordinarily dense description of the historical imagination and its pathos from a time when neither the art of historical writing nor the term "history" is yet in place. The desire to know all that took place, and thus to reestablish in its fullness and truth a genuine connection to the dead, is an overwhelming temptation, but it can also be a route to destruction and death for mortals. Odysseus is a hero of history, whose heroism in these two conjoined adventures is explicitly enacted in the domain of seeing across time in an interaction with the voices and spirits of the dead.

For such a reading, it is important to see that the journey to Hades is not just a journey across an imaginary *space* but also across *time*. Even though Hades is pictured as a distant and hidden *space* at the end of the world, the narrative indicates that it is also a matter of covering a distance in *time*. It is a temporality of *it was* that is enacted in these scenes and that also contributes to their enchanting force. Whereas in the voices of the Sirens this is explicitly the case, it is not always obvious in the Hades episode. But it surfaces there too, as when Odysseus describes how he first stood there waiting for more great souls of the dead "who had perished in times past" (*to prosthen*; XI.629), indicating that the journey is not just a geographical journey to the end of the world but also across time, *into the past.* The narrative construes history as the imaginary temporal space of a *land* of the dead, across a distance that can be traveled and accessed by the hero and poet by means of properly enacted rituals. Once there, the traveler stands again before what was lost but what lives on in a dreamlike and volatile form. It depicts this encounter as both alluring and dangerous. It is this double aspect of the past as both sweet temptation and lethal threat that gives the Homeric narrative its exemplary weight as a poetic anticipation of the historical imagination.

The Dead and the Modern Historical Imagination (Certeau)

Toward the end of his life the great French liberal and anticlerical historian Jules Michelet was working on a new preface to his recently completed magnum opus, *History of France* (1867). In his literary remains there was a text from this project that was found and published much later in 1973 under the title "Heroism of the Spirit."[17] In this text Michelet speaks of his own method as "resurrectionism." He presents himself as a kind of historical child of nature, having been genuinely influenced only by Virgil and Giambattista Vico. Affirming the legacy of the revolution, he condemns the conservatism of the Catholic educational system and its roots in medieval culture. In his own attempt to write anew the history of medieval times, he had sought to resuscitate something of this era that was also forgotten and repressed by its purported inheritors. Describing his approach, he writes that "I would not fight someone who was already dead; first I would make him live again, to see him stand, restored, and warmed by my own life, in order to know what was really the reason for his existence and also the necessary and legitimate reason for his demise." He then likens his work to a "journey to the graves and sepulchers of the dead," a capacity in which he learned to move freely: "I could enter and leave; I did not have to fear becoming trapped in the sepulcher."[18]

Michelet's posthumous note on the ethos and practice of the historian was taken up and quoted at length by Michel de Certeau at the outset of his collection of essays *The Writing of History,* first published in French in 1975. For Certeau this remarkable testimony from one of the great modern secular historians opens the door to a more general characterization and understanding of history as a mode of writing constituted and operating precisely on the threshold of the living and the dead. He writes that "the other is the phantasm of historiography, the object that it seeks, honors and buries."[19] Certeau notes that Michelet posits himself at this border where literature had already erected its fictions of journeys to the land of the dead. But in doing so, and in fantasizing about the possibility of bringing them back, of restoring them to life, and of hearing their voices, he is in fact enacting what for Certeau is the real and fundamental "historical operation," which is not communication with the dead but the effort to "calm the dead who still haunt the present, and to offer them scriptural tombs."[20] What historiography accomplishes, he says, is not the *unification* of the living and the dead but the *separation* between them through writing:

On its own account, historiography takes for granted the fact that it has become impossible to believe in the presence of the dead that has organized (or organizes) the experience of entire civilizations; and the fact too that it is nonetheless impossible "to get over it," to accept a loss of living solidarity with what is gone.[21]

From this viewpoint, the writing of history becomes at once a labor "of death," in affirming that the past is really and irretrievably gone, and a labor "against death" that seeks to restore it to the best of its ability.

At the core of this fundamentally ambiguous relation to the past Certeau situates the art and act of *writing*. To *write* the past is to start anew from an empty space and to take what is given, inherited, and preserved to construe a *representation* of what was. Or as he writes, "of being situated, finally, on this frontier of the present where, simultaneously, a past must be made from a tradition (by exclusion) and where nothing must be lost in the process (exploitation by means of new methods)."[22] The space of historical discourse and writing is always constituted within a present that sets up the conditions for something such as historical writing and historical narrative. It is along these lines that he can also say, in a famous formulation, that "the past is the fiction of the present." In the main essay of the book, "The Historiographical Operation," this operation is described as a "social practice" that creates a space for its readers to inhabit, but as a space that both manifests and hides its constitutive lack; creating narratives of the past that are "the equivalent of cemeteries within cities; it exorcises and confesses a presence of death amidst the living."[23] In another expression he literally speaks of how the historical operation relies on a "ghost" that "insinuates itself into historiography and determines its organization."[24]

Historical discourse will often be organized as knowledge of the *other*, where the different referential practices and methods all serve to produce a "sense of reliability." A "proper name" is presented as a given container to be filled with declarative statements based on historical sources, exemplified by Certeau with the name "Robespierre." However, unlike fictional characters who need to be invented as the narrative progresses, the historical proper names are taken to contain already from the start their own inner stability and fullness that enable them to serve as organizing principles of the historical discourse in a similar way as historical "events." They function as a "hypothetical support for an ordering along a chronological axis" while also hiding their own performative aspect in order to produce the effect of representing *the real*, or simply an *it was*.[25] Historical writing restores, creates, and represents the dead along a chronological axis, and in doing so it is also said to function as a "burial rite" in the sociological sense of "exorcising death by inserting it into discourse." By creating these cemeteries of historical texts, it manages to "establish a place for the living" as a space where the dead are contained in writing to give room for the living.[26] Or as he writes in another of the many striking passages from this essay, "writing speaks of the past only to inter it."[27]

Certeau is writing in the wake of what he refers to as an "epistemological awakening," marked by the names Foucault, Paul Veyne, and Jacques Lacan. The main goal of his analysis is to explore and encircle the writing of history—*historiography*—as a specific linguistic and rhetorical *operation*. Just as in Hayden White's *Metahistory*, published around the same time, Certeau does not explicitly address the issue of *truth* or epistemic validity in historical discourse. Instead he focuses on the *conditions* and *means of the production* of the historical text and the historical discourse as such. In order to isolate and study this domain of historical writing on its own terms, he needs to dislocate it from its primary object, to discharge its affective imaginary core by performing a kind of historical-phenomenological *epoché* (to speak with Husserl). This is at least one way to understand his insistence on reminding the historians of their ambiguous relation to the dead, whom the historical operation is said to both desire and reject. The historian will always start from something that is *lost* and, for this reason, needs or deserves to be re-created and "resurrected." Even though historical discourse often claims to have "resuscitated" its object, Certeau declares that in fact history does not resuscitate anything. Instead, it enacts its discourse in this double and schizophrenic mode, holding out a promise that recoils again back on itself as a partly fictional narrative.[28] History pretends to capture and give life to what is past and gone by enacting a kind of "reality effect," but in the end, it has "become our myth."[29] With the help of numerous formulations like these, Certeau locates the hidden or at least partly concealed passion of historical discourse, while at the same time short-circuiting its rhetorical expression, all in order to situate the historical discourse as narrative and textual operation among the living.

For Certeau, the dead are the lost other around which the historical discourse enacts its operations in the living present. But for him any historical narrative that claims to recall and resuscitate the dead is misguided, since what it really does is create a social space where the dead can be contained. This is what he means by comparing historical discourse to rites of burial and the finished narratives to "cemeteries." Through their focus on the connection between burial, caring for the dead, and the ethos of the historical disciplines, his analyses obviously anticipate many of the themes discussed in the previous chapters. But in the last instance his understanding of the larger phenomenon is impeded by its structuralist formalism, in a way that we should now be prepared to move beyond. His strict separation between an outside (the dead) and an inside (the living) will then have to be renegotiated through what we have explored as the "spectral" or "hauntological" approach on the basis of the existential-historical predicament of a *being with* the dead. Certeau's remarks on burial and cemeteries can here serve as a starting point for a deeper discussion and analysis, because in his use of the metaphors of "burial," "exorcism," and "cemetery," he betrays a theoretical-anthropological bias that also orients his more theoretical argument. Likewise, his strict separation between supposedly earlier (or contemporary) nonhistorical cultures of death and memory and a modern European Enlightenment-style historicism exemplifies a typical dichotomous theoretical-anthropological framework that

ultimately prevents him from seeing and assessing their interconnectedness and thus of visualizing a transcultural phenomenological stratum
and predicament.

For Certeau burial is primarily a social means of *getting rid* of the
dead and of death itself. This is at least what is implied by his use of this
metaphor when he declares, as in the previous quotation, that historical
writing functions as a burial rite in the sociological sense of "exorcising
death" by inserting it into discourse. Yet the metaphorical expression
"exorcising" death is ultimately misleading since it gives to death the status of foreign intruder into a living body that could somehow be assimi-
lated and pacified by ritual means. But if we look at burial practices not
primarily as a way of driving death out of the social body but as ways of
caring for the dead after death, the meaning of the imagery also changes.
Burial is a practice that comes after death, in the wake of and in response
to death as different ways of keeping and holding on to the dead as members of a community, but now as *having-been*. It does not take death away
from the body.

The act of exorcism is supposedly concerned with handling evil
spirits that overtake and threaten the living. In some cultural contexts,
the dead themselves are seen as potentially harmful to the living. And
often a proper burial was seen as a remedy to make sure that the spirits
of the dead would not return, haunt, and harm the living. In this sense
the historiographical operation can be likened metaphorically to an act of
"calming" the dead and thus of making sure that they do not return, that
they remain "in their graves." Historicizing can certainly have the purpose
and effect of containing social unrest by situating and confining violent
and disputed events in the chronological-narrative space of *the past*.[30] But
it does not necessarily imply chasing away or dispelling the dead. It can
just as well also be seen as another way of *being with the dead*, of bringing
them along by providing them with a narrative space that preserves them
in memory.

In Certeau's argument it is decisive that the relation to the dead
has initially been definitively broken and that an irredeemable absence
continues to be operative at the heart of the historiographical enterprise.
Yet his use of the imagery of the cemetery as a metaphor for historical
writing ultimately also becomes misleading, betraying an inner tension

in his argument. In order for the metaphor to fulfill its purpose, the cemetery must be seen as a place where the dead are primarily *hidden* or stored away. But as we know from the long archaeological-anthropological record, human dwellings and entire cultures were often built around and in the vicinity of graveyards and burial grounds. The remains of the dead were not hidden away but instead kept and preserved, sometimes through intricate techniques of maintaining bodily remains. And to this anthropological fact, current modern cultures are no principal exception. The very idea of a home, of a domicile, and of a *sacred* ground, also in its original etymological meaning of a *secured* ground, is very much connected to where the remains of the dead are kept, as also where their *memory* is preserved. Once we accept the extent to which the grave and the burial ground constitute spaces of such personal and social memory, the comparison between historical accounts and cemeteries obtain a more multilayered significance than in Certeau's restricted metaphorical sense of a rejection/abjection of the dead other.

If indeed the historical account is a kind of burial practice and burial ground, then it too constitutes an extension of older practices of *keeping* the dead as also ways for a community and culture to hold themselves together and "ground" themselves. Here the absolute caesura between pre- or nonhistorical cultures and historical cultures in regard to ways of living with the dead becomes less clear and definitive than in the dichotomous structuralist schema of Certeau. In the end, it even becomes counterproductive for the purpose of visualizing the desire, position, and social logic of historical writing and historical culture at large. The act of burial is not just about laying to rest and storing away but rather the center and starting point for a complex set of practices, rituals, and traditions that continue to *care* for and to *be* with the dead, among which *writing* itself from an early stage constitutes an integral part. From this point of view, Certeau's idea of writing the past "*only* to inter it" will ultimately appear redundant. We live in a culture that continues to care for and bury its dead, through numerous and related practices that ultimately also involve historical writing. We are still in the midst of this practice, the full existential and theoretical implications of which we are unlikely to ever fully fathom.

Holding On to the Dead: History and Memory

Certeau is not critical of historical writing as such, nor does he despair about its possibilities and relevance. Even though the historians are said to write "only by combining within their practice the 'other' that moves and misleads them and the real that they can represent only through fiction," his own explicit purpose is to "pay homage" to this writing of history.[31] He awakens the Michelet-type historian from his necromantic reveries, reminding him that his hopes of resuscitating the dead have already been collapsed by the condition of the historical operation itself. Yet in doing so, he also repeats, if yet in more explicit terms, a cut that the historical discourse has already instituted from its very inception. While distancing itself from manifest superstitious and necromantic practices, it has also inherited its affective core as well as its mythical-metaphorical imagery from this domain. In the end, however, the attempt to enact a clear break with the fantasy of retrieving the past, while yet upholding the belief in the historian's craft as a way of reaching the truth of the *other*, leads Certeau into a narrow strait, where the conclusion of his critique seems to be that the historical discourse is either trapped in a presentist constructivism or lost in untenable dreams of heroic journeys to the underworld. By critically exploring his metaphorical means of framing this dichotomous choice, we have seen how the discussion could be brought to another level.

In his views of death and writing, Certeau is guided by the contemporary anthropological literature that sees the *repression* of death as a mark of modernity. But if we consider to what extent historical writing itself is not just the repression of its own original operation but on another level the *affirmation* of itself as a work of memory, and thus also a way of caring for the dead, then we can follow Certeau's basic intuition yet end up with a different conclusion. Then historiography will not be just a burying of the past in the blunt sense of sealing it off in a repression of death but also the operation that inherits and develops an ethos of caring for, keeping, and reenacting the life of the dead. In this way, there is still an inverted way in which the metaphor of burial can be applied to the art of historiography.

For Certeau the question of what the dead really are to the living is never addressed; from the outset, the absent dead are situated outside the space of the historiographical operation, as its topic, foundation, and object of repression. But since the nature of that which is repressed is never discussed as such, it continues to circulate throughout this analysis in an uncertain middle space, where it designates the empty origin of the work of history, unnameable, yet constantly named. History will thus inevitably result in a denial of absence, as it produces narratives of how it *was*, speaking authoritatively of the dead who are no longer. But if history is not the rejection of this absence but rather a mode of inhabiting it, as in fact a mode of living-after as also a living-*with*, then the historian would be someone in whose work absence is not simply denied but where absence is made to surface in the form of a world saturated with the traces of the dead, and through whose operations these traces are given voice. In the struggle to come closer to *how it really was*, the historian could still be said to enact necromantic rituals, the ultimate desire of which is to call forth, through all available technical means of interpretation, the events, actions, and individuals of the past in their self-sameness, as an uncertain and hypothetical present absence. Already in some of Leopold von Ranke's more methodologically oriented notes we can find traces of this disposition, as when he writes to his brother Heinrich in an early letter from 1820 of his aspiration: "How very sweet it is to gorge ourselves with the riches of all the centuries, to see the heroes face to face, almost more impressive and vital, to live again with them all, how very sweet, and how very enticing!"[32] But to historical consciousness also belongs from its very inception the experience of the limits of such necromantic reveries, as in Johann Winckelmann's melancholic and ironic testimony at the end of his monumental *History of the Art of Antiquity* (1764), which shapes the modern discipline of art history and where he likens his own longing to grasp and understand what is lost to those "individuals who wish to converse with spirits and believe they can see something where nothing exists."[33]

In a critical analysis from 2002 of the "memorial turn" in historical discourse, Gabrielle Spiegel addressed the distinction between history and memory in terms that recall Certeau. In her view, the new emphasis on "memory" is leading more and people toward what she sees as a misguided "presentist," and thus in the end "metaphysical," historiography that refuses to recognize that the past is lost and dead and cannot be resurrected.[34] Polemicizing against this new trend, she stresses that according to both Certeau and Pierre Nora, the genuine historian is someone who—on the basis of sources—writes what was *not* written or memorialized before and who thus recognizes and operates on the basis of the fundamental caesura between the living and the dead. She writes, "History re-presents the dead; memory re-members the corpse in order to revivify it." In relation to this basic distinction, the current turn to memory in her view signals what she, with a Freudian expression, speaks of as a certain "desperation" in refusing to "let go."[35]

Spiegel's argument is a response to a historiographical situation that for the last three decades has tended toward sentimentalization, cultural appropriation, and sometimes unreflected and even chauvinistic necromantic identity politics. But in activating Certeau's dichotomy in order to stress the critical independence of the historian vis-à-vis the memory of the dead, Spiegel's remarks also confirm that the fundamental ethos of historiography has to do not with engaging or not engaging with the dead but with *how* one comports oneself toward the dead and what it means to inhabit in authentic ways this space of living *after* those who have been. In her vocabulary, "memory" designates a comportment that is unable to let go of the dead, whereas "history" in a genuine sense is what has accepted the loss. But this clean-cut affective distinction does not mean that the historian is not involved in resuscitating the dead. On the contrary, the historian is someone who is only more attentive to the real challenges of this task, in having passed through the experience of loss. This seems at least to be the conclusion to be drawn if we read her powerful 2009 address to the American Historical Association, "Task of the Historian." It ends with these words: "Our most fundamental task as historians, I would argue, is to solicit those fragmented inner narratives to emerge from the silences. In the last analysis, what is the past but a once material existence now silenced, extant only as sign and as sign drawing to itself chains of conflicting interpretations that hover over its absent presence and compete for possession of the relics, seeking to invest traces of significance upon the bodies of the dead."[36] Thus, even from a Certauean critical standpoint, the discussion will not just end with a reinstalled distinction between the dead and the living. To accept the loss of the lost is not to *cease* to relate and respond to what is lost but rather to orient oneself in a responsible way within the domain of *being-with* those *having-been*. As demonstrated by Spiegel's address, this challenge still continues not only to animate but also to *motivate* history as a supreme form in which this human existential comportment is currently lived and enacted.[37]

The historian holds the keys to the underworld in the form of the means and tools to perform the journey and to decipher the voices of the past. But in seeking to grasp, hold, and hear those who have been, the historian is also someone who experiences most profoundly the volatility and inaccessibility of this domain, as she is torn between the enthusiasm and the ironic sense of loss expressed by Ranke and Winckelmann in the passages quoted previously. Historicism and the whole culture of historical consciousness are enacted on this stage of desire and struggle and of triumph and defeat in relation to the dead. In what follows, I exemplify this situation and *situatedness* by what is and was the single most fiercely debated issue in the historical-human sciences, the "Homeric question," or the question of the historicity of Homer. Our earlier reading of the *Nekya* presented it as a paradigmatic literary anticipation of the historical desire and imagination. As we now move to the second stage of the argument, we look at how the historical debate surrounding the authorship and authenticity of the text itself also provides a concrete example of precisely the tensions pointed out in historical consciousness and imagination. Through this trajectory we perform a hermeneutic loop, as it were, where the text poetically anticipates the structure for both its readability and its unreadability. Because in their search of the historical Homer, the representatives of the historical sciences often found themselves situated—poetically, rhetorically, and philosophically—at the site of the original scene of Odysseus's sacrificial offerings in Hades.

Locating the Dead: History and the Homeric Question

In his commentary on Michelet's essay and its hopes of visiting and resurrecting the dead Certeau writes of how the latter "stakes himself at this border, where from Virgil to Dante, fictions were erected that were not yet history."[38] In his brief list of literary sources he does not include Homer, which is notable, especially in view of the fact that Book XI of the *Odyssey* is the immediate literary background to Virgil (and through

Virgil to Dante).[39] Virgil's description of Aeneas's visit to the land of the dead in Book VI of the *Aeneid* is essentially a pale replica of the *Nekya*, as when the rower Palinurus also pleads Aeneas to provide him with a proper burial and when Aeneas tries in vain to hug the shadow of his father.[40]

The Homeric epic occupies a unique role in the literary-spiritual inheritance of the West, only comparable to that of the Torah in the Jewish-Christian tradition in terms of cultural impact and age of composition. The fate and legacy of the *Iliad* and the *Odyssey* surpass anything known from the ancient world in terms of literary, ethical, and religious influence.[41] The *Odyssey* served as a principal canonical text and reference point for the Greek and Hellenic culture around the Mediterranean into the Christian era, where its culturally guiding function gradually receded within the historical space of a "heathen" world where it was superseded by Virgil as the canonical epic. Seen from this perspective, it is remarkable that the return of Homer at the outset of European modernity literally depicts him as a hero emerging in and from the land of the dead, because this is how Dante finds him in Book IV of the *Divina Commedia*, trapped in the Limbo of Inferno. Here Homer dwells with other great men of the past whose only fault is to have been born before Christ and therefore not to have been baptized. For this reason, they are forever doomed to "live without hope and in longing." Dante knew Homer's work only indirectly since he did not read Greek and there was no available Latin translation at the time. Yet he hails him as the "greatest of the poets," presiding over Horace, Ovid, and Lucan, like a lord with "sword in hand." Together with Virgil they are said to form a group of five savants, to which Dante unblushingly lets himself be invited by Homer himself as the sixth member. In an enigmatic line, he adds that following this unification they conversed of things "of which one should rather keep quiet" (*che 'l tacere è bello*; IV:104).

Dante's necromantic literary encounter with Homer at the outset of European Renaissance culture opens the door to the renewed reception of his work. It is followed by the first complete modern Latin translation half a century later in 1362 by Leontius Pilatus, the first European professor of Greek connected to the University of Florence, at the explicit request of Boccaccio.[42] This translation marks the beginning of the gradual reemergence of Homer as the foremost classical poet in the modern European context. Up until the early eighteenth century, the growing body of modern Homeric scholarship consists mainly of commentaries on the text in the ancient style. They are not historical investigations on its origin and context, and they never voice any doubts concerning the historical reality of a poet with this name. It is only with the Enlightenment historical culture of learning and the development of modern textual-philological criticism that Homer becomes a *historical* problem and quest in his own right and that the paradigmatic historical-philological litmus test is invented: *the Homeric question.*[43]

The enormous efforts spent on establishing and securing the temporal and cultural context of the Homeric epics and their presumed author were not only a fruit of the historical-academic culture but also a major incentive for the establishment and development of this culture in the first place. The pursuit to determine the true historical nature of this enchanting and evasive character gathered all of its different techniques, in Ernst Vogt's words, "to bring Homer back again in his historicalness" (*den Homer in die Geschichtlichkeit zurückzuholen*).[44] Among all the projects that resulted from historicism and the historical turn in the human sciences in general, in particular from the effort to map the inner genealogy of the ancient cultural world, the Homeric question stands out as an exemplary case. This was not incidental. With the gradual rise and reemergence of Homer as the first great ancestor-poet of Western culture from Dante and the Italian Renaissance onward, this specific historical figure became the focal point of the wish to grasp and understand the very emergence of this cultural complex itself over and against its oriental background. Two centuries before Thales and Herodotus, Homer was perceived as marking the great cultural leap from a dark mythical world into the light of pre-Hellenic culture.[45] The desire to fix the historical nature, origin, position, and possibility of this particular poetic voice became an obsession for the historical disciplines devoted to the study of the ancient world, most important, cultural history, philology, and archaeology. Heinrich Schliemann and after him Arthur Evans more or less invented classical Greek archaeology in their lifelong devotion to securing the historical facticity of Troy, the war, and its heroes as the historical context and background of the Homeric narrative.

If we try to survey the research on Homer from this more panoramic perspective, we also discern certain general traits of historicism and its inner tensions. It is characterized by a heroic attempt not simply to stop at the gates of the past in devotion and piety but to really try to *reach* for Homer as a historical-literary figure. For the historians the new techniques of the historical sciences held out the possibility of accessing the *true* nature of the Homeric epic and Homer himself. It was thus their privilege to accomplish the journey back to that hidden source, to retrieve and restore it in its genuine historicity, and to fathom its historical reality. But it was also through them and their efforts that the experience gradually deepened concerning how distant and evanescent this past really is.

Throughout classical times Homer was seen in the same way as he was still seen by Dante and even by Goethe, as an indisputably real and distinct person and poet who had existed but in a somewhat uncertain chronological past (with the dating extending from the ninth to the late seventh century). He was recognized as the author of a great number of narrative poems that continued to be recited by professional rhapsodists, especially people from Chios, who called themselves Homeridae and claimed to be his descendants.[46] But from the outset of the modern era the classicist preoccupation with Homer was both triggered and torn from inside between its poetic and its historical motivation, where the growing poetic admiration for his writing—exemplified not least by Goethe—and the parallel philological textual criticism partly worked in different directions. In the introductory survey to a collection of articles that summarize two centuries of research on Homer, Joachim Latacz, a leading German expert on Homer, writes from the perspective of the historian that the immense respect for the work of the poet even "prevented" the more historically oriented research that sought to determine the emergence, originality, and effect of his work.[47]

The first generations of classicist commentators, mostly British and German, were first of all preoccupied with establishing and securing Homer's role as a poet superior to (the Latin) Virgil. However, over the course of the second half of the eighteenth century, and with the rise of Romantic historicism from Heinrich Heine to Wilhelm von Humboldt, the image gradually emerges of Homer as instead an archaic popular bard who did not himself write and who rested on the shoulders of earlier popular traditions.[48] For the Romantics, Homer became the paradigmatic original, popular genius, comparable to the author of the *Songs of*

Ossian and the *Nibelungen*, a poet who sang from the depths of an original *völkische* culture, unlike an academic, urban poet like Virgil. Here the textual criticism and Romantic fascination with the idea of folk poetry arising from within a culture as its unique expression led to a radical transformation of the historical image of Homer in a way that culminated in Friedrich August Wolf's seminal dissertation in 1795, *Prolegomena to Homer*. This essay basically summarized the results and conclusions of an already ongoing discussion, but it became the emblematic starting point for the Homeric question.[49]

Wolf used all the available tools of historicist thinking to pose the question, What could possibly be the "original" Homeric (oral) text, in view of the realization that it rested on the shoulders of oral predecessors and that it had been filtered through layer after layer of later scribes and commentators? Already Wolf questioned that the *Iliad* and the *Odyssey* had the same author. For more than a century this debate was carried out primarily in terms of philological expertise, where it was believed that textual analysis alone could secure the access to a supposedly *original* text, whether written or oral. It was only with the work of Milman Parry on oral poetry, based on documentation from Serbia in the 1930s, that the debate shifted focus, from the strictly philological to the more sociological study of the preservation and reinvention of oral traditions. Through Parry's analyses of contemporary examples of the preservation and transmission of oral literature, the very idea of securing a definitive situation and person in time where and by whom the Homeric epics were created seemed even less likely to ever bear fruit. In the words of Frank Turner, "At the end of the day the epic existed, but at the beginning of the day there may have been no Homer. Authorship of the Homeric epics has passed from the one to the many."[50]

Uvo Hölscher captures the paradoxical experience of the historical ethos in the 1989 introduction to his book-length study of the *Odyssey*, when he writes of the extent to which the "sheer humanity" of the epic captured the imagination of the German and English classicists in particular, first seemingly "without the mediation of history." While for us, he continues, it "has obtained the element of the historical, it also becomes more distant while also becoming more real."[51] The quotation illustrates a recurring concern in the historical-philological literature, that the specifically *historical* interest and approach itself, while seeking to accomplish to the utmost limits of its capacity the true restoration of and access to its object, also contributes to somehow weakening its original connection to the text, hastening the demise of its original appeal through the critical study of sources and their transmission: in short, that history in a certain sense kills the past that it loves. From the ancient testimony and the preserved written text, the name *Homer* had come down to modernity as the writer of the two great epic poems, and until the age of historicism no one had doubted that it designated a distinct historical individual. But when the philological critique applied its historiographical techniques in the task of filling in the missing information, the very referent of the name began to fade and gradually dissolve into a haze of tradition and transmission.

Supposing Homer was a historical person, under what kind of circumstances was the epic composed? Was it indeed a type of *völkische* culture, as believed by the German Romantics, perhaps comparable to works by the Serbian bards documented by Parry? Or was Homer a court poet-historian, belonging to an aristocratic elite culture, more in the style of Demodocus as the latter is depicted in the epic itself in the scene recalled previously? Were the legends and their poetic form something that this increasingly evanescent Homer had invented as an original Greek genius, or was it the result of a long legacy of similar and much older epics from a neighboring oriental world, as the discovery of the *Gilgamesh* epic indicated? And were the gods depicted in the poem a condensation of long-established religious beliefs, or should Homer be seen as partly an inventor of this particular pantheon and its cults?

In short, was Homer a *link* in a longer tradition, or was he himself a *reformer*, a modernizer and inventor of a new poetic-religious sensibility? And were the tales of which the epic sang mythical events, or did they constitute the remains of a genuine legacy of historical reports transformed into legend, as presupposed and later argued by the archaeological efforts to secure the historical basis of the narratives through the discovery of a lost Troy? During the more than two centuries of intense analysis, interpretation, and archaeological, philological, and paleographical research, all these different hypotheses were formulated, defended, defeated, and again restored in new forms, only to be torn apart again.

The specific question of the enigmatic figure of Homer himself also motivated the more general quest for the Greek-oriental context of the epic that was preserved and transmitted under his name. The beginning of the nineteenth century witnessed remarkable results in the gradual historical reconstruction and recollection of the lost ancient oriental and Mediterranean cultures. From this moment onward, and within only a generation of scholars, old and long-forgotten languages and scripts became legible again, among them ancient Persian, Egyptian, Mesopotamian, Assyrian, and Babylonian. Over the course of only half a century, new doors to a long-lost past that had been sealed for over two millennia were opened through the hard work of philologians and archaeologists. With the excavations of Knossos and the Mycenean culture and with the rediscovery of the legends of Heracles, yet another layer of cultural background became available, continually expanding the historical context of the Homeric epic. And in 1872 the Sumerian *Gilgamesh* epic was discovered, providing an even older background to the Greek heroic narratives, including an earlier version of travel to the land of the dead undertaken by its hero, Enkidu. The Babylonian culture thus emerged as an older framework, and with the discovery and deciphering of the Hittite and Ugarit languages, yet another comparative framework of the Greek myths and rites was made available. Finally, the deciphering of the Mycenaean Linear B in 1952 added a layer to the linguistic history of the Greek Homeric language.

Throughout these remarkable discoveries, the role and position of Homer in the ancient context—the cultural, literary, and linguistic sources of his art—were constantly debated and renegotiated. In his elegant summary of this turbulent hermeneutic enterprise, which was also often motivated and driven by national agendas, Latacz describes the situation as having reached at least some kind of elementary consensus by the time of the early post–World War II era. From that point onward there was general agreement that the Homeric epic should be seen as historically situated within an oriental tradition of originally oral, but also written, literary culture.[52] Yet even this balanced judgment only scratches the surface of still raging debates, such as the deepened interest in later decades concerning the connections between epic, writing, and ritual, especially in relation to the hero cult and ancestor worship.[53]

At the heart of it all, however, we are still confronted with the fundamental historical riddle concerning the proper name of "Homer" and its possible historical referent. Since we know "Homer" only as the name of a presumed writer of a text, the meaning and significance of the text cannot be sought in anything else that is known about its author. Every attempt to secure such information simply returns us to the text and its own questions: oral or written? Greek or oriental? reformed or traditional? The historicity of the writer and what is written thus continues to change with more contextual hypotheses and conjectures added, pitching the "Unitarians" against the "Analysts," that is, the believers in a real and historical Homer as the writer of the two epics against those who see "Homer" only as an inherited label for a gradually evolved and repeatedly grafted narrative tradition.

Homer among the Shadows:
On the Historicity of the Nekya

Perhaps it is not incidental that this hermeneutical vertigo has been particularly intense in relation to the *Nekya*. In an essay from 1988 devoted entirely to the discussion of Book XI and its historical interpretations, Kjeld Matthiessen summarized its extraordinary literary legacy from Plato onward and how it had pitted the Unitarians against the Analysts.[54] For many Unitarians, and notable among them Wilamowitz, it constituted the high point of the entire narrative, whereas for many Analysts it was a clear case of later compilations with little connection to the supposedly "original" text. Through Matthiessen's analysis it surfaces as perhaps the single most dissected part of the entire narrative, questioned at its core, and again restored in its unicity, as if the very life and historicity of its author were more at stake in this particular section than in any other.[55]

At this point there is a strange resonance, where the question of the passage to the underworld and the figure of Homer himself begin to merge. Before the description of this underworld journey, as itself a case of disputable origins, the commentators halt, not knowing if they can truly enter this space as something real, or if indeed the whole scenario is in fact a historically shaped illusion, an illusion of an originality that is already lost and that has been covered over by the very narrative that they are trying to read. In a summary essay on the current state of research on the person Homer, "Homer—a Great Shadow?," Ernst Vogt seeks to capture the vicissitudes of this long debate and its different positions, following the battle between Unitarians and Analysts in regard to the Homeric text.[56] Standing before this frustrating lack of historical certainty concerning an issue that has consumed the efforts of generations of scholars, Vogt turns to a simile from an essay by Erich Bethe, written half a century earlier, where the latter compares the researchers on this field to people who are grasping for a real person only to fathom a shadow (*die nur ein zerinnenden Schatten umarmt*).[57] At this point the entire adventure of the historical quest for the person Homer is thus literally reinscribed into the narrative space of the Homeric epic itself, as a strange and fruitless journey to the land of the dead where only shadows prevail. Throughout his essay Vogt calls for an even deeper integration of all branches of historical disciplines and for an intensified collaboration between history, archaeology, and philology, in order finally to "pull Homer back in his historicity," *den Homer in die Geschichtlichkeit zurückzuholen.* Yet it is with Bethe's earlier melancholic parable that he ends his text.

The 1935 essay by Bethe from which Vogt takes the quotation is a fascinating piece of interpretive historiography in its own right, and one that leads us even deeper into the labyrinth of necromantic hermeneutics. It is one of the fiercest attacks on the school of Unitarians and the belief in a historical Homer ever formulated. Lashing out at Wilamowitz (his own former professor) for having succumbed to the illusion of the existence of an eighth-century writer by the name of "Homer" as the supposed author of both the *Iliad* and the *Odyssey*, Bethe lists all the evidence for seeing the text as instead a compilation from different periods. The very name "Homer," he argues, is not an individual name for a poet but a generic name: "Homer is a concept; he is the historical epic."[58] Bethe accepts that there may have been an actual poet or rhapsodist by this name at an early stage who probably made an impression as a "great personality," even though we can never know exactly in virtue of what he made this impression. But for historical-philological reasons alone, Bethe stresses that the actual collection of texts that were eventually associated with Homer's name could not have been the creation of this hypothetical original Homer. Furthermore, whatever this original Homer sang, it must in turn have been partly inherited from earlier singers of whom we know absolutely nothing. Bethe grants this "Homer" the status of a bard and singer who probably outsang his competitors at one point as a masterful performer of a tradition to which we no longer have any separate access. For all these reasons, Bethe considers the search for an authentic Homeric text to be utterly fruitless and vain. Every interpreter and historian will follow his own conscience, and everyone will bring, he writes, his own "ring of flowers" to the altar. The only thing we possess that has the quality of historical evidence is the written *Iliad* from the early fifth century, a text that Bethe considers to have received its present form around 600 BC. "All this talk of an original Homer," he writes, must finally "come to an end" and give way to a scientific analysis of the transmitted text of the *Iliad*.[59]

Throughout the short and agitated essay, Bethe keeps returning to a sacrificial and necromantic imagery often taken directly from the Homeric text itself. He not only speaks of his colleagues as "hugging shadows"; he also refers to them as performing sacrificial rites, where the shadow of Homer that they call forth is said to correspond to the "sacrificial animal, with whose blood he is forced to speak" and following which he appears either as an "ephemeral representative of Greek folk poetry" or as a genuine "free creative poet" or just as a "collector and editor of older poetry." Whereas his colleagues are thus portrayed as superstitious performers of ancient blood rites in their search for the man behind the literature, Bethe insists that we must look only at the text and learn only through the text of its creator and his style of work. Only on the basis of this strictly applied critical focus on the extant source must something like a "person" behind the text be possible to "grasp," a *faßbare Person*.[60] Who then is this person that Bethe himself ultimately claims to *see* and *grasp* through his own fierce processing of the evidence? Who is it that he can still hold on to after this restriction to historical sources has been meticulously applied, and after which all superstitions and blood rites for the dead have been properly exorcized from the scholarly enterprise? In the end he sees and holds a nameless man, who from the inherited material of the tradition is said to have "built a monument *aere perennius* for the holy name of Homer," a transmitter of cultural memory and a caretaker of those having-been before him. After the most puritan textual-critical historical research has had its say, "Homer" is thus no longer the name of an original writer but of someone who himself, already from the start, inhabits a world of shadows. But precisely through this hermeneutical work, this new Homer nevertheless emerges through the haze of the textual remains as the alias of a nameless but real referent of the expression "the author of our *Iliad*." Thus the name is something more than a mere illusion. It is now the name of a real historical accomplice in the literary transmittance of those who came before him.

After having ferociously expelled all the failed and misconceived attempts to see, touch, and hold the real historical Homer, Bethe ultimately thereby also confirms the historian's desire to touch the real, the really real as it can presumably be perceived only through the sources themselves and not through the deceitful transmission of their original misconstrual. Whereas his competitors are portrayed as necromantic phantasmagorics, only he has managed to truly make the journey and to bring back *that anonymous someone*, who from the outset was hiding in the shadows behind the veils of misnamed and misinterpreted sources. In the end, it was not the palimpsest of a tradition but the original source himself concealed behind the generic name "Homer," who from the very outset had misnamed himself, not to deceive but to display piety and respect toward an ancient Homer, who by then was already long gone.

In this drama of interpretive moves and countermoves around the figure and legacy of "Homer," the historicist culture also stages and makes itself readable as already shaped by a literary text that had provided an original articulation of its ethos. Who can make the hermeneutic journey to the dead? Who is able to perform the adequate rites by means of which they can emerge from the shadows to be heard again? Who can truly hold and *grasp* them and make them speak? Who, in the words of Gabrielle Spiegel, can "solicit those fragmented inner narratives to emerge from the silences"?

Through the example of Homer in general and of the *Nekya* in particular and the tale of the visit to the land of the dead, we are brought closer to a constitutive tension within the whole historicist project. While history emerges from and is maintained within a desire to escape the confines of presentist projections in order to truly know the reality of the past and those having-been, it is also led to confront the deeper experience of how contact with the voices and faces of the dead is dissolved through the layers of their transmission. For this general experience the particular case of the Homeric question is just an example among many. But through its imagery of journeys to the land of the dead and through its depiction of the poet-adventurer as the one who is able to bring back not just tales but true stories of how it really was, it has given poetic shape to the instability of the historical ethos from its inception, as both a rejection and affirmation of the desire to grasp the being of the dead other. Beyond the restricted sense of history as a "mere" burial of the dead, it thus motivates us to view the work of the historian within the larger legacy of spiritual techniques for communicating with the dead and for caring for their afterlife.

7

The Tomb of Metaphysics

Writing, Memory, and the Arts of Survival

> Drive my dead thoughts over the universe
> Like withered leaves to quicken a new birth!
> —Shelley, "Ode to the West Wind"

Introduction

On the chest of a woman buried around 400 BC in Hipponion in contemporary Calabria, in a grave excavated in the early 1970s, a small, thin golden tablet was found that had been folded several times and worn on a necklace. On it was written the following words in Greek:

This is the work of memory [*mnamosynas*], when you are about to die down to the well-built house of Hades. There is a spring at the right side, and standing by it a white cypress. Descending to it, the souls of the dead refresh themselves. Do not even go near this spring! Ahead you will find from the Lake of Memory, cold water pouring forth; there are guards before it. They will ask you, with astute wisdom, what you are seeking in the darkness of murky Hades. Say, "I am a son of Earth and starry Sky, I (masculine) am parched with thirst and am dying; but quickly grant me cold water from the Lake of Memory to drink." And they will announce you to the Chtonian King, and they will grant you to drink from the Lake of Memory. And you, too, having drunk, will go along the sacred road on which other initiates and *bacchoi* travel.[1]

The tablet is one among a total of thirty-eight known examples of similar objects found over the last two centuries on the southern Italian peninsula, on the Greek peninsula, and Peloponnesus, the so-called Bacchic gold tablets, dated between the fifth and first centuries BC. They have been the focus of heated philological-historical debates concerning the role, meaning, and importance of Orphism as a particular Greek religious-mystical cult. The movement goes back to the semimythical poet, cosmogonist, and religious leader Orpheus, who was connected to Dionysus, but also to Pythagoras and supposedly to earlier forms of Egyptian religion. He was reported from early on to have written a poem on the descent into the underworld, which has not been preserved and which is an important background to the later and most famous myth connected to his name of his descent into Hades to save his beloved Eurydice. Lines from the original poem may reverberate in the poetic lines of the golden tablets.[2]

The tablets bear witness to how *writing* at this point has obtained a function in parts of Greek culture as a vehicle and means of communication between the living and the dead, only a few centuries after the introduction of the Phoenician phonetic alphabet in the Greek world. In these golden-leaf burial incantations, the written word is not only taken to carry the voice of the living into the domain of the dead. Writing is also charged with the ability to work *for* the dead in the afterlife, as a "work of memory" (*ergon mnamosynas*) that directs them toward the Lake of Memory where they can drink to ensure them passage to the sacred road. "Memory" is here literally what guards life from its threatening total destruction, and it does so through the means of writing.

In the literature devoted specifically to the interpretation of these artifacts, Egyptian religion is often mentioned as one possible background to Orphism, even though the more specific question concerning the relation between writing and death is rarely thematized as such. But it was with the emergence of the technique of writing in a stricter sense in the semiphonetic alphabets developed around 3500 BC, first in Mesopotamia and then in Egypt, that the forms of mortuary culture also changed and were brought to new levels.[3] It is in Egypt that the tomb for the first time becomes a linguistic entity and a form of literature. Thus, it is a technology that expands and transforms the meaning of mortuary culture and its practices, while also giving shape to their latent aspirations.

As a result of Jan Assmann's pathbreaking interpretations of Egyptian mortuary culture, the depth and implications of these connections have been revealed more fully in recent times. I am referring in particular to his monumental study *Death and Salvation in Ancient Egypt* (2001), which shows how, with the emergence of writing, the very shape and practice of commemoration and cultural memory were transformed.[4] In this book he writes as a historian but also seeks to draw out the speculative implications of this Egyptian development of mortuary culture, ultimately arguing for a new way of looking at the relation between death, memory, and culture. When read alongside his main work on the nature and working of cultural memory, *Cultural Memory and Early Civilization*, first published in German in 1992, it reveals the deep inner connections between cultural memory studies and the study of ancient Egyptian mortuary culture. In the earlier book, the point is stressed that the "primal scene of memory culture" was the desire of the community "not to allow the dead to disappear" and that "death is both the origin and the center of what I mean by memory culture."[5] Here he also distinguishes between two basic temporal dimensions of these practices, the "retrospective" and "prospective." In retrospective acts the living pay tribute to their dead and to their memory in acts that seek to preserve them for posterity. In prospective acts, the living who face death act to preserve themselves across this threshold into another life or simply into another mode of existence, if only in the memories of the living and in posterity. The theory of cultural memory is the study of the technologies and "connective structures" by means of which cultures thus strive and succeed to preserve themselves in their identity over time. From this general perspective, Assmann can compare the study of ancient mortuary ritual with modern hermeneutical techniques for understanding the past. The task of keeping the memory of the dead alive unites the priest of ancient civilizations with the contemporary scholar of culture, who is here literally described as a "later day shaman."[6]

A few years later, Aleida Assmann published her main book on the same topic, *Cultural Memory and Western Civilization: Arts of Memory*, where a similar point was made at the outset that the "anthropological heart" of cultural memory is said to be constituted by the "remembrance of the dead" and that "the rites and practices of the living, and the cult that links them with the dead can be considered the earliest and most widespread form of social memory."[7] She too draws out the connection between these ancient practices and current hermeneutic attempts to maintain contact between the living and the dead, quoting Steven Greenblatt on the scholarly desire "to speak with the dead" and his view of literary scholars as deep down "salaried middle-class shamans."[8] Finally, she also distinguishes two principal modes in which this is manifested, both as the more "secular" aspiration to achieve recognition in the eyes of posterity, as *fama* or *kleos*, and as the more "religious" piety vis-à-vis the dead, echoing the more technical terminology of the "prospective" and the "retrospective" proposed by Jan Assmann. The shaping of time along these two axes and the means employed to maintain them thus form the center of the study of "cultural memory." Especially through the work of the Assmanns, it has come to serve as a general term for *that which survives* over the course of time, through rituals, materials, and technologies, and especially through the technology of writing. Cultural memory studies are explicitly based on a notion of spiritual-cultural *survival* that connects it to a longer legacy of preserving the bond between the living and the dead. Indeed, in the contemporary landscape of cultural theory, it represents the most wide-ranging attempt to understand the possibility of history, tradition, and historical consciousness precisely through the prism of how the living relate to and continue to be with the dead.

Through its emphasis on the *technical-material* side of cultural-spiritual continuity and preservation, and in particular on the role of writing, the study of cultural memory also displays an affinity with the work of Derrida and deconstruction as it was first developed two decades earlier. In the jointly written postface by Jan and Aleida Assmann to the first publication from their group in 1983, they discuss how writing was often given a secondary role in relation to living speech, whereas in fact all culture rests on this technical capacity to reproduce itself in and through symbolization.[9] For this reason, they argue that the conventional image of textual hermeneutics as a way to restore and retrieve life from supposedly dead symbols needs to be reversed. It is only when a space of tradition has been opened up by self-symbolization by means of conventionally fixed signs that hermeneutics even becomes possible and meaningful as a cultural activity. This idea of how *reactivation* of sense presupposes an initial *deposition* of signifiers and symbols is essentially Derrida's argument. In his own contribution to the volume, Jan Assmann also confirms this parallel by beginning with a quotation from the *Grammatology* that "all graphemes are of testamentary essence."[10] He then goes on to present ancient Egypt as the best example of how written literature is literally born in the grave. The grave is the first sign—the *sema*—of the departed person, the present absence of the other.[11] The grave is also the exterior stabilization of social continuity.[12] The idea from Derrida of a structural absence at the very heart of subjectivity is here described as belonging to full literacy through which the subject is deposited from its inception in this sphere of semantization. At this founding stage of cultural memory studies, a link was thus picked up from Derrida's analysis of the relation between subjectivity, writing, and death, in concretizing and contextualizing the argument through a joint history of writing and mortuary culture.

In the subsequently developed theory of cultural memory, Jan Assmann would orient himself more along the line of a Hegelian-Durkheimian conception of a collective survival of culture, meaning, and spirit, where the shared legacy with phenomenology and deconstruction is less apparent. Nor were there any significant attempts from the side of deconstructive thinking to relate philosophically and critically to the work done in cultural memory studies. These intellectual pursuits largely moved along separate but partly parallel tracks in their study of the material, and in particular the graphic, basis of spiritual preservation, memory, and survival. One purpose of this chapter is to bring out these shared theoretical premises, while also critically opposing them to one another, as different ways of conceptualizing the fundamental condition of living both after and with the dead as an essentially *semantic* condition. In different ways, they both understand the phenomenon of burial and the tomb as the making of a *sign* for a present absence that lies at the heart of both metaphysics and history.

I begin with a summary of some of Jan Assmann's observations and analyses of the Egyptian culture of caring for the dead, especially what concerns the relation between writing, burial, and memory, as a preamble to his more general argument concerning the nature of the Egyptian understanding of the role and place of the dead.

Writing for the Afterlife

In Egypt, the use of writing on papyrus in graves is documented from around 1500 BC. These are the texts of the so-called Egyptian *Book of the Dead*, which in ancient Egyptian are known as *Going Forth by Day* or *Going into the Day*.[13] These texts concern the safe and proper way of passage into a life *after* life. They combine liturgical and hymnic writings with instructions to be used by the dead themselves for a safe continued journey. But long before the appearance of texts on papyrus placed in graves, the use of writing in graves had been developed in other ways in Egypt. From around 2000 BC, during the Middle Kingdom, stone coffins have been found whose interiors are decorated with writing. From the design of this writing, it has been interpreted as directed *to* the dead as the presumed *reader* of the text, as *instructions* for use in the successful transition to another mode of being.[14] In some cases it is even the coffin itself that addresses the dead, presenting itself as the body and bosom of a female goddess about to carry and lift the dead into another existence: "I am your mother, who nurses your beauty, I am pregnant with you in the morning and I deliver you as Re in the evening."[15]

The earliest known example of writing inside graves is found in the pyramid of Pharaoh Wenis (or Unis) from around 2200 BC. It contains written formulas, accompanied by the instruction "to be recited." These formulas are often referred to in the scholarly literature as "spells," since they mostly consist of incantations that deal with how the deceased can be transformed into an "ancestral spirit," a process expressed in terms of emerging or *shining* forth and of a movement of *ascent*.[16] The content is considered to date back to even older texts, written on more ephemeral materials that have not survived. In these texts, the deceased appears both as speaker and addressee in appellative declarations such as "May the sky open to you, may the earth open to you, may the ways in the realm of the dead open to you, on which you go forth and enter with Re, striding freely like the lords of eternity."[17] In his interpretations of these writings, Assmann stresses their *ritual* background. The pyramid texts can be read as a continuation of the priestly incantations during the burial ceremony and thus *as technically mediated voices* following the deceased into the sealed burial chamber. With the art of writing, the ritual force of the human voice is then seen as forged in a graphic stable form that permits it to continue to affect the fate of the deceased. With the invention of a (largely) phonetic alphabet comes the idea of how the living voice and breath can be externalized, fixed, and preserved. The sung and spoken rituals for the dead thus become part of how the care for the dead is continued. Through this invention, the interior of the burial chamber becomes a space where *voices* continue to resonate indefinitely, as if emanating from the walls themselves in this speaking-singing tomb.

The most striking aspect of the connection Assmann points out between writing and ritual is the close connection between the act of embalming the body and writing inside the coffin. Of all the contexts in which mortuary liturgies were performed, the most important appear to have been the embalming ritual itself. One tomb inscription even speaks in the first person of how a reading should be carried out in the place of embalming, in order "that recollection of me might endure to the present day."[18]

The making of a well-preserved corpse appears here as a parallel to the act of writing, but the proximity between these two techniques is even more intimate. To seal the body in a stable form is a way of securing that it is saved for a future recollection, but thereby it is also a way of making it into a permanent *sign of and for itself.* To erect a structure that holds and secures it is also a *semantic* procedure: making an indestructible *sign* that can hold its significance over time. The practice of embalming bodies and of building stone burial mounds historically can thus be seen as anticipating the art of (phonetic) writing in its developed form, in Egypt and elsewhere. Nevertheless, the very fact that writing is here so closely linked to the burial ritual, not only as its outer decoration but as an extension of its core practice and purpose, invites us to interpret the mortuary rituals that preceded it as also directed toward such a proto-semantic form. The purpose of the mortuary techniques is connected to a preservation of life over and through times to come, a way to extend the living self across and into a future. The body is here a sign of the living self and a vehicle for its continuation. To extend the life of this body by means of techniques that permit the more stable parts of it to prevail can then also be seen as the craft of shaping a stable sign, not just as a mute materiality but precisely as a carrier and caretaker of its life. To seal it behind and within a stone structure is a continuation of the deeper purpose behind the initial effort.

With the invention of phonetic writing this aspiration reaches a new technical level and dimension. The desiccated body is no longer confined to being a sign of itself. It can also begin to carry its own voice and spirit. Alongside the earliest pyramid writings is the genre of autobiographical tombs, or "sepulchral self-thematizations," as Assmann designates them in an essay on this particular practice.[19] In these texts, engraved on the outside of the tomb so they can be seen and read by passersby, the dead person directs himself to those coming after, recounting in formulaic sentences how his life was lived, how it was carried out according to the norms of justice and good sense, of *maat*. Assmann interpreted this autobiographical literature in stone not just as the extension of or parallel to an earlier oral literature but as generated by writing itself. With the emergence and discovery of this art, the living who are about to die obtain a means through which they may continue to be heard and remembered across death. Thus, the grave and its autobiographical inscriptions can be described as the "breeding ground" or "preparatory school" (*Vorschule*) of literature. The grave becomes a formative "analogy" to the book, where the text makes present a subject that belongs to the world of the dead.[20]

It is important in these examples that the texts are directed toward a *posterior* community. What they aspire to is the preservation of the name and the personal destiny of the dead speaker/writer by and among those who come after. Therefore, Assmann writes, we need not even preoccupy ourselves with which particular (religious) conceptions of an afterlife that the author may have upheld. On a deeper and more principal level the writing constitutes an "appeal to collective memory" and an aspiration toward "social continuation."[21] From this perspective, "immortality" can be understood as a "destiny of reception" (*Rezeptionsschicksal*). Some of these tomb writings from later times even contain instructions to a future reader to copy the name from the stone engraving onto a papyrus. In an early culturally regulative text from the Old Kingdom, the so-called Instruction of Hardjedef, we read: "Make your house in the west excellent, and richly outfit your seat in the necropolis. Heed this, for death is worth little to us, heed this, for life stands tall for us. But the house of death serves life."[22] This conception of a *house of death* that serves life conveys the sense of a space made in solid material that can keep and hold the living for time to come.

That the connection between such structures and written words was not simply an analogy is clearly documented in a text from around 1300 BC that speaks of "the learned scribes from the time of Re," who did not build pyramids and stelae "to keep their names alive" but whose "names are pronounced over the *writings* they produced, for they endure because of their perfection," unlike the temples and altars that have all collapsed. In this extraordinary text, writing speaks of the survival toward which it itself aspires: "More worthwhile is a book than a graven stela or a solid tomb wall. It creates these tombs and pyramids in the hearts of those who pronounce their names."[23]

Interpreting Mortal Signatures: Assmann the Egyptian

In a concluding theoretical and more speculative section of his book on Egyptian mortuary culture, Assmann explicates the conceptual-philosophical underpinning of the different textual remains from Egyptian mortuary culture in terms of two different concepts of *time* and how they relate to language and grammar. The first is the grammatical-temporal form of "resultativity" (*Resultativität*), a future perfect in and through which something is intended as already having become. The corresponding temporal domain is the time of *eternity* that the Egyptians themselves named *djet*. This is contrasted to the temporality of transience and circularity, which they referred to as *neheh*. The equivalent verbs are *wenen* and *kheper*, roughly corresponding to *being* and *becoming*.[24] The former dimension is connected to *remembrance* and thus also to what the mortuary technologies aspire to achieve. The architecture of burial, the techniques of embalming, and the mortuary literature can then be understood as directed toward this temporal dimension of the everlasting *djet*, of *being having become*.

Following his basic interpretive framework, Assmann identifies the unifying formula behind this temporal comportment and orientation as *memory* in the sense that he himself has developed it in the theory of cultural memory: "We have to assume," he writes, "that there was a connection between the desire for immortality and what we are calling here 'cultural memory.'"[25] Through this general matrix it becomes possible to view and interpret the multifaceted phenomenon of Egyptian mortuary culture as essentially preoccupied with the general human predicament of responding to mortality through the creation of culture and tradition, as itself a mode of "self-transcendence." From this conceptual platform he can then explicitly affirm the continuity between the Egyptian cult of the dead and his own scholarly interest in these past remains: the desire to remain in dialogue with "the dead persons who lived more than five thousand years ago." This last argument is presented in passing, but it marks the speculative peak of the book's guiding hypothesis that the Egyptian mortuary culture must be seen as itself a dimension of the larger human endeavor of cultural memory. "We thus hold in our hand," he writes, "not just a key for understanding the ancient Egyptians, but also our own interest in them."[26]

Through this step, the historical enterprise explicitly recognizes itself as an extension of a culture of the dead in that it too seeks to maintain a bond to the past and its dead across the threshold of time, confirming as it were the inner movement and desire of historicism, as discussed in the previous chapter. Through the embalming of their dead and the preservation of their remains in stone structures, and through their discovery and use of the technique to seal and preserve a spiritual content in phonetic writing, the Egyptians opened a trajectory that did not come to an end with this particular ancient civilization and its language. Instead, it opened an avenue of cultural strategies that lead up to the present advanced stage of the human sciences. At the root of the "striving for individual immortality" and the "attachment to the past," Assmann locates a shared "need for tradition" that springs from "a desire for release from transitoriness and for overcoming death."[27]

Through this argument the phenomenon of "cultural memory" is elevated to the general horizon of the interpretation of human culture and tradition. *Memory* becomes the name for a symbolic space that is accomplished by transitory human life by means of various cultural practices and techniques, and in particular by means of *writing*. Through the creation of this structure, life is able to maintain itself over a time span that extends far beyond the limited framework of (oral) social-collective memory that under normal circumstances tends to hold together only for three to four generations. And at the heart of this entire enterprise is not just the aspiration of cultural continuity in general but the desire and aspiration to save and preserve the dead. Memory is a grave or a tomb that is filled with writing through which the dead are maintained in a resting temporality of eternity. We too are part of this space. Indeed, we are held together by it and thus continue to move within it, especially when we seek to approach and decipher the shredded remains of the aspirations of earlier generations. We are them, and they are us as they now become recognizable through our shared pursuit to hold and to save life from destruction and to comfort it in the face of the threat of disappearance and oblivion.

Such at least, seems to be the vision underlying the conclusions drawn by Jan Assmann toward the end of this extraordinarily rich study of ancient Egyptian mortuary culture, when combined with his previously elaborated theory of the workings of cultural memory. Viewed in this light, his overall theoretical pursuit would seem to comprise from its inception the same problem that we have tried to encircle in the preceding chapters: the nature and condition of being with the dead as an existential-ontological basic predicament that is ultimately reflected also in the practice of the human-historical sciences. The *relation* to the dead, the *caring* for the dead and for their continuation, enacted both by those coming after the living and by the living themselves as they face death in the binary intentionality of the "retrospective" and the "prospective," emerges as a general predicament in which we find ourselves beyond every specific cultural stricture, uniting us over and across temporal and cultural-religious domains.

But as the theory of cultural memory coalesces around this fundamental existential condition, it also raises the philosophical stakes of the whole enterprise. It is no longer just a sociocultural theory of the technical underpinnings of tradition but a theory that aspires to a more general existential-ontological truth about human finitude and death and the ontological relation between the living and the dead. For this reason, it also motivates a philosophical critical response that can situate its interpretive claims in a somewhat larger philosophical context. For this purpose, the interrupted dialogue and critical comparison with deconstruction and with Heidegger's existential analytic of historicity will prove helpful.

Situating the Dead: Metaphysics and History

It is Jan Assmann himself who reopens the conversation with Heidegger and the existential analytic by challenging its apriori and general claims. Already in the introduction to the book on Egyptian mortuary practices he recalls Heidegger and the analysis of how the everyday response of *das Man* to death reveals an anxious refusal to recognize and come to terms with finitude and mortality.[28] But Assmann declares this presumably transcultural comportment in regard to death as in fact a culturally specific modern *Western* response. The historically more common way of viewing the interaction between life and death is instead said to be more intertwined and nonexclusive. The ancient Egyptians are described as people who did not shy away from death as "we" presumably do who instead devoted a "massive amount of care and attention to it."[29] Therefore, the "authentic" response to death articulated by Kierkegaard and Heidegger does not capture a timeless existential truth. Instead, it should be viewed as a symptom and an extension of a modern individualist culture that has already lost contact with the deeper *social* sense of death as also continuity and rejuvenation. On the larger scale of cultural comparisons over time, the ancient Egyptian mortuary culture is thus presented as a more adequate, indeed perhaps even a more *authentic*, way of responding to finitude and death than the existential-phenomenological account of being-toward-death.

This contrast is accentuated even further in the concluding coda, "Egypt and the History of Death." Here Assmann explicitly contrasts the Egyptian sense of inhabiting a shared world with the dead with that of Kierkegaard and Heidegger, who are presented as typical examples of a "Western individualism" that understands death only as an "individual experience." In this respect, he writes, "Existentialism represents a position that is the exact opposite of the Egyptian understanding of death."[30] The Egyptian is described as someone who did not necessarily embrace death, but for whom death was not "an existential drama" in the modern existentialist sense since he understood his "social self" as extending beyond the corporeal, individual self into a continued life. Assmann even claims that with the emergence of the Mosaic and Greek religions, the dead were banished from the halls of the living. No religion, he writes, "has renounced the dead and the possibility of communicating with them so thoroughly as our own, Western religion, characterized by its biblical monotheism."[31] The premise for this argument is the observation of how among the taboos erected against "heathendom" by monotheism, the most significant was that against the various ways of contacting the dead. We cannot, Assmann argues, "recross this threshold in the history of consciousness, but we can at least make ourselves aware of what we have left behind, if only not to fall in the error of thinking that our view of the world is in any way natural, self-evident, or even universal."[32]

However, in this attempt to confront Egypt and Egyptian spirituality with a modern cultural ethos that has supposedly lost contact with its understanding of how life is preserved across the threshold of death, Assmann is not breaking new ground theoretically. As noted earlier, in the domain of death studies from the 1970s onward, a recurring trope was that Western modernity had somehow—as in Bauman's words—"killed death."[33] And as we have also noted repeatedly throughout this study, it is a self-assessment of modernity that is already discursively coded. While Western culture clearly sought and achieved a new level of technological mastery over the processes of dying and of caring for the bodies of the dead, it has by no means ceased to *be* with its dead. On the contrary, through its culture of memory and heritage, through its intensified necropolitical endeavors, and not least through the expansion of its human-historical sciences and their institutions, it has opened new modes of inhabiting this domain. That this is so is also recognized by Assmann himself, when he explicitly compares the modern cultural historian with the shamans and priests of the past.

Furthermore, in refuting the existentialist stress on the significance of personal mortality in favor of a diachronic survival of spirit, Assmann is not so much leaving modernity behind as returning to its principal theoretical platform, that is, to Hegel, who remains a hidden ventriloquist for this discourse. This is the same Hegel who not only defined burial as the mark of the survival of spirit beyond the mortal self but in the *Encyclopedia* explicitly compared the sign with the pyramid in which the soul is preserved, making the pyramid into an example of the first inkling of a genuine spirituality precisely in virtue of its ability to aim for and create stable material structures for the preservation of spirit.[34] For Hegel,

Egyptian religion was just a first indication of a mature spirituality, since it was still waiting for its Greek moment of fulfillment of a self-conscious spirit. Seen from this perspective, Assmann's endeavor could be read as a retroactive attempt to reinscribe Egypt as a fully mature member in a Hegelian teleological history of spirit on an equivalent level with Greece.

To simply note the residue of a Hegelian philosophy of spirit in Assmann's conception of cultural memory is of course not in itself a relevant criticism. Assmann is right in questioning the universal reach of the existential-analytical account of being-toward-death. Indeed, it partly recalls the criticism articulated by Levinas and Derrida that the existential analytic tends to leave aside the role of the death of the other and the phenomenon of *afterlife* as only inauthentic digressions in relation to the principal problem of individual mortality. But when stating that Kierkegaard and Heidegger represent an extreme contrast to an Egyptian understanding of death, Assmann is suggesting that the latter can somehow provide a tenable philosophical alternative to understanding the possibility of life after death. Thereby we are led back to the point that in his book on cultural memory was suggested only obliquely, that ancient mortuary culture anticipates cultural memory as a connective structure that ultimately also serves the continued communication with the dead. What modern individualistic, disenchanted philosophy and science have somehow presumably lost contact with could then be retrieved through a careful study of the long-term cultural practices of ancient civilizations in general and of ancient Egypt in particular. The earlier reference to the "testamentary essence" of writing has here become an affirmation of how the production of material-symbolic legacies generates a stable lineage of cultural memory as a connective framework and as a redemption from mortality. But at this point we must pause the conclusions and return to the initially posed philosophical challenge involved in thinking the death of the other and the inner connection between history, historicity, and those having-been.

In my discussion of the philosophical background to this question, I stressed that Heidegger and the existential analytic did not simply take the side of the living; instead, its conclusions invite us to contemplate the existential-ontological problem of survival and living-on as the very premise for human historicity. By focusing on how the death of the other distorts our ability to see the true fate of our mortality as a this-worldly experience, Heidegger bypasses the significance of *after-life* as an onto-logical question in its own right. But in coining the term "being-with the dead" and thereby showing that the phenomenality of the death of the other requires us to think beyond the strict separation of life and death, and in arguing for how the very possibility of history and historical aware-ness implies the category of *Dasein* as having-been, he also opens the exis-tential analytic to the dimension of its own "spectrality" and "hauntology" as later developed by Derrida. Ultimately it is toward the inner dynamics of this intergenerational finite sharing of being that we need to look. Only then can we grasp the social-ontological phenomenon of being with the dead in its inner tension and possibility, where survival is not simply the antipode and reversal of finitude, but where finitude is what makes the phenomenon of survival of the dead possible and meaningful in the first place. Every survival is impregnated with the finitude that conditions it. Therefore, the ethical and political interaction between the dead and the living will always remain an open challenge, not just a case of being either with or without the dead.

Assmann is correct in having noted that the inability to recognize and think the relation to and being with the dead as a human existential apriori has produced artificial barriers to understanding and conceptu-alizing the many cultural practices that arise from this form of social-ity. Instead of being seen as different ways of shaping a cultural memory over time, they have been described and then disparaged as expressions of superstitious religious *beliefs* in an afterlife. And still, in the end Ass-mann does not do justice to the deeper implications of his own explora-tions. By insisting on the strict separation between cultural epochs, he anthropologizes not only the Egyptian (as presumably entirely differ-ent from us) but also his own cultural context, as it is sealed within its presumably culturally conditioned refusal to see the other side of death. To take the Egyptian example of mortuary writing and architecture as a philosophical-anthropological paradigm ultimately leads to a confusion of conceptual levels that does not result in a better understanding of the gen-eral predicament that is also exemplified by the Egyptian material. Instead of establishing the general and shared condition that could permit us to think these cultural expressions in their differences, it alienates them. The result even runs counter to his own aspirations to create a general theoretical framework for understanding the continuity and communication between the dead and the living as a theory of cultural memory.

The deeper purpose of a theory of cultural memory is to account for the general shared and underlying "connective" structures that enable the living to remain in contact with the dead, and vice versa. But when the theory is presented as a critical alternative to an existential-philosophical affirmation of finitude, the project instead results in a metaphysical reaffirmation of a temporality beyond time and of a supraindividual spirituality. In doing so, it inadvertently returns the discussion to the same Hegelian conceptual foundations that continue to orient much of the modern social and human sciences in their conceptualization of death and finitude.

Metaphysics of Survival

Instead of seeing the post-Hegelian criticism of metaphysics as a neglect of the supraindividual connective structures, we should assume this criticism as a premise for continuing to think the inner logic of the "hauntological" sociality of being with the dead in its different forms. In the section "On Redemption," from the second part of Nietzsche's *Thus Spoke Zarathustra*, the protagonist describes how the "spirit of revenge" will respond to suffering with a will to punish time and transience itself as of lesser worth than eternity. In his commentary on *Zarathustra* in the essay "Who Is Nietzsche's Zarathustra?" Heidegger makes this same point in a more systematic fashion. Here he gathers and concentrates the analyses from his long previous work on Nietzsche into a comprehensive thesis.[35] The problem of the spirit of revenge is said to be not just a moral and psychological issue but something that points to the fundamental metaphysical question of how to understand being. If being is understood from the viewpoint of refusal and resentment in regard to time, as becoming, destruction, and change, then the spirit of revenge will inevitably put its mark on the conception of being. It will place the absolute and permanent as superior to the contingent and transitory. Heidegger writes that Nietzsche defines revenge as "the will's aversion to time and its 'it was,'" resulting in a view of the earthly and all that is part of as devoid of true being. Plato had already called it *me on*, non-being."[36] Later on in the same essay Heidegger states, "Metaphysical thinking rests on the distinction between that which truly is and that which, by comparison, does not constitute true being."[37]

Assmann's description of the Egyptian temporal category of *resultativity* almost literally overlaps with how *metaphysics* is defined by both Nietzsche and Heidegger. Indeed, the articulation of how the actual transitory world and time are inferior to eternity was never described in clearer terms than in some of the early testimonies from Egyptian spiritual literature quoted in his study. More explicitly than in the later Greek and Jewish sources, this eternity is also connected to death and the care for the dead. From the tomb writing of Amenuser (fifteenth century BC), we read: "Only a little of life is this world, eternity is in the realm of the dead." A striking illustration of how this "nihilistic" (in Nietzsche's sense) conception also guided everyday life in Egypt in later pharaonic times is preserved in a fragment from the early Greek historian Hecataeus, writing in the fourth century BC: "For the Egyptians regard the time spent in this life as completely worthless; but to be remembered for virtue after one's demise they hold to be of the highest value. Indeed, they refer to the houses of the living as 'inns' (*katalyseis*), since we dwell in them but a short time, while the tombs of the dead they call 'everlasting homes' (*aidioi oikoi*), since in Hades we remain for an endless span. For this reason, they trouble themselves little about the furnishing of their houses, but betray an excess of ostentation concerning their places of burial."[38]

In the first part of *Zarathustra*, Nietzsche has his protagonist lash out against the "preachers of death," those who reject life and lure people away from this life with words of "eternal life." With these words he brings out the new and critical ethos of a post-Christian Western humanity for whom the very conception of eternal life and being is just a mask over a nihilistic affirmation of death as more true than life. If we confront the Egyptian mortuary culture as presented and discussed by Assmann to this familiar modern criticism, it would seem as if the ancient Egyptians, not the Persians, and certainly not the Hebrews or the Greeks, were the first genuinely *metaphysical* people, precisely through their elaborate construction of a parallel, cultural, and cultivated time beyond the transitory time of mortal life. In Assmann's reading, this metaphysical understanding of a time in which the dead and living are united also holds a redemptive promise. After having made the claim that with Mosaic and Greek religions the dead were banished from the halls of the living and taboos erected against the various ways of contacting the dead, he suggests that it is only through a deeper confrontation with Egyptian cultural memory and its mortuary practices that we can reach into a more general apriori of culture, which also constitutes a positive inheritance of the human-historical sciences themselves.

Assmann's goal is to make the Egyptian cultural mortuary practices accessible and readable from a modern perspective. By interpreting them as ultimately having to do with the shaping of social and cultural memory, where the embalming of corpses, the burial architecture, and the mortuary literature all have the same purpose—serving the survival of the dead—the material becomes accessible from a contemporary cultural-theoretical perspective in ways that more traditional references to ancient religious beliefs fail to accomplish. Yet in its dual attempt to restore the legitimacy of the Egyptian mortuary culture as in fact devoted to the maintenance of cultural memory, and thus to reestablish the bond between ancient religious practices and the practices of the cultural-historical sciences, the argument ultimately bypasses the most difficult challenge of thinking *the inner finitude of the being with the dead and its technical mediation* as a persistent challenge of how to live and uphold this predicament in the present. The fact that life seeks to reach into the temporality of permanence through the technical means at its disposal, and that it through this process objectifies this pursuit in images and myths, does not mean that life in general simply prevails. Mortality and finitude do not go away with the symbols that are created in the service of their transcendence; instead, they continue to bear witness to the inner mortality of this aspiration.

Instead of making the culturally relative shape of Egyptian metaphysics into a new general pattern for cultural interpretation, we could focus on how the *semantic* approach to burial shows that not only the act of burial but the event of death itself as the passage from living to nonliving transforms the living into a *sign* of himself or herself, generating the temporality of a having-been as also a having lived. As grieving survivors, those who live *after* become responsible for the continuation of this temporality in its inner tension. It is a temporality that relies on their actions, but it is also a temporality that encompasses their being and in relation to which their finite existence will appear as only a fleeting moment. This is not just a phantasmatic dimension but a *lived* dimension of *continuing* and of coming *after*, as a predicament within which life is called to orient and shape its future. To stand in this predicament is to stand within the historical, as having to act not just before an empty future but in the shared space of having-been, as responsibility and responsiveness vis-à-vis others.

As we look at the Egyptians from the vantage point of this way of inhabiting time, we need not choose between affirming the redemptive powers of their cultural memory or refusing the temporal metaphysics of an everlasting having-become. Instead, the continued challenge is to think and act in a nonreactive and nonreactionary way to this condition. In doing so, we have to continue to respond to these questions: How far do we *carry* the dead, and when do we cease to carry them? What monuments do we create for the dead, and which of their monuments do we allow to perish or even destroy? Through what means and technologies and through which artifacts do we seek to continue to live? Where do we draw the border between our dead and the dead of the others, and to what consequence? The different responses given to such questions will structure the material and intellectual landscape of the living, not only in terms of their archives, memorials, and graveyards but also in their rituals and means of learning, and ultimately in the shaping of their political communities.

Concluding Remarks

The premise for the argument developed throughout this book is that if we are to understand the inner nature and possibility of historical consciousness and ultimately of history as known to us, we must explore the existential-ontological category of being with the dead. That humans are social beings, whose subjectivity, awareness, and expressive and communicative abilities are constituted within an intersubjective space is obvious, if yet not philosophically simple or innocent, as demonstrated in the vast literature on social ontology. But to describe how humans also exist in a historical and temporal social space with others no longer there or others having-been poses a more difficult challenge.

Today, we normally think of the presence of the past and of the dead through the category of *memory*, be it individual or collective, be it immaterial or material. But through this concept we also risk objectifying what it means to inhabit the irreducible temporal and existential domain of *being-with* the dead. Throughout this book we have traced this tendency toward objectification of the other (and consequently of the self) in the human-historical sciences that preoccupied themselves with mortuary culture as the study of the means through which humans care for, preserve, and communicate over the threshold of death. The very prospect of such attempts—in all their exuberance and excesses—attracted their attention, perhaps more than any other dimension of human cultural expression. Yet when confronting the hopes and ambitions of such endeavors in the past, they also recoiled as before a spectacle that they could watch in fascination but in which they were no longer able to participate. After having first observed, collected, and analyzed the remarkable death rites of the other as a sign and symptom of cultural primitiveness, they were also pulled in the other direction, partly through a longing for a presumably lost enchanted existence but also as a result of the necropolitical activism of the marginalized other. But throughout these turbulent attempts to grasp and contain the rites and monuments of death as a cultural expression, the human sciences largely refrained from thinking their own philosophical and existential complicity as themselves caretakers of the dead.

In the analyses presented here we have explored some of the ways in which the human sciences, notably sociology, anthropology, archaeology, and philology, through their own attempts to gather, hold, and organize the dead also exposed their own situatedness within a larger domain of living with the dead, in the face of which the theoretical gaze often found itself solicited and compelled to act and respond. Throughout this trajectory we focused in particular on the phenomenon of *burial*, insisting that it was not just a question of placing or disposing of bodies for reasons of social utility. In burial, the phenomenon of being with the dead is concentrated as a question of how to care not for oneself or for the living but for the dead themselves. As we move closer to the domain of burial, it exposes its volatile and unpredictable temporality. In locating the dead, space is transformed into time, and the time of history is revealed as the time of the dead other, or of the other as having-been.

As a social space and as a space essentially shared among the dead and the living, it is also a political space, indeed a necropolitical space. In Sophocles's *Antigone* we have a paradigmatic literary example of a necropolitical heroine, who risks her life to bury her brother. But instead of reducing her to either an unconscious vehicle of spirit or to revolutionary heroine defending her rights, a reading was proposed that focuses on the dialogue and conflict between the sisters, for whom the claims of the dead and the duties toward the dead expose the inherent ethical and political ambiguity of this very loyalty and commitment.

There is no social space entirely outside the shared space with the dead. To learn to live is to learn to inhabit this space in a responsible way. Life is a life after, as inheritance, ancestry, legacy, and fate. All wounds are not healed by time. Time itself is a wound within which life prevails. We do not overcome the finitude of death; we share it with the living to which we give birth and for which we too will one day belong to those having-been.

Coda

Grave men, near death, who see with blinding sight
Blind eyes could blaze like meteors and be gay.
Rage, rage, against the dying of the light.
—Dylan Thomas, "Do Not Go Gently into That Good Night"

Late in life and shortly before his death, Sophocles returned a third time to the story of the royal house of Thebes and the cursed fate of King Laius and his descendants with the tragedy *Oedipus at Colonus*. It was performed only posthumously as his ultimate literary legacy. This entire drama, which is less often staged, read, and discussed than the previous two, *Oedipus Rex* and *Antigone*, is centered on a remarkable necropolitical plot, involving the dying body and grave of Oedipus himself. Here we encounter the blind beggar king, who has been driven away from Thebes, supported by his two daughters, Antigone and Ismene, wandering through the countryside in search of a place where he can lie down and die. He stumbles upon a sacred grove protected by Eumenides in Colonus, a village outside Athens, which he chooses for his final resting ground. He calls on Theseus, the ruler of Athens, pleading with him to be granted refuge there, offering his "own shattered body" with the promise that when buried, it holds gains "greater than great beauty."[1]

The scene is interrupted twice, first by Creon and then by Polyneices, who both come to claim him and his body for their causes. Creon wants to convince him to return to Thebes to die and be buried there outside the city wall but under its protection for the purpose of good fortune. But Oedipus scorns this false invitation, recalling how he was treated earlier, cursing him and Thebes. Then comes Polyneices, who has already organized his attack on the city that will result in the disastrous events depicted in *Antigone*, seeking his father's blessing. Oedipus discards and curses him too, prophesying what will take place if he does not refrain from his attempted coup. Polyneices realizes that he is doomed, and as he leaves, he asks his sisters at least to make sure that he is properly buried. Thus, the entire terrible course of events that we know from the earlier drama is projected by Sophocles, in retrospect as it were. All the characters are set for destruction. And the whole scene is accompanied by the dark undercurrent from the choir, which here sings the words that for the young Nietzsche in *The Birth of Tragedy* marked the epitome of Greek pessimism: "Not to be born is best when all is reckoned in, but once a man has seen the light, the next best thing, by far, is to go back, back where he came from."[2]

In the final scene Oedipus asks Theseus to accompany him to the place where he "must die."[3] The words that directly follow this pledge contain the mystical core of the drama. He promises Theseus that he will reveal a "power that age cannot destroy, the heritage [*choron/chora*] stored up for you and Athens" and a "bulwark stronger than many shields."[4] The secret of this power Theseus alone shall learn as they reach the site, and it must never be revealed to anyone, not even to Oedipus's own children, but only transmitted from the king to his son and onward as a knowledge guarded by the ruler for the preservation of the community. As Oedipus walks away toward his final resting place, he suddenly no longer needs the support of Antigone and Ismene; instead, he moves on his own as if equipped with an inner sight. After having performed the ordained cleansing rites on his still-living body with the help of his daughters, he takes his farewell from them through tears of love. He is then received by the "lightless depth of the Earth" with Theseus as his only silent witness and under circumstances that the text explicitly refrains from revealing. When Antigone and Ismene realize that he is really gone, they are both struck by uncontrollable grief and ask Theseus in turns to tell them where the grave is so that they can join him in death. But Theseus keeps his promise not to reveal it, and he calms the sisters, who then return together to Thebes to try to prevent the fight between their brothers (in vain, as we know).

The story draws its power and significance from a long preceding history of necropolitical practices in the Greek world and elsewhere, where the graves of heroes would serve as foundations for the establishment of political communities and cities. To dwell in the vicinity of an important grave was to find support and protection, by resting on a stable past. But Oedipus's is far from the model of a hero's life. He is an outcast who has suffered the most disgraceful and pitiable destiny. He is a *homo sacer* in an original sense, a stateless destitute who cannot even touch the hands of the king to thank him since he is contaminated by guilt. Yet he holds a power through his sorrowful body that he can confer as protection under the concealed circumstances only indicated in the narrative. Furthermore, his last resting place is not an actual grave expected to be made the center of a new cult. On the contrary, the site of his descent into the underworld will always have to be kept secret. Not even his grieving daughters are permitted to know the place and exact circumstances of his death. The grave is not created, marked, or kept by anyone. Nor is Oedipus properly buried, since he buries himself. He himself participates in the bathing and libations that would normally be performed on the body of the dead. And he walks to his death to a place where he is *received* by a god or perhaps by the earth itself. He *enters* the other side freely, but at the same time as a gift to the Athenian community that has granted him refuge.

Colonus was Sophocles's own birthplace, where he would also be buried a few years after completing the drama. He wrote the play at a time when the power of Athens was crumbling following the long Peloponnesian Wars, and where its very existence as a free and democratic city-state was threatened, not least by the actual historical Thebes. In this situation, he lets the characters from his two most famous tragedies reappear one last time to partake in a celebration of the generosity and high-mindedness of his own city at a time of crisis and peril. Sophocles has Oedipus, his literary protagonist, return to offer himself and his body as a foundation for the continuation of the city. He lets him come there to die and to enter its earth at the very site of his own birthplace and future grave, not to create a physical monument of his bodily remains but to work from the other side of life for its continued protection.

Oedipus at Colonus is clearly a drama about death as legacy and inheritance, as well as about foundations and justice and living with the dead. But is it not also a drama about *writing* and *literature*? Is not the figure of the dying Oedipus also a metonym for the writing that he himself is? As the author approaches his end, he brings his protagonist with him, as someone who will prevail, who by means of the secret force of his legacy seeks to secure that neither he nor Athens will perish, even under overwhelming pressure. Was this Sophocles's legacy? Was he also speaking of the capacity of literature to hold a future and to shape an inheritance as a protective space and domicile beyond death? Is this strange final scene, surrounded by its secrets and silences, thus also a scene that literally depicts how the dead can act on the living through writing? We do not know. We will not know. But written from within a culture where ancient death rites and beliefs in the power of the dead encounter an advanced literary-historical sensibility, the Sophoclean drama here brings itself to a close in the shape of a self-enacted burial for the sake of a future, leaving itself behind as a written legacy.

Notes

INTRODUCTION

1. *The Phenomenology of Spirit* is here quoted in the English translation by A. V. Miller (Oxford: Oxford University Press, 1977), §445, 266.

2. Ibid., §451, 269.

3. Ibid., §452, 271.

4. Ibid.

5. The same point is made in one of the very few texts that explicitly addresses what Hegel has to say about burial: David Ciavatta, "On Burying the Dead: Funerary Rites and the Dialectic of Freedom and Nature in Hegel's *Phenomenology of Spirit*," *International Philosophical Quarterly* 47, no. 3 (2007): 279–296.

6. Sophocles, *The Three Theban Plays: Antigone, Oedipus the King, Oedipus at Colonus*, trans. Robert Fagles (New York: Penguin, 1982), 63.

7. Martin Heidegger, *Being and Time*, trans. J. Staumbaugh (Albany: SUNY Press, 2010), 238.

8. Zygmunt Bauman, *Mortality, Immortality and Other Life Strategies* (Cambridge: Polity Press, 1992), 152.

9. The article "Necropolitics" was published in *Public Culture* 15, no. 1 (2003): 11–40. Sovereignty, in Mbembe's words, amounts to "exercising control over mortality and to defin[ing] life as the deployment and manifestation of power" and the "instrumentalization of human existence" (14). For the term in Agamben, see *Homo Sacer: Sovereign Power and Bare Life*, trans. D. Heller-Roazen (Stanford, CA: Stanford University Press, 1998), 142. Another related term sometimes used in current archaeology and anthropology is "dead body politics." See, e.g., Craig Young and Duncan Light, "Corpses, Dead Body Politics and Agency in Human Geography: Following the Corpse of Dr Petru Groza," *Transactions of the Institute of British Geographers* 38, no. 1 (2013): 135–148.

10. Mbembe, "Necropolitcs," 40.

11. Robert Hertz, *Death and the Right Hand*, trans. R. Needham and C. Needham (New York: Routledge, 1960), 28.

CHAPTER I

1. Jan Patočka, "Phénomenologie de la vie après la mort," French translation from Czech original by E. Abrams, in *Papiers phénoménologiques* (Grenoble: Jérome Millon, 1995), 145–156. The following English quotes are my own translations from Abram's French edition. For a reading of this text that situates it at the heart of the problem of *tradition* as the in-between of death and birth, see Marcia Sá Cavalcante Schuback, "The Hermeneutics of Tradition," in *Rethinking Time: History, Memory, and Representation*, ed. A. Ers and H. Ruin (Huddinge, Sweden: Södertörn Academic Studies, 2011), 63–74.

2. Jacques Derrida, *Memoires for Paul de Man*, trans. C. Lindsay, J. Culler, E. Cadava, and P. Kamuf (New York: Columbia University Press, 1986).

3. Ibid., 32.

4. *Specters of Marx*, trans. P. Kamuf (New York: Routledge, 1994).

5. In 1976 he published a long preface to their analysis of Freud's Wolfman case: "*Fors*: The Anglish Words of Nicholas Abraham and Maria Torok," trans. B. Johnson, in *The Wolf Man's Magic Word: A Cryptonomy*, by Abraham and Torok, trans. N. Rand (Minneapolis: University of Minnesota Press, 1986).

6. For a more extensive presentation of their theories, see the collection of articles in Nicholas Abraham and Maria Torok, *The Shell and the Kernel*, trans. N. Rand (Chicago: University of Chicago Press, 1994), especially the last essay.

7. Derrida, "*Fors*," xvi.

8. *God, Death, and Time*, trans. B. Bergo (Stanford, CA: Stanford University Press, 2000).

9. Ibid., 8.

10. Ibid., 15.

11. See, e.g., ibid., 36.

12. Ibid., 86.

13. Jacques Derrida, *Aporias*, trans. Thomas Dutoi (Stanford, CA: Stanford University Press, 1993). Ariès's book was published in English as *The Hour of Our Death*, trans. H. Weaver (New York: Knopf, 1981).

14. Derrida, *Aporias*, 57–58.

15. Ibid., 42.

16. Ibid., 43.

17. Ibid., 60.

18. Ibid., 61–62.

19. Derrida, *Specters of Marx*, 237.

20. In 1999 the results of a symposium on Derrida's book were published, with responses from contemporary neo-Marxist thinkers, such as Frederic Jameson, Terry Eagleton, and Antonio Negri, and with a long reply to his critics by Derrida. See *Ghostly Demarcations*, ed. M. Sprinker (London: Verso, 1999). For an important book on this topic, see Colin Davis, *Haunted Subjects: Deconstruction, Psychoanalysis and the Return of the Dead* (New York: Palgrave, 2007). It

brings together Derrida and Abraham and Torok with analyses of contemporary popular cultural interest in ghosts, vampires, and zombies, but it leaves out most of the phenomenological background. For a collection of articles that demonstrates the scope of this theme and its metaphors in current cultural and literary theory, see *The Spectralities Reader: Ghosts and Haunting in Contemporary Cultural Theory*, ed. M. del Pilar Blanco and E. Peeren (London: Bloomsbury, 2013). See also Lorenz Aggermann, Ralph Fischer, Eva Holling, Philipp Schulte, and Gerald Siegmund, *"Lernen, mit den Gespenstern zu leben": Das Gespenstische als Figur, Metapher und Wahrnehmungsdispositiv in Theorie und Ästhetik* (Berlin: Neofelis Verlag, 2015), in particular the essay by Christian Sternad that discusses the underlying phenomenological debates: "Die Zeit ist aus den Fugen: Auf der Jagd nach sterblichen Gespenstern mit Emmanuel Levinas und Jacques Derrida" (59–71). For two important recent books that demonstrate the relevance of Derrida's analysis of spectrality for the understanding of contemporary historical-political phenomena, see Berber Bevernage, *History, Memory, and State-Sponsored Violence: Time and Justice* (London: Routledge, 2013); and Alexander Etkind, *Warped Mourning: Stories of the Undead in the Land of the Unburied* (Stanford, CA: Stanford University Press, 2013). For a very recent important argument in defense of the relevance of Derrida's analysis of spectrality for both the theory and practice of history and historical research, see also Ethan Kleinberg, *Hauntings: For a Deconstructive Approach to the Past* (Stanford, CA: Stanford University Press, 2017).

21. Robert Pogue Harrison, *The Dominion of the Dead* (Chicago: University of Chicago Press, 2003), is a broadly construed meditation on the "humic foundations of our life world" (x), which also explores the role of burial for creating a historical dwelling space. The study takes its point of departure from Vico, but the philosophically most significant section of the book is chapter 6, which also addresses Heidegger's analysis of historicity. Harrison shows that the topic of repetition (*Wiederholung*) contains an implicit recognition of the power of inheritance and tradition, and ultimately of the dead. He does not refer explicitly to Derrida or the topic of spectrality, nor does he address the more complex necropolitical implications of this way of conceptualizing the past. But his careful way of approaching Heidegger's text on this topic is exemplary.

22. The relevant sections are §§46–53, in Heidegger, *Being and Time*. The following page references are to the standard original German pagination, which is also provided in the margins of the English translation.

23. Ibid., 250.

24. Ibid.

25. Ibid., 238.

26. Ibid.

27. Ibid., 239.

28. Ibid., 238.

29. Ibid.

30. The chapter covers pages 372–404 in the original pagination, and the central definition of historicity is presented on 383–384.

31. The term "ancestral" should not be confused with how Quentin Meillassoux uses it to refer to a commonsense "objective past" that precedes subjectivity and human cognition altogether. See Meillassoux, *After Finitude*, trans. R. Brassier (London: Continuum, 2008). Here it refers instead to the phenomenological quality of that which in the present recalls and reaches back into what presents itself as "past."

32. In the Acknowledgments I mentioned how this correlation between the problem of the death of the other and the analysis of historicity first captured my interest when working on a monograph on historicity in Heidegger. See Hans Ruin, *Enigmatic Origins: Tracing the Theme of Historicity through Heidegger's Works* (Stockholm: Almqvist and Wiksell, 1994), 131n40; see also chapter 3 in *Enigmatic Origins* for a longer discussion and analysis of these sections in *Being and Time*.

33. Heidegger, *Being and Time*, 386.

34. Karl Löwith, *Mein Leben in Deutschland* (Stuttgart: Metzler, 1986), 56.

35. For a more extensive and critical discussion of the theme of "destiny" in Heidegger's work and its relation to the theme of historicity, see Hans Ruin, "Ein geheimnisvolles Schicksal—Heidegger und das griechische Erbe," in *Heidegger und die Griechen*, ed. Michael Steinmann (Frankfurt am main: Klostermann, 2007), 15–34. For a more recent critical assessment of the *Black Notebooks* and the larger issue of Heidegger's relation to Judaism, see Hans Ruin, "In the Spirit of Paul: Thinking the Hebraic Inheritance (Heidegger, Bultmann, Jonas)," in *Heidegger's Black Notebooks and the Future of Theology*, ed. M. Björck and J. Svenungsson (Cham, Germany: Palgrave Macmillan, 2017), 49–76.

36. For an updated and comprehensive survey of the origin and development of the concept and theme of "historicity" from Dilthey to Heidegger to Derrida, see Hans Ruin, "Historicity," in *Oxford Handbook of the History of Phenomenology*, ed. D. Zahavi (Oxford: Oxford University Press, 2018).

37. For a text that specifically links the hermeneutical problem of historicity to the topic of memory and cultural memory, see Hans Ruin, "Memory," in *The Blackwell Companion to Hermeneutics*, ed. N. Keane and Ch. Lawn (Oxford: Blackwell), 114–121.

38. See Martin Heidegger, *Hölderlins Hymne "Der Ister,"* in *Gesamtausgabe*, vol. 53 (Frankfurt am Main: Klostermann, 1984), where the full second part of the lecture is devoted to Sophocles's *Antigone*, on 63–154, with the discussion of the dialogue between the sisters on 122–129. Martin Heidegger, *Hölderlin's Hymn "The Ister,"* trans. W. McNeill and J. Davis (Bloomington: Indiana University Press, 1996).

39. In Robert Fagles's translation, the first lines read "Numberless wonders / terrible wonders walk the world but none the match for man— / that great

wonder crossing the heaving gray sea . . .", in Sophocles, *The Three Theban Plays*, 76. The Ode also occupies a central role in Heidegger's interpretation of the play in his 1935 lectures, *Introduction to Metaphysics*, but there Antigone herself is less important.

40. Heidegger, *Hölderlin's Hymn*, 100.

41. In the English translation of the lecture course, it reads: "You have a fiery heart, though turned toward the cold (dead). Ibid., 98.

42. See Heidegger, *Being and Time*, 384.

CHAPTER 2

1. Peter Metcalf and Richard Huntington, *Celebrations of Death: The Anthropology of Mortuary Ritual* (Cambridge: Cambridge University Press, 1991), 24.

2. For a more extended discussion of this question, see Robert Garland, *The Greek Way of Death*, 2nd rev. ed. (Ithaca, NY: Cornell University Press, 2001), 34, which remarks that the two practices in fact seem to have been used interchangeably, with one taking precedence over the other at different times.

3. Philippe Ariès, *The Hour of Our Death*, trans. H. Weaver (New York: Knopf, 1981). For the analysis of the establishment of the modern necropolis and the gardenlike memorial grounds, see 531–533. For a longer analysis of the same topic, see Thomas Laqueur, *The Work of the Dead* (Princeton, NJ: Princeton University Press, 2015), chap. 5. For a summary and critical discussion of Laqueur in a contemporary theoretical context of mortuary studies, see also Hans Ruin, "History and Its Dead," *History & Theory* 56, no. 3 (2017): 407–417.

4. This point is made by Edward Evans-Pritchard in his preface to the English translation of Hertz's study, where he comments that this circle of "Jewish and Catholic atheists" showed an almost "obsessive interest in religion." See Robert Hertz, *Death and the Right Hand*, trans. Rodney Needham and Claudia Needham (Aberdeen, Scotland: Cohen and West, 1960), 16.

5. Metcalf and Huntington pay their respects to Hertz, as do numerous studies in the growing literature on mortuary practices, including the other modern classic in the field, Maurice Bloch and Jonathan Parry, eds., *Death and the Regeneration of Life* (Cambridge: Cambridge University Press, 1982), which focuses explicitly on the figure of rebirth and rejuvenation in mortuary culture. Ariès is actually one of the few important writers in the field who does not recall Hertz, which is notable in view of the fact that Hertz basically invented theoretical anthropology of mortuary culture in France more than half a century earlier.

6. Hertz, *Death and the Right Hand*, 29–88.

7. Hertz's essay often shares its status as the founding document of anthropological death studies with Arnold van Gennep's *Les rites de passage* (Paris: Emile Nourry, 1909), a text of lesser philosophical interest but to which I return later in this chapter.

8. The parenthetical page references in this chapter are all from Robert Hertz's essay "A Contribution to the Study of the Collective Representation of Death," in *Death and the Right Hand,* trans. Rodney Needham and Claudia Needham (New York: Routledge, 1960).

9. Hertz's main informants, judging from his footnotes, were the German linguist August Hardeland, who had published a grammar and a dictionary for the Dayak language in 1858, and the German zoologist Friedrich Grabowsky, who did field work in Borneo in the early 1880s. By the time of Hertz's study, most of the more extreme practices documented in these reports had already been forbidden and uprooted by the Dutch Christian colonists and missionaries.

10. The time of writing the thesis was also a time of increasing debates in Europe on the topic of cremation. In the largely Catholic France it was still mostly anathema, but in the northern Reformed part of Europe it was propagated by a growing movement, connected to Enlightenment ideals of both intellectual-spiritual and hygienic nature. For a detailed discussion of this debate, see Laqueur, *The Work of the Dead,* pt. 4, 492–548.

11. This is quoted from an earlier study by Edward Shortland, *Maori Religion and Mythology* (London, 1882).

12. At the time of the study, the French colonial name "Huron" was used to designate the people now recognized as the Wyandot, who mostly reside in Quebec.

13. Among the peoples mentioned in the footnotes are the Arawaks from southern Orinoco.

14. See van Gennep, *Les rites de passage,* chap. 8, 211.

15. The story of Hertz's family and life is found in Robert Parkin's intellectual biography, *The Dark Side of Humanity: The Work of Robert Hertz and Its Legacy* (Chur, Switzerland: Harwood Academic, 1995), 1–2.

16. "In Memoriam," *L'anneé sociologique,* n.s., 1 (1925): 7–29. For the obituary for Hertz, see 23–25.

17. Ibid., 28–29 (my translation).

18. Terry Pinkard, *Hegel: A Biography* (Cambridge: Cambridge University Press, 2000), 660.

19. Émile Durkheim, *Durkheim on Religion* (Atlanta: Scholars Press, 1994), 103.

20. Ibid.,106.

21. In recent discussions of Hertz's model in the archaeological literature, the need to expand its reach in the direction of such a temporal ontology of the living and the dead is also suggested. See Gordon F. M. Rakita, Jane E. Buikstra, and Lane A. Beck, *Interacting with the Dead: Perspectives on Mortuary Archaeology for a New Millennium* (Gainesville: University Press of Florida, 2005). Hertz is cited throughout the book, and in their own contribution the editors speak of

the need to expand his model toward a deeper understanding of how the dead and the living interact. They exemplify this with the culture of mummies in the Andean culture, where the dead appear to continue to "act through the living" and where the mummies thus represent an example of an "extended or permanent liminality," where "the power of these ancestors is derived from their continued state of *communitas* with both the society of the living and the realm of the dead" (106). In Chapter 4 I discuss this book and its arguments in the larger context of burial archaeology.

CHAPTER 3

1. *Encyclopedia of Religion and Ethics*, ed. James Hastings (Edinburgh: T & T Clark, 1908), 1:425–467. Its article "Ancestor Worship and Cult of the Dead" runs more than forty double-column pages and is written by ten different authors. Together they cover twenty different regions of the world throughout history, from ancient Babylonia, Egypt, and Greece, to contemporary India, Japan, North America, and China, demonstrating the extraordinary weight ascribed to this particular phenomenon and the effort spent on exploring it among the first generations of social and cultural anthropologists of religion.

2. For some examples, see Nicola Harrington, *Living with the Dead: Ancestor Worship and Mortuary Ritual in Ancient Egypt* (Oxford: Oxbow Books, 2013); and William Lakos, *Chinese Ancestor Worship: A Practice and Ritual Oriented Approach to Understanding Chinese Culture* (Newcastle, UK: Cambridge Scholar Publishing, 2010). For an earlier classic study on China in this respect, see Maurice Freedman, *Chinese Lineage and Society: Fukien and Kwangtung* (New York: Athlone Press, 1966), which contains a remarkably rich chapter on the relation between ancestral worship and the art of finding a proper place for graves, as the core meaning of *fêng-shui* or geomancy (118–154). For an analysis of the *Confucian Analects* along the lines of the argument in the present book, see my "Death, Sacrifice, and the Problem of Tradition in the *Confucian Analects*," *Comparative and Continental Philosophy*, DOI: 10.1080/17570638.2018.1488353. For an earlier and shorter conference-paper version of this article, see also "Rituals of death, ancestrality, and the formation of historical consciousness—comparative philosophical reflections on the *Analects* of Confucius," *The European Journal of Sinology* 7 (2016).

3. For a scathing criticism of the connection between ancestor claims and cultural heritage, see David Lowenthal's modern classic, *The Heritage Crusade and the Spoils of History* (Cambridge: Cambridge University Press, 1998). The discourse of heritage is said to rest on fatalism and chauvinism; it disguises "authority as authenticity" and fails to recognize that our history is "not imposed on us

by the dead hand of remote ancestors" (250). Even though I sympathize with many of the concrete criticisms that he voices in this book and elsewhere, my following discussion runs counter to his more general argument in that I show how the very practice of history need not be seen as the pure opposite of heritage claims and ancestor piety, but that it can be interpreted instead as an *existential modification* of a more fundamental social-ontological predicament of being with the dead.

4. We should not fail to note that already from the very start of this theoretical enterprise the term "ancestrality" thus begins to duplicate and fold around itself, as it conditions the form of its own exploration. Etymology is concerned precisely with ancestry, with the ancestral of and within language itself.

5. In modern German, the term *Ahnenkult* is perceived as somewhat dated, and the phenomena that it describes are more often referred to in terms of *Todenkult* or having to do with *Vorfahren* or *Familienkult*. See *Der Neue Pauly: Encyklopädie der Antike*, ed. Hubert Cancik and Helmuth Schneider (Stuttgart: Metzler, 1996), 303.

6. *Encyclopedia of Religion*, ed. M. Eliade (New York: Macmillan and Free Press, 1987), 1:263.

7. Sylvie Poirier, "The Dynamic Reproduction of Hunter-Gatherers' Ontologies and Values," in *A Companion to the Anthropology of Religion*, ed. J. Boddy and M. Lambek (Oxford: Wiley Blackwell, 2013), 50–68. In the *Encyclopaedia of Global Religion*, ed. Mark Juergensmeyer and Wade Clark Roof (Thousand Oaks, CA: Sage, 2012), there is no entry on ancestor worship, but Aaron Sokoll's article "Ancestors" states that "in multiple religious traditions, living relatives call on ancestors to provide aid, guidance, and intercession. Ancestors are generally beneficent, domesticated, and deceased relatives or prominent community figures. They may also be seen to punish those who do not act properly toward them or their guidance. And the living show reciprocity for ancestors by honouring them through memorials, caring for the resting place of the ancestor, making prayers for and to ancestors, offering goods to ancestors that are needed in the afterlife, and holding feasts for ancestors" (31–32).

8. Georg W. F. Hegel, *The Philosophy of History*, trans. J. Sibree (Mineola, NY: Dover Publications, 1956), 91–99.

9. Ibid., 99.

10. For the German text, see Georg W. F. Hegel, *Werke*, vol. 12, *Vorlesungen über die Philosophie der Geschichte* (Frankfurt am Main: Suhrkamp, 1970), 123. Susan Buck-Morss's interpretation of Hegel and the question of slavery shows that Hegel followed and philosophically conceptualized the Haitian revolution in his master-slave dialectic but that he never recognized it as such. In line with the hypocrisy of many leading Enlightenment thinkers, he never spoke out in public against the slavery of his own time. See Susan Buck-Morss, "Hegel and

Haiti," in *Hegel, Haiti, and Universal History* (Pittsburgh: University of Pittsburgh Press, 2009), 3–78.

11. Hegel, *The Philosophy of History*, 94.

12. Ibid., 95.

13. Ibid.

14. Translated as *The Ancient City: A Study on the Religion, Laws, and Institutions of Greece and Rome* (Baltimore: John Hopkins University Press, 1980).

15. He also writes: "This belief and these rites are the oldest and the most persistent of anything pertaining to the Indo-European race. . . . Before men had any notion of Indra or Zeus, they adored the dead; they feared them and addressed them through prayers." Ibid., 14.

16. Ibid., 19.

17. In his recent attempt to trace the origin of political order as such, Francis Fukuyama returns to Fustel de Coulanges's thesis as one of his historical sources. See Fukuyama, *The Origins of Political Order: From Prehuman Times to the French Revolution* (New York: Farrar, Straus and Giroux, 2011). Fustel de Coulanges is recalled initially in order to support the basic thesis of the book that "the reason for social organization was religious belief, that is, the worship of dead ancestors," and that it is the "belief in the power of dead ancestors over the living and not some mysterious biological instinct that causes tribal societies to cohere" (59–60).

18. Herbert Spencer, *The Principles of Sociology* (New York: Appleton, 1897), esp. chap. 20.

19. Ibid., 286.

20. Ibid., 294.

21. "No more, then, of Semites than of Aryans can ancestor-worship be denied" (ibid., 299).

22. Ibid., 300.

23. Ibid., 301.

24. Erwin Rohde, *Psyche: The Cult of the Souls and Belief in Immortality among the Greeks*, trans. W. B. Hillis (Eugene, OR: Wipf and Stock Publishers, 2006). Originally published in 1925 by Kegan Paul, Trench, Trubner. See in particular chapter 1 on Homer, 3–54; introductory remarks on Spencer and contemporary discussions in comparative anthropology of religion, 6–7.

25. Ibid., 217. Rohde usually puts quotation marks around "savages" when referring to this term, perhaps to distance himself from its most obvious derogatory implications. In Chapter 7 I return in detail to the specific question of Homer and to Odysseus's journey to the land of the dead.

26. James Frazer, *The Fear of the Dead* (London: Macmillan, 1933), 4–5.

27. Ibid., 13. The topic had in fact preoccupied Frazer throughout his life, as early as his 1886 article, "On Certain Burial Customs as Illustrative of the

Primitive Theory of the Soul," *Journal of the Anthropological Institute of Great Britain and Ireland* 15 (1886): 63–104. There he contrasts, in a derogatory tone, the modern English way of caring for the dead with the superstitious practice of securing that the souls or ghosts of the dead do not return and haunt the living.

28. For an excellent discussion of Frazer's ambiguous position within the anthropological canon, which situates him in the context of the colonial and imperialist discourse on the "savage," see Patricia Lorenzoni, *Att färdas under dödens tecken: Frazer, imperiet och den försvinnande vilden* (Göteborg: Glänta, 2008).

29. *Totem and Taboo*, in *The Standard Edition of the Complete Psychological Works of Sigmund Freud* (London: Hogarth Press, 1953), 13:1.

30. Ibid., 4–5.

31. "The taboo upon the dead is—if I may revert to the simile of infection—especially virulent among most primitive people" (ibid., 51).

32. Ibid., 56.

33. Ibid., 57.

34. Ibid., 61.

35. See Peter Jay, *Freud: A Life for Our Time* (New York: Norton, 1988), 88–89. Jay also discusses the persistently troubling implications for psychoanalysis that several of Freud's most far-reaching ideas had on this deeply personal and individual background. In this particular case his own struggle with death of his father and with the continued presence of the figure of the father blended with his readings of Frazer and cultural anthropology to form his conception of the original totemistic community, with its death wish, ritual killing, and pathological response to the death of an ancestral paternal figure.

36. See especially the work of Graham Harvey, notably *Animism: Respecting the Living World* (London: C. Hurst, 2005), and his edited *Handbook of Contemporary Animism* (Durham, UK: Acumen Publishing, 2013). For an important critical intervention, see Armin Geertz, "Can We Move beyond Primitivism? On Recovering the Indigenes of Indigenous Religions in the Academic Study of Religion," in *Beyond Primitivism: Indigenous Religious Traditions and Modernity*, ed. Jacob K. Olupona (New York: Routledge, 2004), 37–68.

37. Jack Goody, *Death, Property and the Ancestors: A Study of the Mortuary Customs of the Lodagaa of West Africa* (Stanford, CA: Stanford University Press, 1962).

38. Igor Kopytoff, "Ancestors as Elders in Africa," *Africa* 41 (1971): 229–242.

39. Ibid., 140. For a more recent analysis in a similar vein, see Kwasi Wiredu, "African Religions from a Philosophical Point of View," in *Blackwell Companion to the Philosophy of Religion*, ed. Ph. Wuinn and Ch. Taliaferro (Cambridge: Blackwell, 1997), 34–42, which argues that the very concept of "religion" is misleading in regard to Africa, where the spiritual culture is strongly connected to

ancestors and spirits. Ancestors are the most important and appreciated, they do not belong to an entirely "abstract sphere," and the greatest that one can aspire for is to be taken up in this circle as a guiding ancestor. Peter Geschiere argues from a different perspective in *Witchcraft, Intimacy and Trust: Africa in Comparison* (Chicago: University of Chicago Press, 2013), showing that this spiritual complex often works in a destructive way, undermining civil society and fostering distrust and suspicion within families.

40. Kopytoff, "Ancestors as Elders," 236. Kopytoff's later work is also important for our topic. In the edited volume *The African Frontier: The Reproduction of Traditional African Societies* (Bloomington: Indiana University Press, 1987), he gathered an impressive amount of data to support the idea of the so-called frontier society as a model for understanding the development of African societies. He dismantles the image of solid, timeless tribes, showing instead that these communities are constantly renewed through migration, branching, and encounters, calling forth an image of the continent as essentially mobile and multiethnic. Rootedness is not connected to a "ground" or territory as much as in the sense of "a kin group, in ancestors, in a genealogical position," which can also be renewed through new establishments. Unlike the Chinese, Kopytoff writes here, "Africans take their ancestors with them when they move, regardless of where these ancestors are buried" (22–23).

41. Sylvie Poirier, "The Dynamic Reproduction of Hunter-Gatherers' Ontologies and Values," in *A Companion to the Anthropology of Religion*, ed. J. Boddy and M. Lambek (Oxford: Wiley Blackwell, 2013), 50–68.

42. Ibid., 56.

43. See Johannes Fabian, *Time and the Other—How Anthropology Makes Its Object* (New York: Columbia University Press, 2002).

CHAPTER 4

1. The speech was published as a separate booklet the following year: *Wissenschaft als Beruf* (Munich: Duncker and Humblot, 1919). In English, it was published in *From Max Weber: Essays in Sociology*, ed. and trans. H. H. Gerth and C. Wright Mills (New York: Oxford University Press, 1946), 129–156.

2. Ibid., 139–140.

3. Ibid., 156.

4. Benedict Anderson, *Imagined Communities: Reflections on the Origin and Spread of Nationalism* (London: Verso, 2006), 9–10.

5. For the remarkable story of the burial and reburial of Marx in London and the struggle for his body, including an unsuccessful attempt by Russia in 1922 to have it moved to the Kremlin, see Thomas Laqueur, *The Work of the Dead: A*

Cultural History of Mortal Remains (Princeton, NJ: Princeton University Press, 2015), 18–19.

6. Reinhart Koselleck and Michael Jeisman, eds., *Der politische Totenkult: Kriegerdenkmäler in der Moderne* (Munich: Wilhelm Fink Verlag, 1994), 9–10.

7. Ibid., 15–16; see also the essay that especially focuses on this topic: Volker Ackerman, "'Ceux qui sont pieusement morts pour la France . . .': Die Identität des Unbekannten Soldaten," in ibid., 281–314.

8. Katherine Verdery, *The Political Lives of Dead Bodies—Reburial and Postsocialist Change* (New York: Columbia University Press, 1999), 29–31.

9. Ibid., 109–111. Following the "successful" reintegration of Nagy into the public space of the dead, a similar restoration of the body of Imre Horthy was also later performed, restoring the fascist national leader to the rank of national hero, an act that has since been followed by a series of monuments throughout the country celebrating this figure in Hungarian history, a necropolitical strategy orchestrated and encouraged by the increasingly nationalist-conservative government.

10. Laqueur, *The Work of the Dead*, 18, 81.

11. Ibid., 8. The overall argument is cast in the form of an ambition to explore "a more enchanted view of politics" in Verdery, *The Political Lives of Dead Bodies*, 126.

12. Bioarchaeologist Bettina Arnold, in another article on postmortem agency, voices this idea when noting that dead bodies and their parts constitute "one of the most potent and poignant bridges between past and present," speaking of bioarchaeology itself as "a primary reanimation nexus." At the same time she also recognizes that while the discipline itself is increasingly tempted to use the language of "agency" to refer to these phenomena, deep down it still is mostly agreed "that the dead are not actors in the literal sense and once dead are incapable of primary agency." Instead, it is a question of something like "symbolic capital" and "secondary agents" that may be possessed by some bodies or parts of bodies, which thereby obtain "extremely active afterlives." See Bettina Arnold, "Life after Life: Bioarchaeology and Post-mortem Agency," *Cambridge Archaeological Journal* 24 (2014): 523–529, 524.

13. Paul-Laurent Assoun, *Tuer le mort: Le désir révolutionnaire* (Paris: Presse Universitaire de France, 2015).

14. Thesis VI, in *Illuminations: Essays and Reflections*, by Walter Benjamin, trans. H. Zohn (New York: Schocken Books, 1968), 255.

15. For one version of the story of the body of Voltaire, see Laqueur, *The Work of the Dead*, 193–195. Laqueur speaks of these battles, when Voltaire's bones at one point were stolen by monarchists, as a "counter-revolutionary politics of the body" (197).

16. The last chapter in *The Social Contract* describes the idea of so-called civil religion (*religion civile*). Rousseau's basic point is that there can be no state

without some sort of religious commitment to its existence and principles. The literature on the notion and phenomenon of civil religion is large, most notably perhaps the work by Robert Bellah. For an excellent study of Comte and his program, see Andrew Wernick, *Auguste Comte and the Religion of Humanity: The Post-theistic Program of French Social Theory* (Cambridge: Cambridge University Press, 2001).

17. An important dimension of the question of religion and the cult of the dead concerns the relation between Catholicism and the Reformation. The long history of the Christian cult of dead saints and their body parts is told in Robert Bartlett's impressive historical study, *Why Can the Dead Do Such Great Things?* (Princeton, NJ: Princeton University Press, 2013). The title is a quotation from Augustine, and the book recapitulates the history of this cultural practice from the early saints up through the Reformation, which defines itself partly through the critique and open iconoclastic violence against the cult of body relics and their shrines. For Bartlett's analysis of Luther's position on this practice, see 85–91. The modern "rational" ethos in regard to necropolitical phenomena clearly also draws from this aspect of the Reformation.

18. Friedrich Nietzsche, *Thus Spoke Zarathustra*, trans. G. Parkes (New York: Oxford University Press, 2005), 64.

19. Zygmunt Bauman, *Mortality, Immortality and Other Life Strategies* (Cambridge: Polity Press, 1992), 152.

20. This is addressed in a compelling way by Alexander Etkind in *Warped Mourning: Stories of the Undead in the Land of the Unburied* (Stanford, CA: Stanford University Press, 2013), 129–131, 211.

21. Verdery, *The Political Lives*, 41.

22. George Ritzer, *Sociological Theory* (Boston: McGraw-Hill, 2008).

23. Schütz continues a line of thought from the fifth of Husserl's *Cartesian Meditations*, where the topic is the constitution of objectivity and a shared objective world through the emergence of an elementary I-thou intersubjectivity. He elaborates, in greater detail than Husserl himself, the steps toward the life world of social meaning, being, and interaction, in order to demonstrate how a genealogy of subjective life is relevant and a necessary foundation for the social sciences. Despite his project of moving transcendental phenomenology in the direction of the ontology of the life world, Schütz never seriously followed or commented on the work of Heidegger or that of Merleau-Ponty, as he remained committed to the basic epistemological premise of Husserlian transcendental and egological phenomenology. He failed in his attempts to convince Talcott Parsons and the dominant strain of sociological thinking in the United States of the relevance of a phenomenology for sociology, but his work was rediscovered in the late 1960s as a forerunner to a new generation of more hermeneutically minded social scientists. In his *Interpretation of Culture* (New York: Basic Books, 1973), Clifford

Geertz, e.g., refers to the distinctions from the *Aufbau* in the seminal essay "Person, Time, and Conduct in Bali," which argues for "a scientific phenomenology of culture" in the spirit of Schütz (364).

24. Alfred Schütz, *The Phenomenology of the Social World*, trans. G. Walsch and F. Lehnert (Evanston, IL: Northwestern University Press, 1967). The categories are first introduced on 8, and then the analysis resumes on 142.

25. Ibid., 143.

26. Ibid., 144.

27. Ibid., 146.

28. Ibid., 166.

29. Ibid., 181.

30. Ibid., §41, 207–214.

31. Ibid., 207.

32. Ibid., 208.

33. Ibid.

34. Ibid., 214.

35. Ibid., 144.

36. Ibid., xxxi.

37. Alfred Schütz, *Collected Papers I: The Problem of Social Reality* (The Hague: Martinus Nijhoff, 1962), 318.

38. While I was finalizing this manuscript, the Polish parliament passed a bill to legislate against the use of the formulation "Polish death camps," again igniting the ongoing battle of how to describe and live with the events of the war and the history of anti-Semitism in Poland.

39. For reference to this work, which is funded by the Polish cultural ministry and other donors, see Witold Wrzosiński, "Why I am Writing a Field Guide to Jewish Cemeteries—for Poles," July 3, 2016, http://www.jewish-heritage-europe.eu/have-your-say/why-i-am-writing-a-field-guide-to-jewish-cemeteries-for-poles. There are currently several similar parallel projects under way, both in Poland and in other parts of former Eastern Europe, the largest initiative being the recently established European Jewish Cemetery Initiative (http://esjf-cemeteries.org), founded in 2015 and funded by Germany and the Council of Europe.

40. For the database, see http://www.memorializeamericanslavery.com. For the article, see "Why Slaves' Graves Matter," *New York Times*, March 4, 2016.

CHAPTER 5

1. For a good introduction to the general history of archaeology, see Bruce Trigger, *A History of Archaeological Thought* (Cambridge: Cambridge University

Press, 1989), especially chapter 3, which gives the story of the emergence of "scientific archaeology" from the early nineteenth century.

2. Or as stated by Adam Stout, "In Britain as elsewhere, the archaeology of death and burial grew out of tomb robbery and the boundaries are appropriately murky." "Cultural History, Race, and Peoples," in *The Oxford Handbook of the Archaeology of Death and Burial*, ed. S. Tarlow and L. Nilsson Stutz (Oxford: Oxford University Press, 2013), 17.

3. In a recent article on the position of the discipline, French archaeologist Laurent Olivier summarizes its transformation during the last half century, from (positivist) "process" archaeology to (postmodern) "post-processual" theorizing toward a position that he names "post-post-processual" but that should rather be labeled "neomaterialist," as he argues for its specific identity as the caring for and interpretation of material cultural objects, inspired by the work of Latour and others. "The Business of Archaeology Is the Present," in *Reclaiming Archaeology. Beyond the Tropes of Modernity*, ed. A. Gonzáles-Ruibal (London: Routledge, 2013), 117–129.

4. See Geoffrey Scarre and Robin Coningham, eds., "Introduction," in *Appropriating the Past: Philosophical Perspectives on the Practice of Archaeology* (Cambridge: Cambridge University Press, 2013), 1.

5. For a good summary of the earliest examples of burial excavations from the first half of the eighteenth century onward, and for the principal interpretive themes in burial archaeology, see Fredrik Ekengren, "Contextualizing Grave Goods: Theoretical Perspectives and Methodological Implications," in Tarlow and Stutz, *Oxford Handbook of the Archaeology of Death and Burial*, 173–192.

6. The so-called Red lady is a famous grave finding, routinely mentioned in most surveys of the development of European archaeology. For a good summary and analysis of this particular case, see Paul Pettitt, *The Palaeolithic Origins of Human Burial* (London: Routledge, 2011), chap. 6.

7. The discussion concerning Neanderthal burial is a fascinating story in itself in the burial-archaeological literature (see ibid., 78–79, for a good summary). The first findings have been disputed until recently. An important step in the debate was a consecutive finding in La Chapelle-aux-Saints, which from 1908 led to the more generally held conception that Neanderthals buried their dead.

8. The interpretation of this deposit is still disputed, but if it is indeed some form of burial ground, it means that the emergence of this practice moves drastically further back in Paleolithic, prehistorical, and prehuman times.

9. Pettitt, *The Palaeolithic Origins*, 2.

10. Ibid., 8–10.

11. Ibid., 45.

12. See also Erella Hovers and Anna Belfer-Cohen, "Insights into Early Mortuary Practices of Homo," in Tarlow and Stutz, *Oxford Handbook of the Archaeology of Death and Burial*, 635.

13. Pettitt, *The Palaeolithic Origins*, 11, 4.

14. Ibid., 39.

15. For the original article and documentation, see Tetsuro Matsuzawa, "Jokro: The Death of an Infant Chimpanzee," published by the Kyoto Primate Research Institute, 2003, http://hdl.handle.net/2433/143350. For the later observation, see Dora Biro, Tatyana Humle, Kathelijne Koops, Claudia Sousa, Misato Hayashi, and Tetsuro Matsuzawa, "Chimpanzee Mothers at Bossou, Guinea Carry the Mummified Remains of Their Dead Infants," *Current Biology* 20, no. 8 (2010): 351–352, https://www.pri.kyoto-u.ac.jp/press/20100427/index-e.html.

16. Biro et al., "Chimpanzee Mothers."

17. Mike Parker Pearson, *The Archaeology of Death and Burial* (Stroud, UK: History Press, 2009), 148, refers to Cynthia Moss, *Elephant Memories: Thirteen Years in the Life of an Elephant Family* (New York: Fawcett Columbine, 1988), which describes a group of elephants that put dirt and branches on the corpse of a fallen member, presumably to prevent scavenging.

18. Pettitt, *The Palaeolithic Origins*, 39.

19. Ibid., 56.

20. Ibid., 265, 262.

21. Ibid., 266–268.

22. Ibid., 269.

23. It is generally recognized as the inception of what is referred to as "mortuary archaeology," "burial archaeology," or just "archaeology of death" as a subdiscipline of the general field of archaeology. For a good survey of the development, see Robert Chapman, "Death, Burial and Social Representation," in Tarlow and Stutz, *Oxford Handbook of the Archaeology of Death and Burial*, 47–58.

24. Lewis R. Binford, "Mortuary Practices: Their Study and Their Potential," *Memoirs of the Society for American Archaeology* 25 (1971): 6–29, 6.

25. See Arthur Saxe, "Social Dimensions of Mortuary Practices" (PhD diss., University of Michigan, 1970). See also his contribution "Social Dimensions of Mortuary Practice in a Mesolithic Population from Wadi Halfa, Sudan," in *Approaches to the Social Dimensions of Mortuary Practices*, ed. James Brown (Salt Lake City: Memoirs of the Society for American archaeology, 1971), 39–57.

26. For a good summary of the earlier position and its legacy, see the most recent volume from the same series: Gordon F. M. Rakita, Jane E. Buikstra, and Lane A. Beck, eds., *Interacting with the Dead: Perspectives on Mortuary Archaeology for a New Millennium* (Gainesville: University Press of Florida, 2005), 3–5.

27. Ian Hodder, *Symbols in Action—Ethnoarchaeological Studies of Material Culture* (Cambridge: Cambridge University Press, 1982), 11–12. Some of the

points had been published previously in "Social Structure and Cemeteries: A Critical Appraisal," in *Anglo-Saxon Cemeteries*, ed. P. Rahtz, Tania Dickinson, and Lorna Watts (Oxford: British Archaeological Reports, 1980), 161–169.

28. Hodder, *Symbols in Action*, 221. In Hodder's own extended interpretation of this material, which had by then been widely discussed, he also questions previous assumptions by Gordon Childe and Collin Renfrew that these early Neolithic societies were egalitarian, reading instead signs of male lineage and proposing that graves are concerned with establishing relations to ancestors and with legitimizing authority.

29. Ian Hodder, *Present Past: An Introduction to Anthropology for Archeologists* (Barnsley, UK: Pen & Sword Archaeology, 2012), 139–146, 140.

30. Christopher Tilly, *Interpretative Archaeology* (Oxford: Berg, 1993), 7.

31. Richard Bradley, *The Significance of Monuments: On the Shaping of Human Experience in Neolithic and Bronze Age Europe* (London: Routledge, 1997).

32. For a long time, it was generally believed that the earliest large stone burial architecture in Europe was a result of the new social organization that came with agriculture, as argued in a famous paper by Claude Meillassoux: "From Reproduction to Production," *Economy and Society* 1 (1973): 93–105.

33. An important empirical basis for this interpretation are the Neolithic barrows at Barkaer in Denmark. When they were first excavated in the 1930s, they were believed to be remains of huge dwelling houses for the living, but later it appeared that they had been houses for the dead, erected in a landscape with very limited traces of previous farming activity. This realization and its implications are part of a larger ongoing debate within archaeology and evolutionary anthropology on how to understand the so-called Neolithic revolution, the gradual transition from hunter-gatherer to agricultural societies. For Bradley, the explanation is not only to be found in the economic-material transformation of human life as such but also in the transformation in "beliefs, values, and ideals, about the place of people in the scheme of things, about descent, origins and time, and about relations between people." An important precursor to Bradley was Alisdair Whittle, *Europe in the Neolithic* (Cambridge: Cambridge University Press, 1996), whom Bradley is here quoting.

34. Bradley, *The Significance of Monuments*, 51–53.

35. Ibid., 53.

36. Ibid., 54. Bradley's book is one example of a large and growing literature that focuses in new ways on the emergence of Neolithic burial architecture from the viewpoint of time, memory, ancestrality, and the relation to the dead. See, e.g., Mark Edmonds, "Interpreting Causewayed Enclosures in the Past and the Present," in Tilly, *Interpretative Archaeology*, 99–142. To this we should also add the important work that has grown from this line of inquiry that seeks to reinterpret these monuments as the creation of social "memory." See in particular Howard

Williams, ed., *Archaeology of Remembrance: Death and Memory in Past Societies* (New York: Kluwer, 2003), especially the contribution by Vicki Cummings, "Building from Memory: Remembering the Past and Neolithic Monuments in Western Britain," which states that "memory is a social process, embedded in a specific cultural context" (34). See also Andrew Jones's chapter, "Technologies of Remembrance: Memory, Materiality and Identity in Early Bronze Age Scotland" (65–85), which interprets burial practices and their different forms of materiality as correlated to the formation of "subjectivity" or "identity," where the different forms of burial practices contribute to situating the individual in a social/historical space. For further important contributions in this line of interpretation that now seek to interpret burial architecture as "fields of memory" and "technologies of remembrance," see Dorthe Christensen Refslund and Rane Willerslev, *Taming Time, Timing Death: Social Technologies and Ritual* (Farnham, UK: Ashgate, 2013); and Avril Maddrell and James Sidaway, eds., *Deathscapes: Spaces for Death, Dying, Mourning and Remembrance* (Farnham, UK: Ashgate, 2010).

37. Bradley, *The Significance of Monuments*, 63.

38. Parker Pearson, *The Archaeology of Death and Burial.*

39. Rakita, Buikstra, and Beck, *Interacting with the Dead*, 5.

40. Ibid., 11.

41. Gordon Rakita and Jane E. Buikstra, "Corrupting Flesh: Reexamining Hertz's Perspective on Mummification and Cremation," in Rakita, Buikstra, and Beck, *Interacting with the Dead*, 97–106, 100.

42. Ibid., 105–106.

43. Mike Parker Pearson has a good summary of the whole issue and its development in *The Archaeology of Death and Burial*, 173–175; see also Joe Watkins, "How Ancients Become Ammunition: Politics and Ethics of the Human Skeleton," in Tarlow and Stutz, *Oxford Handbook of the Archaeology of Death and Burial*, 701.

44. From the late 1990s, the literature on this topic has grown rapidly, demonstrating the complexity, richness, and profound implications of this issue for the human sciences generally and for archaeology and anthropology in particular. Among the many important books and collections are Nina Swidler, ed., *Native Americans and Archaeologists: Stepping Stones to Common Ground* (Walnut Creek, CA: AltaMira Press, 1997); David Hurst Thomas, *Skull Wars: Kennewick Man, Archaeology, and the Battle for Native American Identity* (New York: Basic Books, 2000); T. Bray, ed., *The Future of the Past: Archaeologists, Native Americans, and Repatriation* (New York: Garland 2001); C. Fforde, Jane Hubert, and Paul Turnbull, eds., *The Dead and Their Possessions: Repatriation in Principle, Policy and Practice* (London: Routledge, 2002); P. Turnbull and M. Pickering, eds., *The Long Way Home: The Meanings and Values of Repatriation* (New York:

Berghahn 2010); Laurent Daville, *Repatriation of Indian Human Remains: Efforts of the Smithsonian Institution* (Hauppauge, NY: Nova Science Publishers, 2013).

45. See Tamara Bray, "Introduction," in Bray, *Future of the Past*, 1.

46. For references to this story, see Parker Pearson, *The Archaeology of Death and Burial*, 173; and Thomas, *Skull Wars*, chap. 20, 209–210. The desecration and plundering of Native American graves for curiosity and treasures have a much older history documented among the very first Pilgrims. See Watkins, "How Ancients Become Ammunition," 695.

47. Mike Parker Pearson states that along with social anthropology, archaeology had been "merely one arm of the colonial administration's control over the colonized." Parker Pearson, *The Archaeology of Death and Burial*, 171.

48. For a report on the proceedings and its background, see Tamara Bray and Thomas W. Killion, eds., *Reckoning with the Dead: The Larsen Bay Repatriation and the Smithsonian Institution* (Washington, DC: Smithsonian Institution Press, 1994).

49. The story of the NAGPRA and its legal aftermath, with the complex battles over its interpretation that followed in its wake, surfaces in several of the books and articles listed in note 44. But see especially Larry Zimmermann, "On Archaeological Ethics and Letting Go," in Scarre and Coningham, *Appropriating the Past*, 98–118. For a summary of the parallel discussion in the Australian context, and from a more critical perspective, see Colin Pardoe, "Repatriation, Reburial, and Biological Research in Australia: Rhetoric and Practice," in Tarlow and Stutz, *Oxford Handbook of the Archaeology of Death and Burial*, 733–762.

50. For the full text of the Vermillion Accord, see, e.g., World Archaeological Congress, 1999, http://worldarch.org/code-of-ethics/.

51. See Zimmermann, "On Archaeological Ethics and Letting Go," esp. 102, 116.

52. See Geoffrey Scarre, "Archaeologists and the Dead," in *The Ethics of Archaeology: Philosophical Perspectives on Archaeological Practice*, ed. Chris Scarre and Geoffrey Scarre (Cambridge: Cambridge University Press, 2006), 181–216, 184.

53. Ibid., 197–198.

54. Liv Nilsson Stutz and Sarah Tarlow, "Beautiful Things and Bones of Desire: Emerging Issues in the Archaeology of Death and Burial," in Tarlow and Stutz, *Oxford Handbook of the Archaeology of Death and Burial*, 9.

55. Ibid., 2–3.

56. Liv Nillson Stutz, "Contested Burials: The Dead as Witness, Victims, and Tools," in Tarlow and Stutz, *Oxford Handbook of the Archaeology of Death and Burial*, 811.

57. Vermillion, South Dakota, is located about four hundred miles from Wounded Knee, the site where in December 1890 the American cavalry killed

around two hundred Lakota Indians, half of which were women and children, following a conflict that erupted after they had sought to escape the reservation. The dead were then placed in mass graves at the site. In February 1973, at the height of the AIM movement's activities, the small town of Wounded Knee was occupied by Lakota activists in a conflict that involved demands for new treaty negotiations. During the standoff between activists and police, several people were killed. The location had originally been chosen for its place in the memory of Native Americans, but through the violent incident it was reactivated as a necropolitical site of struggle and sacrifice.

58. During the same ceremony, a skull from Madagascar was also returned to representatives from the country of origin. See, e.g., Parker Pearson, *The Archaeology of Death and Burial,* 172.

59. In a retrospective commentary on the event, one of the participants, the Australian biological anthropologist Colin Pardoe, ridicules its pretensions and concludes that in the end it "signified nothing." However, a central point in this criticism is that it was not a *genuine* reburial, since it was carried out through rituals that were inappropriate for the occasion and for the body in question. See Pardoe, "Repatriation, Reburial, and Biological Research in Australia," 747.

60. In the literature I have consulted concerning this event there are different accounts of the origin of these remains. Some say they are the bones of a Lakota who died in the Wounded Knee massacre; others say that it was the body of a Seminole from Florida who had incidentally ended up in storage in Dakota. In any case, they were the bones of an unknown individual who in this case served as a representative of the dead.

CHAPTER 6

1. This indirect narrative covers most of Books IX–XII. The quotes are from Robert Fitzgerald's translation of *The Odyssey* (New York: Anchor Books, 1963).

2. Hannah Arendt, *Between Past and Future* (New York: Viking, 1954), 45.

3. Ibid., 43.

4. François Hartog, "The Invention of History: The Pre-history of a Concept from Homer to Herodotus," *History and Theory* 39, no. 3 (2000): 384–395.

5. François Hartog, *Memories of Odysseus: Frontier Tales from Ancient Greece,* trans. J. Lloyd (Chicago: University of Chicago Press, 2001), 4. The significance of Homer for Herodotus has also been explored in the scholarship on Homer, notably by Gregory Nagy, who devotes several chapters to this relation in *Pindar's Homer: The Lyric Possession of an Epic Past* (Baltimore: Johns Hopkins University Press, 1990). See also Uvo Hölscher, *Die Odyssee: Epos zwischen Märchen und Roman* (Munich: Beck, 1989), 142–144. Hölscher stresses the importance of

travels and of witnessing. Yet none of these studies has taken a particular interest in the significance of the ultimate journey to Hades as a comparison to the
task of the historian.

6. See, e.g., Homer, *The Iliad*, trans. Robert Fagles (New York: Penguin,
1990). All references are to standard pagination.

7. In later Attic Greek this would be the *martus*. For the etymology of *histor*, see Pierre Chantraine, *Dictionnaire étymologique de la langue grecque* (Paris:
Klincksieck, 1974), 779: "Du point de vue fonctionel, le nom d'agent *histor* . . . se
rattache à *oida* plus qu'à *idein*, c'est celui qui sait pour avoir vu ou appris" (779).

8. Michel de Certeau, *The Writing of History*, trans. T. Conley (New York:
Columbia University Press, 1988), 1–3.

9. For an excellent survey article on two centuries of scholarship and different
readings of the *Nekya*, see Kjeld Matthiessen, "Probleme der Unterweltsfahrt des
Odysseus," *Grazer Beiträge* 15 (1988): 15–45.

10. The section that even the most generous philological critics take to be non-
original are lines X.568–627, which describe Minos, the son of Zeus, as "dealing
out justice among the ghostly pleaders," a religious imagery unanimously considered to be un-Homeric and hence as belonging to a later editorial layer of the text.

11. Chapter 2 recalled several studies of ancient Greek religion on this fundamental significance of a proper burial, many of which rely precisely on the
depiction of the role that this theme has in the Homeric epic, especially the
extraordinary burial of Patroclus, but also the plea of Elpenor. To these analyses
can also be added a study by Jasper Griffin, *Homer on Life and Death* (Oxford:
Clarendon Press, 1980), which insists not only on the role of securing a proper a
burial but also on the idea of preventing one's enemies from being properly buried as the ultimate punishment, since "to deprive the dead of a grave is to abol-
ish his memory, to make him as if he had never been" (46). Achilles's disgraceful
treatment of Hector's body compared to his lavish burial rites for Patroclus illustrates this struggle in a concentrated form, as he even ridicules Hector that he
will become prey for "birds and dogs," in an affect that literally anticipates Antigone's later concerns for her dead brother (116; Il. XXII.335).

12. The oldest preserved examples of writing in Northern Europe, from the
later fourth century onward, are runes written on stones raised as memorials for
the dead, sometimes for the dead who have been lost and never returned from
their travels in distant lands.

13. This failed attempt to embrace the shadow of Anticlea also has its poetic
preamble in the description of Achilles's dream encounter with the ghost of
Patroclus in the *Iliad* (XXIII.114–116), addressing him thus: "'Oh come closer!
Throw our arms around each other, just for a moment—take our fill of the tears
that numb the heart!' In the same breath he stretched his loving arms but could

not seize him, no, the ghost slipped underground like a wisp of smoke . . . with a high thin cry." Homer, *The Iliad*, 562.

14. See, e.g., Hölscher, *Die Odyssee*, 22.

15. Hecataeus, *Hecataei Milesii, Fragmenta*, Test, introduzione, appendice e indici a cura ti Giuseppe Nenci (Firenze: La nuova Italia, 1954).

16. The Sirens are mentioned only in this particular passage in Homer and in no other older Greek sources. They are generally believed to have been part of a common mythical heritage. The explicit link to the land of the dead surfaces only in later ancient sources, where they are connected to Demeter and Persephone, as well as to Orpheus. See, e.g., "Seirenes," in *Der Kleine Pauly: Lexikon der Antike* (Munich: Alfred Druckenmüller Verlag, 1975), 79–80. From the fifth century BC onward, they also appear on graves and sarcophagi as Angels of Death, which through music and song lead and accompany the dead to the afterworld.

17. Jules Michelet, "L'heroisme de l'esprit," *L'arc* 52 (1973): 3–19, with commentaries by Jacques le Goff and Pierre Nora. The editors added the title, but it was based on a quote from Vico on *mens heroica* that Michelet had written on the manuscript page.

18. Ibid., 8., in my translation: "Je ne combattrai pas un mort; d'abord, je le ferai revire et c'est en le voyant debout, refait, réchauffé de ma vie, que je saurai loyalement quel fut vraiment son droit de vivre et quelle est légitimement sa nécessité de mourir. . . . Avec cette clef, j'étais libre; je pouvais entrer, sortir; je n'avais pas à redouter de m'enfermer dans le sépulcre."

19. Certeau, *The Writing of History*, 1–2. Certeau's book was favorably reviewed and translated from early after publication, but his influence remained limited in the English-speaking world, as it was eclipsed by the enormous impact of his contemporary Michel Foucault and his somewhat younger colleague Derrida. This is illustrated not least in Nancy Partner and Sara Foot, eds., *SAGE Handbook of Historical Theory* (London: SAGE, 2013), which is crowded with references to the latter two but mentions Certeau only in passing. For a good summary of his standing in the research literature generally and in the Anglophone debate in particular, see Wim Weyman, "Certeau and the Limits of Historical Representation," *History and Theory* 43 (2004): 161–178, which focuses on his different ways of engaging with "the other" as historian and as theoretician. For more recent examples of how Certeau is returning in the historiographical debate, see Gabrielle Spiegel, "Revising the Past / Revisiting the Present: How Change Happens in Historiography," *History and Theory* 46 (2008): 1–19, especially 6–7, which builds its analysis of recent transformations in history writing on Certeau's account of history as inhabiting a site of absence and death to account for the impact of poststructuralism as a response to the Holocaust. In her presidential address to the American Historical Association in 2009, Spiegel also returns to Certeau and his fundamental distinction according to which discourse about the past "has as

the very condition of its possibility the status of being discourse about the dead," filling a void created by "history's founding gesture of rupture." See "The Task of the Historian," *American Historical Review* 114 (2009): 1–15, 4. See also Joan Scott, "On the Incommensurability of Psychoanalysis and History," *History and Theory* 51 (2012): 63–83, esp. 78–79, where she takes Certeau as a witness to the paradoxical desire vis-à-vis the (dead) other, and the workings of language and its inner ambivalence as both "a structure of subjectivation . . . and as a vocabulary."

20. Certeau, *The Writing of History*, 2.

21. Ibid., 5. Certeau mentions a number of different ways in which various indigenous cultures presumably preserve their past through oral memory, citing an unpublished thesis by Alain Delivré on the interpretation of oral tradition and the sense of history; see 15n11.

22. Ibid., 6.

23. Ibid., 87.

24. Ibid., 91.

25. Ibid., 96.

26. Ibid., 100.

27. Ibid., 101.

28. Ibid., 44.

29. Ibid., 45.

30. See, e.g., Berber Bevernage, *History, Memory, and State-Sponsored Violence: Time and Justice* (London: Routledge, 2013).

31. Certeau, *The Writing of History*, 14.

32. Leopold von Ranke, *The Secret of World History: Selected Writings on the Art and Science of History*, trans. R. Wines (New York: Fordham University Press, 1981), 240. In a later remark with the title "The Historian's Ideal," he gives another powerful image of this aesthetical-ethical desire as the heroic aspiration to open oneself to and to give voice to the full impact of the past: "To look at the world, past and present, to absorb it into my being as far as my powers will enable me; to draw out and appropriate all that is beautiful and great, to see with unbiased eyes the progress of universal history, and in this spirit to produce beautiful and noble works; imagine what happiness it would be for me if I could realize this ideal, even in a small degree" (259).

33. Johann Joachim Winckelmann, *History of the Art of Antiquity*, trans. H. Mallgrave (Los Angeles: Getty Research Institute, 2006), 351. The same ideas are expressed in his famous meditation on the truncated Belvedere Torso, whose magnificent but fragmented physical properties are ultimately described as just a carrier for an "immortality" and for a "higher spirit," which takes the place of the "mortal limbs." See Johann Joachim Winckelmann, *On Art, Architecture, and Archaeology*, ed. and trans. D. Carter (Rochester, NY: Camden House, 2103), 143–148.

34. Gabrielle Spiegel, "Memory and History: Liturgical Time and Historical Time," *History and Theory* 41 (2002): 149–162.

35. Ibid., 162.

36. Spiegel, "The Task of the Historian," 15. This renewed commitment to the task of letting the dead speak and to hear the silenced voices is the more remarkable since Spiegel begins her lecture by recapitulating Certeau's argument concerning the condition of history as the separation between the living and the dead.

37. In this chapter, the main idea is to explore and show the interconnectedness between the imagery of the journey to the land of the dead and the emergence and pathos of *historiography*. There is, however, another trajectory, which I can only briefly indicate here and to which I hope to return in a different context, the one that concerns the relation between the *Nekya* and the origin of *philosophy*. It is well known that Plato was especially fascinated by this theme, and he returns in several of his myths to the image of journeys to the land of death, notably the story of Er in the *Republic*. The connection is discussed by Radcliff Edmond in *Myths of the Underworld Journey: Plato, Aristophanes, and the "Orphic" Gold Tablets* (Cambridge: Cambridge University Press, 2004), which connects the figure of Socrates in *Phaedo* with earlier journeys to the land of the dead. See especially 180–185, which address how earlier religious rites of purification were taken up by philosophy. His interpretation points toward the larger question of a transition that takes place at this time in history, connected to the gradual abandonment of sacrifice and the interiorization of spirituality, where a historical-humanist culture replaces the mythical experience of a contact with the dead.

38. Certeau, *The Writing of History*, 2.

39. There are of course other older narratives of journeys to the land of the dead, notably that of Enkidu in *Gilgamesh*, and also the legends of Heracles and the tales of Hermes and Orpheus, although the textual support for the latter are all from a later date.

40. Virgil is writing from within the imperial Roman context and under the rule of Augustus, explicitly seeking to create a literary-poetic monument to his own cultural present. The journey to the underworld, undertaken in the sixth song, also located at the very center of the narrative, is made explicitly for the reason that Aeneas wants to meet his father, Anchises, one last time. Their encounter first repeats the poetic effect of Odysseus's meeting with his mother, as Aeneas tries to hug his father three times, only to see him disappear: "The phantom sifting through his fingers, light as a wind, quick as a dream in flight." Virgil, *The Aeneid*, trans. R. Fagles (New York: Penguin, 2008), Book 6, lines 700–702. The encounter with the father also includes being shown in detail the future that awaits their family, as the founders of imperial Rome, its cities and provinces, and being shown their stroll around the Elysian Fields as purified souls waiting

to be called back to new deeds of greatness. If the *Odyssey* can be said to found a historical imagination in the form of an imagined journey to the land of the dead, the *Aeneid* uses this fictionalized past to create a living historical myth, a tale of origins, authority, and foundations. In this way, it illustrates another side of the historical imagination, not just the longing to restore what is lost or to hold on to the dead across the irrevocable river of time but to recall past greatness to secure a genealogical legitimacy in the present.

41. For a concise formulation on this topic, see Jan Assmann, *Cultural Memory and Early Civilization: Writing, Remembrance, and Political Imagination* (Cambridge: Cambridge University Press, 2011), on the culturally foundational nature of the *Iliad*, as the "priceless national treasure" and the "secret that made Hellas into a nation" (47–48).

42. For a detailed reconstruction of the remarkable story of how Boccaccio and Petrarch organized this translation, see Bruce Ross, "On the Early History of Leontius' Translation of Homer," *Classical Philology* 22 (1927): 341–355. For the reference to Leontius as "the first professor of Greek in Western Europe," see Gilbert Highet, *The Classical Tradition: Greek and Roman Influences on Western Literature* (Oxford: Clarendon Press, 1949), 16.

43. As Frank Turner writes, it quickly became "a vehicle whereby philologists worked to assert their cultural authority in European and more particularly German intellectual life." "The Homeric Question," in *A New Companion to Homer*, ed. Ian Morris and Barry Powell (New York: Brill, 1997), 23–145, 123.

44. Ernst Vogt, "Homer—ein großer Schatten? Die Forschung zur Person Homers," in *Zweihundert Jahre Homer-Forschung: Rückblick und Ausblick*, ed. Joachim Latacz (Stuttgart: B. G. Teubner, 1991), 365–337.

45. For a good discussion of how this image of Homer as the turning point in ancient Greek culture, see Fritz Graf, "Religion und Mythologie im Zusammenhang mit Homer: Forschung und Ausblick," in Latacz, *Zweihundert Jahre Homer-Forschung*, 331–362, esp. 343–344. Graf recalls the British scholar Gilbert Murray, who in *Four Stages of Greek Religion* (New York: Columbia University Press, 1912), had described Homer as the leap from "original stupidity" to the clarity of the Hellenic world (*Der Quantensprung von der primitiven "Urdummheit" zur hellenistischen Klarheit*), to which Graf adds the comment: "schöner kann sich die klassizistische Grundlage des victorianische Imperialismus kaum äußern." Murray also provides an unusually concise and telling example of how the reception of Homer was projected onto the religious politics of modern-day Europe, torn between Catholicism and Protestantism, as he explicitly refers to him as seeking a "religious reformation," coming from an "aristocratic," "patriarchal," and "conquering race" opposed to the southern backward societies dominated by "polygamy and polyandry, their agricultural rites, their sex-emblems and fertility goddesses" (78–79).

46. For a good summary of the ancient *testimonia*, see J. A. Davison, "The Homeric Question," in *A Companion to Homer*, ed. Alan J. B. Wace and Frank Stubbings (New York: Macmillan, 1962), 235–236.

47. Latacz, *Zweihundert Jahre Homer-Forschung*, 1.

48. Ibid., 3–4.

49. The original was published in Latin as *Prolegomena ad Homerum*, in English translation by A. Grafton, G. Most, and J. Zetzel (Princeton, NJ: Princeton University Press, 1985).

50. Turner, "The Homeric Question," 128.

51. Hölscher, *Die Odyssee*, 21 (my translation): "Wenn es für uns das Element des Geschichtlichen hinzugewonnen hat, entfernt es sich uns in demselben Maße, als er wirklicher wird."

52. Latacz, *Zweihundert Jahre Homer-Forschung*, 167: "Die homerische Dichtung steht nunmehr doch wohl unwiderrruflich in einem vorderasiatisch-ägäischen Horizont."

53. For a good survey of such open questions that concern in particular the religious-ritual context of the narrative, see Fritz Graf, "Religion und Mythologie im Zusammenhang mit Homer: Forschung und Ausblick," in Latacz, *Zweihundert Jahre Homer-Forschung*, 331–362.

54. Matthiessen, "Probleme der Unterweltsfahrt des Odysseus," 15–45.

55. At the same time Matthiessen also stresses that certain parts of the *Nekya* are sections where Unitarians and Analysts can unite, especially concerning the core theme of sacrificial rites for the dead and the encounter with Teiresias. Against the Analysts, Matthiessen's motive is to secure the originality and inner coherence of the text primarily by means of narratological and compositional arguments, showing how different characters and episodes fit within an imagined whole of the text. And after having gone through and cataloged the entire scholarly interpretive tradition and its suggested emendations, he comes out defending the originality of the entire text, with the only exception the description of Heracles in lines 602–604.

56. Vogt, "Homer—ein großer Schatten?," 365–377.

57. Ibid., 375. The quotation is taken from Erich Bethe, "Homerphilologie heute und kunftig," *Hermes* 70 (1935): 46–58, 58.

58. Bethe, "Homerphilologie Heute und Künftig," 46–58: "So meinte und meint man, wenn man 'Homer' sagt, nich ihn, sondern *Ilias* und *Odyssee*. Homer ist Begriff, ist heroisches Epos. Bis ins Ende des 5. Jh.s war dieser Begriff noch viel weiter: er umfaßte die ganzen Epen des troischen und thebanischen Sagenkreise und manches andere. Dies ist die älteste Überlieferung, von ihr muß vorurteilsfreie Forschung ausgehen, nicht vom Ergebnis antiker Kritik" (52).

59. Ibid., 58.

60. Ibid.

CHAPTER 7

1. For the translation, see Fritz Graf and Sarah Iles Johnston, *Ritual Texts for the Afterlife: Orpheus and the Bacchic Gold Tablets* (London: Routledge, 2013), 5. The same volume contains an excellent essay by Graf, "A History of Scholarship on the Tablets," that gives background on the interpretation of these artifacts (50–65).

2. For more details on the question of the poem on the descent to the underworld ascribed to Orpheus, see ibid., 176.

3. The historical *origin* of the art of writing is of course disputable, since it is not possible to pinpoint in time its emergence as a distinct technique. Rather, it is a question of a gradual emergence of something that on the basis of a series of criteria can be defined as "writing", e.g., that it should consist of artificial graphic marks on a durable surface that have a communicative purpose and relate conventionally to articulate speech. For a good overview of the topic and a discussion of these criteria, see Steven R. Fischer, *A History of Writing* (London: Reaktion Books, 2001), especially the introduction.

4. Jan Assmann, *Death and Salvation in Ancient Egypt*, trans. D. Lorton (Ithaca, NY: Cornell University Press, 2005); the German original is *Tod und Jenseits im alten Ägypten* (Unich: Beck, 2001). Assmann mentions the orphic tablets as a later parallel to the Egyptian mortuary writing, adding that "nowhere else has the use of speech and writing in connection with the cult of the dead assumed such forms as it did in Egypt" (238). See also 207 and 392 for comparisons between the orphic tablets and Orphism and Egyptian religion generally.

5. Jan Assmann, *Cultural Memory and Early Civilization: Writing, Remembrance, and Political Imagination* (Cambridge: Cambridge University Press, 2011), 19, 45. Together with Aleida Assmann, he shaped the field of cultural memory studies from the outset by coining the term itself. In doing so, they built on Maurice Halbwachs's earlier theory of "collective memory" but expanded it to encompass the larger exploration of the formation and maintenance of cultural traditions. This work first took shape within their Heidelberg group Archeologie der literarischen Kommunikation beginning in the late 1970s, which comprised experts in several ancient civilizations whose initial focus was the study of the techniques and means through which a culture signifies, communicates, and thus preserves itself over time, among which mortuary culture stands out as a paradigmatic case.

6. Ibid., 4.

7. Aleida Assmann, *Cultural Memory and Western Civilization: Arts of Memory* (Cambridge: Cambridge University Press, 2011), 23.

8. Ibid., 170. She quotes here from Stephen Greenblatt, *Shakespearean Negotiations: The Circulation of Social Energy in Renaissance England* (Oxford:

Clarendon Press, 1988), 1. Assmann's book was first published in German as *Erin-nerungsräume: Formen und Wandlungen des kulturellen Gedächtnisses* (Munich: Beck, 1999).

9. Aleida Assmann and Jan Assmann, with Chr. Hardmeier, "Schrift und Gedächtnis," postface in *Schrift und Gedächtnis: Archäologie der literarischen Kommunikation*, ed. Aleida Assmann and Jan Assmann, with Chr. Hardmeier (Munich: Fink, 1983). This was the first volume in a series of books under this general heading that would subsequently be issued by this group.

10. Jan Assmann, "Schrift, Tod, Identität: Das Grab als Vorschule der Litera-tur im alten Egypten," in Assmann and Assmann, *Schrift und Gedächtnis*, 64–93. Marek Tamm suggests a connection between Assmann's concept of a "mnemo-history" and Derrida's idea of "hauntology," but he does not refer it back to the original point of contact around the question of the sign. See Marek Tamm, ed., *Afterlife of Events: Perspectives on Mnemohistory* (New York: Palgrave Macmillan, 2015), 4.

11. Jan Assmann, "Schrift, Tod, Identität,"64.

12. Ibid., 67.

13. See Jan Assmann, *Death and Salvation*, 209–211, for a good introduction to this body of writing and its general title; the transcribed Egyptian reads *pr .t m hrw*. For the classic English edition of this material, see E. A. Wallis Budge, *The Egyptian Book of the Dead* (Penguin: London, 2008), xxii; first published in 1899 and reissued with a new introduction by John Romer. Romer largely confirms Budge's older translations, which had a profound impact on the anthropological and literary life of his time, from Frazer to Joyce, and he presents it as "a kind of passport to the afterlife." For a more updated version of the text and intro-duction in English, see Erik Hornung, *Altägyptischer Jenseitsbücher*, published as *The Ancient Egyptian Books of the Afterlife*, trans. D. Lorton (Ithaca, NY: Cornell University Press, 1999).

14. For this interpretation, which has to do with how they imitate bureau-cratic manuscripts, see Jan Assmann, *Death and Salvation*, 248.

15. Ibid., 165. Usually it would be the goddess Nut speaking, but in this par-ticular example, highlighted by Assmann as representative of the genre, the god-dess speaking in the coffin to the embalmed is Neith.

16. Ibid., 240.

17. Ibid., 242.

18. Ibid., 260.

19. Jan Assmann, "Schrift, Tod, Identität," 64. This is the same essay that con-tains the reference to Derrida.

20. Jan Assmann, *Death and Salvation*, 65 (my translation).

21. Ibid., 67.

22. Ibid., 373. The same lines are recalled in a slightly different translation on 13.

23. The text is from the so-called Chester Beatty papyrus IV, quoted in ibid., 376.

24. See Jan Assmann, *Death and Salvation*, 372–374.

25. Ibid., 377.

26. Ibid., 379.

27. Ibid.

28. Ibid., 12.

29. Ibid.

30. Ibid., 409.

31. Ibid., 407.

32. Ibid.

33. Zygmunt Bauman, *Mortality, Immortality and Other Life Strategies* (Cambridge: Polity Press, 1992), 190.

34. Hegel, *Enzyklopädie der philosophischen Wissenschaften III* (Frankfurt am Main: Suhrkamp, 1986), 260. Hegel is never mentioned in this book, but when looking for a modern resonance with the Egyptian experience, Assmann recalls—in passing—Hegel's older contemporary, the poet Christoph Wieland, whose text "Living On in the Memory of Posterity" (1812) is said to "touch directly on the Egyptian mystery of the 'social self' and of its presence, which lasted beyond the boundary of death." Jan Assmann, *Death and Salvation*, 408.

35. Martin Heidegger, "Who Is Nietzsche's Zarathustra?," trans. B. Magnus, *Review of Metaphysics* 20, no. 3 (1967): 411–431. Original German: "Wer ist Nietzsches Zarathustra?," in *Vorträge und Aufsätze* (Pfullingen, Germany: Neske, 1954), 97–122.

36. Heidegger, "Who Is Nietzsche's Zarathustra?," 423.

37. Ibid., 428.

38. Jan Assmann, *Death and Salvation*, 375.

CODA

1. *Oedipus at Colonus*, trans. Robert Fagles, in *The Three Theban Plays*, by Sophocles (New York: Penguin, 1984), 319.

2. Ibid., 358.

3. Ibid., 375.

4. Ibid.

Index

Abraham, Nicholas: vs. Derrida, 19–20, 22, 208n5, 209n20; on mourning, 19; on the psychic phantom, 19

Abrams, Erica, 17

Africa: eldership complex in, 79–80, 216n39, 217n40; Hegel on, 68–70

African American slaves, 110–11

Agamben, Giorgio: *Homo Sacer*, 7; on thanatopolitics, 7

agency of the dead, 87–89, 102, 107–8, 218n12

AIM. *See* American Indian Movement

Amenuser: tomb writing of, 197

American Indian Movement (AIM), 136, 138, 226n57

American Indians Against Desecration, 136

ancestor worship, 87, 101–2, 175, 214n7; vs. burial customs, 64, 65; in China, 66, 213n2, 217n40; defined, 67; vs. eldership complex in Africa, 79–80, 216n39, 217n40; Frazer on, 10, 72–73; Fustel de Coulanges on, 70, 71, 72, 215nn15,17,21; Hegel on, 68–70, 96; relationship to cultural conservatism and authoritarianism, 65; relationship to evolution of human spirituality, 6, 10, 49, 64–65, 72–73; relationship to historical consciousness, 65, 67, 75, 76, 77–78, 82; relationship to mourning, 77; relationship to nationalism, 65; relationship to religion, 66–67, 68, 70, 71–72, 82; Schütz on, 101;

Spencer on, 70–72, 79–80; term, 66–67, 214nn4,5

Anderson, Benedict: on ghostly national imaginings, 85, 108; *Imagined Communities*, 85–86; on Marxists and liberals, 85–86, 92; on nationalism and religion, 85, 89–90; on nationalism and Tomb of the Unknown Soldier, 85–86, 89–90

animism, 77

L'année sociologique, 43, 54–55

Antiquities Act of 1906, 137

Archaeologie der literarischen Kommunikation, 233n5

archaeology: bioarchaeology, 218n12; and colonialism, 136, 137, 145, 225n47; conceptualization of graves and burials, 11–12; as discourse on origins, 116, 118; emergence as modern academic discipline, 115–18, 220n1; evolutionary anthropological approach to mortuary culture, 11, 119–26, 128; graves in, 112, 113, 115, 116, 128, 146–47, 222n23; and historical consciousness, 112–13, 135; historicity of materials, 116; humanist-hermeneutic ethos in, 11, 128, 130–32; and inheritance, 137–38; megalithic monuments in, 132–33; *Memoirs of the Society for American Archaeology*, 128, 222n23; and necropolitics, 6, 11, 12, 114, 116, 135–47; *New Perspectives in Archaeology*, 128; *Oxford Handbook of*

Harrington, Nicola: *Living with the Dead*, 213n2
Harrison, Robert Pogue, 209n21
Hartog, François: *Memories of Odysseus*, 150; on Odysseus and sight, 150
hauntology, 5, 13–14, 23, 163, 196; Derrida on, 195, 234n10
Hecataeus, 12, 150, 156, 197
Hegel, Georg W. F., 7, 117, 185; on Africa, 68–70; on ancestor worship, 68–70, 96; Jan Assmann, 185; vs. Jan Assmann, 193–94; on burial, 1–3, 9, 21, 36, 40–43, 44–45, 54, 56, 58, 120, 126, 193, 207n5; and Christianity, 44, 56, 73; dialectic of Freedom, 3; on Egyptian religion, 193–94; *Encyclopedia*, 193; on family obligation, 1–3; vs. Frazer, 72; vs. Freud, 75, 76; funeral services for, 56; vs. Heidegger, 22; vs. Hertz, 43, 44–45, 50–51, 52, 54, 57, 58; on human law vs. divine law, 1–3; legacy in human sciences, 10, 57, 97, 196; vs. Levinas, 21; master-slave dialectic, 214n10; vs. Pettitt, 126–27; *The Phenomenology of Spirit*, 1–3, 36, 40–41; *The Philosophy of History*, 68; *The Philosophy of Right*, 3; on the pyramid, 193; on slavery, 68, 214n10; and Sophocles's *Antigone*, 2–3, 9, 36, 40–41, 44, 45; vs. Spencer, 71–72; on spirit, 1–3, 9, 13, 21, 36, 40, 44, 52, 54, 56, 58, 71–72, 75, 96, 126, 193–94, 196; on the state, 1–3
Heidegger, Martin: on artifacts, 30–31; Jan Assmann on, 192, 194; on authentic historicity, 24, 32–36, 38–39; *Being and Time*, 4–5, 6–9, 20, 21, 23–35, 38–39; on being with the dead, 4–5, 9, 24, 27–28, 29, 31–32; on care for the dead, 27, 31–32; on collective destiny, 33, 35, 36, 38, 210n35; on *Dasein*/human existence, 4–5, 9, 25–27, 29–35, 38–39, 107, 191, 194–95; on death and finitude,

5, 8–9, 13, 20, 21–22, 23–24, 26–29, 32, 38–39, 192; on death of the other/*Dasein* as having-been (*Dagewesen*), 4–5, 9, 24, 26–28, 31–32, 33, 34–35, 194–95; Derrida on, 5, 8, 21–22, 23–24, 28, 29, 38; vs. Hegel, 22; on historicity, 4–5, 9, 24, 29–36, 38–39, 107, 191, 194–95, 209n21, 210n32; influence of, 36; *Introduction to Metaphysics*, 211n39; Levinas on, 5, 8–9, 20, 21, 22, 23–24, 28–29, 38; on metaphysical thinking, 197; and mourning, 24, 27–28, 38–39; and National Socialism, 35; vs. Schütz, 107; on Sophocles's *Antigone*, 9, 24–25, 36–39, 211n39; on temporality, 25–26, 32–33; on tradition, 32–36; "Who Is Nietzsche's Zarathustra?", 196–97
Heiner, Heinrich, 172
Heracles, 157, 175, 230n39, 232n55
Heraclitus, 87
Hermes, 230n39
Herodotus, 12, 150; Hartog on, 149; vs. Homer, 149
Hertz, Robert: vs. Binford, 128, 129; on body of the deceased, 46–50, 52; on burial, 9–10, 44–54, 55, 56, 57–58, 59, 128, 129, 134; "Contribution à la représentation collective de la mort", 43–58, 59–60, 61, 211n7; on death and collective consciousness, 10, 44, 45, 50–51, 52, 53, 54, 60; death in WWI, 43, 54–56; on deaths without end, 52–54, 60; on double/second burial, 10, 45–52, 54, 56, 134; vs. Durkheim, 10, 53–54, 57, 128; on Egyptian mummification, 48; vs. Hegel, 43, 44–45, 50–51, 52, 54, 57, 58; informants for, 45, 212n9; Mauss's obituary for, 10, 54–56, 58, 59, 60–61; on needs of society, 120; vs. Pettitt, 119, 120; Rakita, Buikstra and Beck on, 212n21; on social status and burial, 129; on soul of the

Cultural Memory *in the Present*

Jacques Derrida and Catherine Malabou, *Counterpath: Traveling with Jacques Derrida*

Martin Seel, *Aesthetics of Appearing*

Nanette Salomon, *Shifting Priorities: Gender and Genre in Seventeenth-Century Dutch Painting*

Jacob Taubes, *The Political Theology of Paul*

Jean-Luc Marion, *The Crossing of the Visible*

Eric Michaud, *The Cult of Art in Nazi Germany*

Anne Freadman, *The Machinery of Talk: Charles Peirce and the Sign Hypothesis*

Stanley Cavell, *Emerson's Transcendental Etudes*

Stuart McLean, *The Event and Its Terrors: Ireland, Famine, Modernity*

Beate Rössler, ed., *Privacies: Philosophical Evaluations*

Bernard Faure, *Double Exposure: Cutting Across Buddhist and Western Discourses*

Alessia Ricciardi, *The Ends of Mourning: Psychoanalysis, Literature, Film*

Alain Badiou, *Saint Paul: The Foundation of Universalism*

Gil Anidjar, *The Jew, the Arab: A History of the Enemy*

Jonathan Culler and Kevin Lamb, eds., *Just Being Difficult? Academic Writing in the Public Arena*

Jean-Luc Nancy, *A Finite Thinking*, edited by Simon Sparks

Theodor W. Adorno, *Can One Live after Auschwitz? A Philosophical Reader*, edited by Rolf Tiedemann

Patricia Pisters, *The Matrix of Visual Culture: Working with Deleuze in Film Theory*

Andreas Huyssen, *Present Pasts: Urban Palimpsests and the Politics of Memory*

Talal Asad, *Formations of the Secular: Christianity, Islam, Modernity*

Dorothea von Mücke, *The Rise of the Fantastic Tale*

Marc Redfield, *The Politics of Aesthetics: Nationalism, Gender, Romanticism*

Emmanuel Levinas, *On Escape*

Dan Zahavi, *Husserl's Phenomenology*

Rodolphe Gasché, *The Idea of Form: Rethinking Kant's Aesthetics*

Michael Naas, *Taking on the Tradition: Jacques Derrida and the Legacies of Deconstruction*

Herlinde Pauer-Studer, ed., *Constructions of Practical Reason: Interviews on Moral and Political Philosophy*

Jean-Luc Marion, *Being Given That: Toward a Phenomenology of Givenness*

Theodor W. Adorno and Max Horkheimer, *Dialectic of Enlightenment*

Ian Balfour, *The Rhetoric of Romantic Prophecy*

Martin Stokhof, *World and Life as One: Ethics and Ontology in Wittgenstein's Early Thought*

Gianni Vattimo, *Nietzsche: An Introduction*

Jacques Derrida, *Negotiations: Interventions and Interviews, 1971–1998*, edited by Elizabeth Rottenberg

Brett Levinson, *The Ends of Literature: The Latin American "Boom" in the Neoliberal Marketplace*